THE
RESURRECTION
OF
JESUS CHRIST

THE
RESURRECTION
OF
JESUS CHRIST

EXPLORING ITS THEOLOGICAL SIGNIFICANCE
AND **ONGOING RELEVANCE**

W. ROSS HASTINGS

JB
Baker Academic
a division of Baker Publishing Group
Grand Rapids, Michigan

Published by Baker Academic
a division of Baker Publishing Group
PO Box 6287, Grand Rapids, MI 49516-6287
www.bakeracademic.com

Printed in the United States of America

Library of Congress Cataloging-in-Publication Data
Names: Hastings, W. Ross, author.
Title: The resurrection of Jesus Christ : exploring its theological significance and ongoing relevance / W. Ross Hastings.
Description: Grand Rapids, Michigan : Baker Academic, a division of Baker Publishing Group, [2022] | Includes bibliographical references and index.
Identifiers: LCCN 2021030948 | ISBN 9781540965295 (casebound) | ISBN 9781540964922 (paperback) | ISBN 9781493434800 (ebook) | ISBN 9781493434817 (pdf)
Subjects: LCSH: Jesus Christ—Resurrection.
Classification: LCC BT482 .H38 2022 | DDC 232/.5—dc23
LC record available at https://lccn.loc.gov/2021030948

Baker Publishing Group publications use paper produced from sustainable forestry practices and post-consumer waste whenever possible.

22 23 24 25 26 27 28   7 6 5 4 3 2 1

Dedicated to the memory of
J. I. Packer,
Supervisor, Mentor, Friend,
Fellow Consumer of Hot Food

Contents

Acknowledgments

This book had an unusual birth. On a summer day in 2020 I turned the radio on between the grocery store and home, and it just so happened that an oratorio called *The Resurrection*, composed by George Frideric Handel (1685–1759), was playing. It is a magnificent piece. I had listened to Handel's *Messiah* many times but had never heard this piece before. It suddenly lifted my spirit, and the brain cells started to come alive. When I arrived home, I went to my desk and in ten minutes or so wrote a ten-chapter outline of a book on the theology of the resurrection. This is the book, and the chapter titles have more or less stayed intact. So, I am grateful first to God for his gracious work in giving me the vision for this book and enabling its completion.

I am thankful also to Regent College for the gift of sabbatical time in which to write. When the COVID-19 pandemic struck the world in March 2020, just as I was about to go on sabbatical, I offered to postpone my sabbatical, given the challenges the pandemic brought. However, our dean, Paul Spilsbury, urged me to move forward with it. I am grateful for his urging and his constant, selfless encouragement and work on our behalf as a faculty at Regent College. I am grateful also for a number of theological influences that have helped shape this book. Their names will be apparent in the text and the bibliography. I wish to express thanks also for the help of my teaching assistants, Jacob Raju, Chris Agnew, and Noah Collins. I am grateful also to Robert Hosack and Tim West of Baker Academic for their expert editorial assistance, and for the work of copyeditor Melinda Timmer.

My wife, Tammy, has been a huge source of emotional support during this summer and fall season of writing and has also helped with proofreading and welcome breaks walking around this beautiful Ladysmith area of Vancouver Island. FaceTime calls during this pandemic with our grandchildren, Ada,

Carlos, Jayden, Keiden, Lucia, Makayla, Mario, and Rhys, have also brought great joy. This book has special significance for both Tammy and me. We both lost our first spouses to cancer in 2008. The hope of resurrection grounded in the bodily resurrection of Jesus is more than academic for us. He is risen! He is risen indeed!

Introduction

Christians everywhere value the resurrection of Jesus Christ from the dead two thousand years ago. Often they do so because they have heard that it is a historic fact and therefore a sound foundation for their faith. The first chapter of this book certainly confirms all of this to be true. The resurrection of Jesus Christ *is* one of the best-attested facts in history. Many books have been written on this theme. This book, however, is not really about that. It is not apologetics. Rather, it is theology. It answers the question, So what? What did and what does the resurrection mean? What does it mean for God? For Jesus? For humanity? For creation? For science? For the arts?

I recently traveled in a small plane piloted by my bonus-son[1] Brandon Carrillo. When I told him what this book was going to be about—that we know and value the fact that Jesus rose from the dead but that we don't often think deeply about its meaning—he said, "You mean it's like the buttons on the cockpit of my plane? You can't just flick one of them on without knowing what it does, what it's going to do to the engine or the wings. You have to know its meaning." "Exactly!" I responded. "We Christians flick the switch of the resurrection because we know we have to believe it (Rom. 10:9) or because it makes for credible witness to our faith, but we often don't know its meaning, all that it has done, what it continues to do now, for us and for creation."

Chapter 1 briefly revisits the question of the historicity of the resurrection, emphasizing that it was a bodily event and looking at the distinct emphases of the Gospel writers. Chapters 2–6 as a whole focus on what the resurrection has accomplished—that is, what it means *for our salvation*. Chapter 2 begins the exposition of the meaning or theological significance of the resurrection

---

1. This term seems better to me than the formal "stepson." My wife and I lost our spouses to cancer in 2008 and married three years later, and we determined we would call each other's kids bonus-daughters and bonus-sons.

by exploring the question, What does the resurrection have to do with the atonement, our salvation, and, in particular, our regeneration and our justification? Chapter 3 asks the question, What does the resurrection of the *person* of Christ and his personal history have to do with our history, and so with our salvation? This chapter focuses on the significance of the resurrection for three great themes of the Christian tradition: Christ's participation in humanity, recapitulation, and the *Christus Victor* (Christ the Victor) model of the atonement. Chapter 4 asks the pertinent question, What does the resurrection have to do with our actual transformation as persons—that is, our progressive sanctification? This chapter includes a discussion of the relationship between justification and sanctification as *theosis*, or deification, a term that has been used for centuries to speak of our transformation to become like God in character as a result of being in union with Christ. Chapter 5 moves to the question, What does the resurrection of Jesus have to do with our vocation or mission as humans, as the church, and as individual Christians? In light of who Jesus is as resurrected in a body and as the last Adam, we will gain a sense of the integral depth and width of what mission really is, including the role that our everyday work plays. Chapter 6 moves on from consideration of what the resurrection means for us in the kingdom that has come to ask the question, What does the resurrection mean for the kingdom when it is fully come? What is the future of Christians after we die, or when Christ returns? This chapter involves discussion of the glorification of the believer, bodily resurrection, and what we can know about resurrected bodies in light of Jesus's postresurrection body.

In chapter 7, the theme of the book shifts from an emphasis on the saving efficacy of the resurrection to questions regarding *being*—sometimes called ontological (*ontos* = being) matters. The saving nature of the resurrection is grounded in who the risen Christ was and is. So what does the resurrection have to say about the person of Christ, his identity? In other words, what does the doctrine of the resurrection contribute to Christology, the doctrine of the person of Christ? Chapter 8 explores what the resurrection means for his office as our Great High Priest, who is also King-Priest-Prophet, leading to a discussion of the importance of the resurrection for the worship of the church, including its preaching, seen as a participation in Christ's preaching. Chapter 9 poses the crucial question, What does Jesus's resurrection in a body mean for creation? Does it perhaps reaffirm God's commitment to his creation? If this is so, what does this means for ethics, and what does it mean for the study of science and the arts? The final chapter explores the nature of the second coming of Christ in light of the resurrection. Here we look at the literal, personal nature of that coming and what the new creation might bring.

The Resurrection as Good History

This [the resurrection of Jesus Christ from the dead] is a historical happening not of the kind that fades away from us and crumbles into the dust, but of the kind that remains real and therefore that resists corruption and moves the other way, forward throughout all history to the end-time and to the consummation of all things in the new creation. Jesus remains live and a real historical happening, more real and more historical than any other historical event, for this is the only historical event that does not suffer from decay and is not threatened by annihilation and illusion.

—T. F. Torrance[1]

This book is about the theological significance and ongoing relevance of the resurrection of Jesus Christ in the twenty-first century, including and maybe especially in its times of crisis. It seeks to offer a message of defiant hope for the Christian, for the church, for all humanity, and for all creation. The words of Scottish theologian T. F. Torrance above set the tone for the message of this entire book, first because they establish the historicity of the resurrection of Jesus, and second because they express what is at stake in the historical reality that the real person of the Son of God, who became fully and truly human for us and for creation, really died and really rose again from the dead. We can enter into the consequences of that resurrection through faith in Jesus, which brings us into union with Jesus by the fellowship of the Holy Spirit.

1. T. F. Torrance, *Space, Time and Resurrection*, 95.

But this "experience" is not ungrounded subjectivity. Rather, it is grounded in the historical reality that Jesus of Nazareth rose again from the dead, is alive today, and enters into living relationship with every believing person by the power of the Holy Spirit.

This book is primarily about the theological meaning and consequences of the resurrection. All subsequent chapters major on that theme: the theological meaning of the resurrection for our salvation and our being as human persons. This book is about the significance of the resurrection for the atonement, for our justification and sanctification and vocation, for the high priesthood of Jesus, for creation, for science and the arts, and for the future resurrection of humanity and the renewal of creation. It is not intended, therefore, to be a book about the apologetics for the veracity of the resurrection. It assumes the veracity of the bodily resurrection of Jesus. Nevertheless, just to establish confidence in its meaning and consequences, we begin with a brief summary of the evidence that Jesus really did rise from the dead.

Examining the evidence is important simply because the New Testament apostles gladly staked their claim about the truth of the Christian gospel on this historical reality. The fact that the Christian faith is a historical faith, dependent on a historical reality, already provides evidence of the importance of the incarnation and the resurrection of Jesus. Paul, for example, made no bones about the fact that if you could disprove the resurrection, you could toss Christianity aside as a fable not worth following and simply live it up in a hedonistic way: "Let us eat and drink, for tomorrow we die" (1 Cor. 15:32). He based his entire exposition of the gospel and his entire life on the fact that Jesus had risen. He staked his claim about the uniqueness of Jesus Christ precisely on this one historical point because he was convinced that it was true. Paul had, after all, actually encountered the risen Christ and had his view of God and the world upended. The most significant evidence that the resurrection happened is the transformation of the disciples of Jesus, their lifelong commitment to it, and their martyrdom for it. The accusation that they stole the body of Jesus and hid it somewhere is not logically tenable. Nobody allows themselves to be martyred for something they know to be a lie. The swoon theory—that is, the idea that Jesus merely swooned on the cross and then recovered—not only is untenable but also would not and could not have generated the zeal and faithfulness of apostolic witness.

When we fast-forward to the twentieth century, one of the most convincing accounts of the evidence for the real, bodily resurrection of Jesus was that given by the great professor of English literature at both Oxford and Cambridge, C. S. Lewis, who is known best by some for *The Chronicles of Narnia*. Lewis was baptized in the Church of Ireland but drifted away from the faith. His conversion at the age of thirty-two was due in part to the influence of J. R. R. Tolkien, but a significant cornerstone of his faith came from his investigation into the historicity of the resurrection of Jesus from the dead. And Lewis, like the apostle Paul, knew what was at stake with this claim. One cannot be neutral about Jesus's claim that he was the Son of God and his promise that he would rise again.

> I am trying here to prevent anyone saying the really foolish thing that people often say about [Jesus]: I'm ready to accept Jesus as a great moral teacher, but I don't accept his claim to be God. That is the one thing we must not say. A man who was merely a man and said the sort of things Jesus said would not be a great moral teacher. He would either be a lunatic—on the level with the man who says he is a poached egg—or else he would be the Devil of Hell. You must make your choice. Either this man was, and is, the Son of God, or else a madman or something worse. You can shut him up for a fool, you can spit at him and kill him as a demon or you can fall at his feet and call him Lord and God, but let us not come with any patronizing nonsense about his being a great human teacher. He has not left that open to us. He did not intend to.[2]

Lewis went on to say that to "preach Christianity meant primarily to preach the Resurrection."[3] In a letter written in May 1944, Lewis expressed his belief in the veracity and the importance of the resurrection:

> It is very necessary to get the story clear. I heard a man say, "The importance of the Resurrection is that it gives evidence of survival, evidence that the human personality survives death." On that view what happened to Christ would be what had always happened to all men, the difference being that in Christ's case we were privileged to see it happening. This is certainly not what the earliest Christian writers thought. Something perfectly new in the history of the universe had happened. Christ had defeated death. The door, which had always been locked, had for the very first time been forced open.[4]

What Can Be Proved?

Any investigation of the resurrection of Jesus must include consideration of the historical sources and documentation; and once the reliability of the documents has been established, consideration must be given to what they

2. Lewis, *Mere Christianity*, 53.
3. Lewis, *Miracles*, 234.
4. Lewis, *God in the Dock*, 170.

record—the empty tomb, eyewitness accounts of Jesus's postresurrection appearances, and the ongoing witness of the church. How dubious all proposed alternative explanations to what happened (the swoon theory, for example) have been must also be considered. But before we discuss some of these lines of evidence, I want to preface this discussion of apologetics by indicating what it is we can and cannot "prove" about the resurrection. "Proof" is probably the wrong word. We can discover much *evidence* for the resurrection. We can show that the historical events are best made sense of by the proposal of resurrection. But we cannot offer proof. Proof requires reproducibility. We cannot reproduce the resurrection of Jesus in a laboratory. This is a discussion within the realm of history, not the natural sciences. We can show that the resurrection is a historical fact on the basis of *critical realism* as it applies to history, but not on the basis of *logical positivism*. And actually, even science itself functions on the same basis: critical realism rather than logical positivism. Let me explain.

Trying to convince someone of the veracity of the resurrection by seeking to show absolute proof actually reveals an uncritical enculturation to modernity, in which reason and faith are considered to be separate. Seeking proof—as opposed to evidence—is in keeping with a philosophy regarding scientific discovery that arose out of modernity, one known as logical positivism or verificationism. This was an influential school of thought in the philosophy of science that emerged from the Berlin Circle and the Vienna Circle in the late 1920s and 1930s. It asserted that only statements that are verifiable through direct empirical observation or logical proof are actually meaningful. Only scientific knowledge is real knowledge, it was thought. One can easily see how this would make for a rift between theology and science and create the way for scientism of the kind that Richard Dawkins has exhibited in recent times, for example. The resurrection of Jesus accounts well for all the historical evidence, and there is a considerable amount of that historical evidence. But on the basis of the criteria of verificationism, since we cannot reproduce this event, "proof" of the resurrection of Jesus does not exist, and theological knowledge based on it does not exist either.

Enter the philosopher of science Karl Popper (1902–94), who attacked this premise for knowledge and offered falsificationism as a better way of establishing scientific knowledge than verificationism. He exposed true empirical verification as logically impossible. The more realistic aim of science, he suggested, is corroboration of a scientific theory such that there can be reasonable confidence that it accounts for the data and that what is being proposed actually bears a resemblance to reality as it is. Its goal is a rational realism or a scientific realism that recognizes that we have to, at best, settle for strong "truthlikeness" or "corroborated verisimilitude."[5] For example, proposing a theory about what electrons are and where they are situated must involve hypotheses and a model that can be tested. Or stated positively, when all the data has come in, these hypotheses must account well for all the evidence and be self-consistent. But at the end of the day, we cannot assume that the proposed model represents exactly what electrons look like. There remains an element of mystery. No one has actually seen an electron or a gluon. This falsification epistemology makes room for knowledge that is not strictly scientific, such as historical knowledge. On Popper's account, therefore, the resurrection of Jesus can be considered "scientific" in that it accounts well for all the evidence and because there has been no evidence to render it false.

The evidence for the resurrection does not stand or fall on rationalistic apologetics, therefore. I wish to stress that theology, including resurrection theology, is done by "faith seeking understanding," or critical realism, and not by logical positivism. Theology functions properly in an epistemological sense when it encounters mystery, responds in faith, and then pursues understanding. The order is mystery, faith, understanding, and not the other way around. Separating reason from faith and disallowing all mystery is the epistemology of modernity. Christian apologetics, if we are not careful, can sometimes be *of* modernity, and I want to avoid this while still engaging the historical evidence well and fruitfully. I believe that the road to convincing people of the resurrection of Jesus is actually explaining what the significance of the resurrection is, theologically speaking. When they grasp this and gain a sense of wonder about it, which is the core purpose of this book, they will rise in faith to accept the history and, even more, to believe in the Lord of history.

Another way to come at this is to say that, yes, reasonable (as opposed to rationalistic) apologetics has a work it can do here, but the awakening and revealing work of the Spirit is still required for people to believe. Logic and evidence and so-called general revelation are not enough for people to be convinced. Saving revelation is provided by the revealing God, and in the very act of revelation by God, communion with him is established. Stating this the other way around, it is only as relationship is begun that revelation can be imparted. Revelation understood in a theological way is not just a knowledge category; it is a *communion* category. God is the triune revealer as the Revealer, the Revealed, and the Revelation—that is, as Father, Son, and Holy Spirit. The Father reveals himself in the person of the Son objectively, and we receive that revelation subjectively through the person of the Holy Spirit. We can consider this in the opposite direction. The Holy Spirit

5. Popper, *Conjectures and Refutations*, 253–92.

awakens those who are seeking truth even as they seek, and he opens their eyes to truth as it is proclaimed. But they are already in relationship with the Spirit by the time their eyes are opened. The *substance* of what the Spirit reveals is the person of the Son, and in the very act of receiving revelation, people are already receiving the Son—they come into union with him as persons in Christ. And as such, they are now in relationship to the Father as children of God. There is, in other words, a trinitarian hermeneutical circle into which seekers must enter to find the truth about the resurrection and life in God. This is why evidence for the resurrection has its place within a critically realistic, "faith seeking understanding" framework. It makes sense of what happened. It is, as we have said, a critically realistic approach that leaves room for God.

What Is the Evidence?

With these provisos, we can now examine the historical evidence for the resurrection of Jesus and find that the facts as they are known are best made sense of by this great central claim of the Christian faith that makes Jesus unique among all religious leaders, the Son of God and the Lord of the cosmos.

Reliable Reporting?

It is not surprising that each of the four Gospels describes in vivid detail, though from a different perspective, the unexpected reality that Jesus rose from the dead. The event was unexpected even though Jesus had informed his disciples beforehand on a number of occasions that he would rise. Either his words did not register in their minds, and/or they still did not fully believe who he was. One may argue that it is not surprising that these Gospel writers mention and make much of the resurrection, and one may also argue that they were "of the church" and therefore biased and unreliable. Bible authors arguing for the Bible may seem like circular reasoning. This is, of course, unfair to these writers—one of whom, Luke, is an irenic and careful physician and historian, for example. What is more, these four writers agree on the major events that occurred during and around the resurrection.

Furthermore, it is highly improbable that early Christians would have invented the crucifixion event and therefore its sequel, the resurrection. The cross was a "stumbling block to Jews and foolishness to Gentiles" (1 Cor. 1:23), so why invent something like that? Jewish people knew that to hang on a tree meant to be under a curse (Deut. 21:23; Gal. 3:13), so this was no way to glorify their Messiah.[6] In an unemotional and historically conscious way, these Gospel writers describe the eyewitness accounts of the disciples and many others and so give a dispassionate and convincing account of the historical reality that Jesus was risen.[7]

In response to doubters who say that the Gospel records were written too many years after the fact to be reliable, New Testament critical scholar Craig Blomberg has insisted that a strong case may be made "that all three [Synoptic] Gospels were composed within about thirty years of Christ's death . . . and well within the period of time when people could check up on the accuracy of the facts they contain."[8] Other historical documents that are considered reliable do not have anything like the turnaround time that the Gospels do. The Gospel writers also frequently make statements that ground their writings in history, such as which Caesar was ruling in Rome, suggesting that they knew they were writing history and not wishful narratives.

The fact that there may be some inconsistencies regarding details in the four accounts (number of women at the tomb, number of angels, location of appearances) on the one hand suggests that the authors naturally had slightly different purposes for how they used the accounts of events in their narratives. On the other hand, it confirms how recent the events were when described by the writers. As New Testament scholar N. T. Wright has suggested, "surface inconsistencies," which may make the accounts appear to be "careless fiction," rather constitute "a strong point in favor of their early character." He goes on to say that these "stories exhibit exactly the surface tension which we associate, not with tales artfully told by people eager to sustain a fiction and therefore anxious to make everything look right, but with hurried, puzzled accounts of those who have seen with their own eyes something which took them horribly by surprise."[9] Critiques of the historicity of the resurrection offered by liberal "historical Jesus" scholars abound, guided by a presupposition against the miraculous. Most of these objections, including the notion that the resurrection does not belong in the actual narrative of the life of Jesus but was added later by the church, arise from an unfortunate severing of history from theology.

But for the sake of the skeptic, the question may be asked, What *external* evidence is there for the resurrection? Do Jewish or Roman historians of the time who were not Christians speak of Jesus and his cross and resurrection? Michael J. Wilkins and J. P. Moreland state that "when mutually accepted

---

6. This is a point made in Habermas and Licona, *The Case for the Resurrection of Jesus*, 282.
7. See Fuller, *The Formation of the Resurrection Narratives*, 37.
8. Blomberg, "Where Do We Start Studying Jesus?," 28.
9. Wright, *The Resurrection of the Son of God*, 612.

standards of historiography (the science of historical investigation) are applied to ancient religious records, the Jesus of history fares well historically." They suggest further that when "records of religious history are compared—such as Zoroaster, Buddha, and Mohammed—we have better historical documentation for Jesus than the founder of any other religion."[10] Edwin Yamauchi, in particular, has provided evidence in the form of ten writers who make references to Jesus outside of the New Testament.[11] These include the Roman historian Tacitus (*Annals* 15.44) and the Jewish historian Josephus (*Jewish Antiquities* 18.63–64),[12] who respectively refer to early Christian belief in the death by crucifixion and the resurrection of Jesus specifically.

Having given a nod to the historical reliability of the New Testament records and having noted references to the resurrection in some nonbiblical sources, we may now examine the evidence in the substance of these records. The following realities are *best accounted for* by the hypothesis that Jesus rose from the dead on the third day after his death, and they form a self-consistent and reasonable account[13] with better explanatory power than any other options: the crucifixion that preceded the resurrection; the empty tomb and the postresurrection appearances of Jesus; the transformation of the eyewitnesses; the Pauline witness to the appearances; and the centrality of the resurrection in the teaching of the early church. As strong as this evidence may be, we must confidently *proclaim* rather than *defend* the resurrection, trusting the revealing God to work in the power of the resurrection to convince and convert people.

The Crucifixion That Preceded the Resurrection

The events of Jesus's death by crucifixion and his resurrection are inseparable. The crucifixion of Jesus is therefore part of the core historical data surrounding the resurrection, as Gary Habermas has suggested.[14] That Jesus was executed by crucifixion is recorded not only in all four of the Gospels but also in a significant number of non-Christian sources of that period, includ-

---

10. Wilkins and Moreland, *Jesus under Fire*, 3.

11. Yamauchi, "Jesus outside the New Testament," 207–30.

12. One must not press this too far, however. Josephus scholar Paul Spilsbury states, "As to being a witness to the resurrection of Jesus, I would say the evidence is equivocal. The famous *Testimonium Flavianum* has undoubtedly been corrupted by Christian scribal tradition. At best we could say that Josephus was aware that early Christians believed that Jesus had been raised." Personal email communication, October 6, 2020.

13. For fuller treatments of the evidence for the resurrection, see Wright, *The Resurrection of the Son of God*; Craig, *Assessing the New Testament Evidence for the Historicity of the Resurrection*; Habermas, *The Risen Jesus and Future Hope*; and Habermas and Licona, *The Case for the Resurrection of Jesus*.

14. Habermas and Licona, *The Case for the Resurrection of Jesus*, 48–49.

ing the writings of Josephus, Tacitus, and Lucian of Samosata, as well as the Talmud.[15] Even John Dominic Crossan, a highly critical liberal scholar, acknowledges, "That he was crucified is as sure as anything historical can ever be."[16] As noted above, the disciples concocting a story about Jesus dying a death by crucifixion would have made no sense.

In addition to providing corroborating evidence for the historicity of the resurrection, the crucifixion also sets the tone for overcoming the objection that perhaps Jesus did not actually die on the cross and so was resuscitated rather than resurrected. According to the now-famous sentiments of the nineteenth-century German liberal New Testament scholar David Strauss,[17] it is unthinkable, given the brutal nature of scourging and crucifixion, that Jesus could survive them without medical help, roll back a heavy stone, beat off the armed guards, walk some distance on pierced feet, and convince his disciples in this pathetic state that he was the Lord of life. What's more, the Gospel writers provide a number of details that indicate Jesus was really dead: the wound in his side, the emission of blood and water, the witness of an experienced centurion. Further, the Jewish leaders and Pilate used overt strategies to anticipate and prevent a possible claim of resurrection by the disciples. The assertion that Jesus had not really died was not one of them. It simply wasn't a reasonable possibility. And certainly the swoon theory would not have led to the prevailing teaching of the early church that Jesus rose victorious from the dead. It seems clear that Jesus must really have been dead, since Christianity is not likely to have been birthed from the "apparent-death" hypothesis.

The Empty Tomb and the Postresurrection Appearances of Jesus

It is important to understand the expectations and worldview of the disciples who witnessed and then proclaimed the resurrection of Jesus. New Testament scholars such as N. T. Wright have made us aware that their context was Second Temple Judaism, which "supplied the concept of resurrection" but most certainly did not spontaneously generate it. Something happened that was *permitted* within their Judaistic worldview—that is, resurrection. But

15. These and other references may be found in Habermas and Licona, *The Case for the Resurrection of Jesus*, 49. One example will suffice. Cornelius Tacitus, in discussing Nero and his crucifixion of Christians, writes, "Christus, from whom the name had its origin, suffered the extreme penalty during the reign of Tiberius at the hands of one of our procurators, Pontius Pilatus" (*Annals* 15.44, ca. AD 115).

16. Crossan, *Jesus*, 145, cited in Habermas and Licona, *The Case for the Resurrection of Jesus*, 49, 257.

17. Strauss, *A New Life of Jesus*, 1:412.

the actual teaching on resurrection that followed Jesus's resurrection—that is, the "striking and consistent Christian mutations" regarding resurrection—surpassed the teaching of Judaism. When asked where this teaching came from, the early Christians would have responded by relaying two sets of stories, says Wright. The stories that spawned the awareness that Jesus was the Son of God, and that God was working in a radically new way, were those of an empty tomb and of the postresurrection appearances Jesus made to his disciples. And they must go together, for an empty tomb on its own could represent tragedy and loss, and appearances on their own could have been construed as visions. But considered together, they were "a powerful reason for the emergence of the belief" in the resurrection.[18] And indeed, they did go together. The disappearance of a body and then the discovery of that person fully alive account for the only reasonable explanation for the disciples' shift from their Judaistic view of resurrection.

All the postresurrection appearances Jesus made, taken together, also constitute strong evidence for his resurrection. This is true with respect to the number of the appearances that are recorded and how detailed they are, the numbers of people in addition to the apostles who saw him—five hundred people don't see the same hallucination all at once (1 Cor. 15:6)—and the sheer physicality of these encounters: the apostles saw his hands and his side, Thomas touched his wounds (John 20:27), and the risen Jesus even ate fish, according to the account of Luke the doctor (Luke 24:39–43). This was no ghost. The resurrection's "explanatory power"[19] outguns alternative explanations for what might have happened.

Christ did not rise in the minds of the disciples but in real time and space, and this immediately establishes Christianity as a religion based on history that can be assessed by critical historical scholarship. And, according to the best historians, Jesus's resurrection stands as a well-attested fact of history. It is important to note that this central tenet of Christianity is grounded in story and in history. George Eldon Ladd, in his *A Theology of the New Testament*, states, "God did not make himself known through a system of teaching nor a theology nor a book, but through a series of events recorded in the Bible. The coming of Jesus of Nazareth was the climax of this series of redemptive events; and his resurrection is the event that validates all that came before."[20] The resurrection is for Christianity the ultimate apologetic that is the validation of all the miracles of the Bible. And it is the climax of all

18. Wright, *The Resurrection of the Son of God*, 686.
19. Wright, *The Resurrection of the Son of God*, 687.
20. Ladd, *A Theology of the New Testament*, 354.

of God's redemptive acts. If the resurrection did not occur, as Ladd goes on to say, "the long course of God's redemptive acts to save his people ends in a dead-end street, in a tomb. . . . Christian faith is then incarcerated in the tomb along with the final and highest self-revelation of God in Christ—if Christ is indeed dead."[21] But the empty tomb and the postresurrection appearances of Jesus together comprise in part the explanatory power of the proposal that Jesus Christ rose from the dead in glorious triumph.

The Transformation of the Eyewitnesses

The disciples of Jesus certainly claimed to have seen and encountered Jesus. If there is a ring of authenticity regarding the witness of the apostles to the resurrection, it is corroborated by the transformation they underwent as a result of their encounters with the resurrected Christ. In general, the disciples were transformed from fearful to bold, from aimless to missionally focused, and these changes were permanent, for they remained faithful to the end of their lives, through persecution, hardship, and martyrdom. Peter is just one example. After denying his Lord three times, he became the greatest of the Jewish apostolic preachers, and tradition tells us that he was martyred in Rome by being crucified upside down. The intestinal fortitude, the intellectual awakening, the steady, faithful leadership of this man following his post-resurrection encounters with Jesus are in stark contrast with his weak-kneed denials, his lacunae concerning the cruciform nature of the Messiah, and his boastful claims to leadership. The Jewish authorities did not know how to deal with the persuasive and intelligent preaching of Peter even within days of his receiving the Spirit at Pentecost (Acts 4:13).

The transformation of the hardheaded, persecuting, Christ-blaspheming Pharisee Saul into the brilliant, persecuted, Christ-proclaiming apostle Paul is best explained by an unusual encounter, one that is in fact described three times in the book of Acts. The defender supreme of the Jewish religion became the apostle to the Gentiles! This evidence is best explained by an encounter with the living, resurrected Christ.

And then there is the conversion of James the brother of Jesus, who was skeptical about his brother's identity—until he saw the risen Lord. It is interesting that the Gospel writers do not hide the fact that Jesus's brothers did not initially believe in him—interesting because it is a potentially embarrassing fact. One of the hallmarks that authenticates these writers is that they do not mask these realities. Mark (3:21; 6:2–6) and John (7:5) both record

21. Ladd, *A Theology of the New Testament*, 354.

this filial unbelief. First Corinthians 15:7 is Paul's record that James had an encounter with the risen Jesus. The extent of James's transformation is measured by the fact that he became a "pillar" of the early church (Gal. 2:9) and was martyred for his faith. The scholar Reginald H. Fuller suggests that the evidence surrounding James's conversion was so convincing that "it might be said that if there were no record of an appearance to James the Lord's brother in the New Testament we should have to invent one in order to account for his post-resurrection conversion and rapid advance."[22]

The Pauline Witness to the Appearances

According to Gary Habermas and Michael Licona, evidence for the claims of the disciples that Jesus appeared to them lies in "early and independent sources" of three kinds: the testimony of Paul about the disciples, the oral tradition passed on through the early church, and the written works of the early church.[23] Our focus here is on the appearances as validated by Paul. The next section addresses the teaching of the early church.

Paul claimed his own authority as an apostle on the same grounds as those of the other apostles: he had seen the risen Christ. Paul's conversion is itself a strong apologetic for the resurrection, but his attestation of the witness of the other apostles has weight in light of his recognition by the church as an apostle. Paul's authority as an apostle was acknowledged by the apostolic fathers (including Polycarp, Eusebius, and Ignatius), including two who were disciples of the apostles (Polycarp was a disciple of John and cited Paul sixteen times; Papias, also taught by John, cited Paul twice).[24] The book of Acts records that Paul met Peter and the other apostles and fellowshipped with them (Acts 15). And in 1 Corinthians 15, Paul asserts the veracity of his own witness to the resurrection but also corroborates that of the other disciples, including Peter, the Twelve, James the brother of Jesus, "all the apostles," and the "five hundred" (vv. 3–8, 11).

The Centrality of the Resurrection in the Teaching of the Early Church

With regard to the preaching of the resurrection, there is evidence from critical New Testament scholarship that it began very quickly after the resurrection event. For example, James D. G. Dunn, in his book *Remembering*

---

22. Fuller, *The Formation of the Resurrection Narratives*, 37.
23. Habermas and Licona, *The Case for the Resurrection of Jesus*, 51.
24. Habermas and Licona, *The Case for the Resurrection of Jesus*, 258n18.

Jesus, asserts that the words of 1 Corinthians 15:3–4 ("For what I received I passed on to you as of first importance: that Christ died for our sins according to the Scriptures, that he was buried, that he was raised on the third day according to the Scriptures") are an early Christian creed that was formalized and preached within months of Jesus's death.[25] Paul, it is agreed, *received* this tradition three years after his conversion (Gal. 1:18–19) during a visit to Jerusalem, where he met with Peter and James. If, as seems reasonable, the appearance of Jesus to Paul happened about two years after Jesus's resurrection, and the tradition preceded this event, then the tradition was extant within five years of Jesus's resurrection, which is very early by the standards of ancient literature.[26]

Accounts of how the appearances claimed by the apostles were communicated in both the oral tradition and the written works of the early church have been documented carefully and extensively by various scholars.[27] Notably, church fathers Irenaeus and Tertullian both bear witness to the passing on of the resurrection tradition from the apostle Peter to Clement of Rome (AD 35–99), who fellowshipped with and then succeeded Peter in his position as bishop of Rome. The oral tradition was then written down by Clement, who references the resurrection in a letter to Corinth: "Having therefore received a charge, and having been fully assured through the resurrection of our Lord Jesus Christ and confirmed in the word of God with full assurance of the Holy Ghost, they went forth with the glad tidings that the kingdom of God should come."[28] Irenaeus also provides evidence of the fellowship of Polycarp (AD 69–155) with the apostles and the transmission of the faith to him from them. From Clement, Ignatius, and Polycarp, on to the apologists like Justin Martyr, Athenagoras, and Theophilus, and on to the great early theologians like Tertullian, Irenaeus, Hippolytus, and Origen,[29] the resurrection was asserted and assumed as an accepted fact of history, as the pillar of orthodox Christian faith, and as that which distinguished it from dualistic Gnostic thought systems. "Something perfectly new in the history of the universe had happened." Truly, "Christ had defeated death. The door, which had always been locked, had for the very first time been forced open."[30]

25. Dunn, *Remembering Jesus*, 855.

26. For more on this, see Habermas and Licona, *The Case for the Resurrection of Jesus*, 160–61.

27. For example, Habermas and Licona, *The Case for the Resurrection of Jesus*, 53–63; and Wright, *The Resurrection of the Son of God*, 480–532, 587–99.

28. *1 Clement* 42.3, http://www.earlychristianwritings.com/text/1clement-lightfoot.html, accessed October 7, 2020.

29. See Wright, *The Resurrection of the Son of God*, 484–528, and references therein.

30. Lewis, *God in the Dock*, 170.

The care taken in the providence of God over the event of the resurrection of his Son signals its importance. The remainder of this book is an exposition of the resurrection's *meaning*, which may hopefully explain why it was revealed in the careful way it was.

Discussion Questions

1. Do we have proof of the resurrection based on logical positivism? Or do we have strong evidence that the historical facts are best made sense of by what the early church proclaimed: that Jesus rose from the dead (critical realism)?

2. Summarize the evidence with six brief bullet points.

3. Engage in the spiritual practice of resurrection by reading one of the accounts of the resurrection in the Gospels and celebrating its reality with a prayer or song that expresses worship to the risen Son and your response to this great historical reality.

PART 1

Christ's Resurrection Has *Saving* Efficacy

The Resurrection as the Seal of the Atonement

> God will credit righteousness [to] us who believe in him who raised Jesus our Lord from the dead. He was delivered over to death for our sins and was raised to life for our justification.
>
> —Romans 4:24–25

Why does the resurrection of Jesus from the dead in a body matter? The first reason is that it is the climax and the seal of the saving work of Jesus. In fact, the atonement is not complete without the resurrection.

Resurrection and Forensic Justification

Paul makes it clear in the Romans 4 passage quoted above that Christ's death was "for our sins" and that his resurrection was "for our justification." This is what we might call legal or forensic language. Its setting is the divine court of law. The idea is that the God of justice has raised his Son Jesus from the dead to ratify or endorse the atoning efficacy of his vicarious, substitutionary death for sinners. In so doing, God has proved himself to be faithful to his covenant with his people—his commitment to being their God and his commitment to making them his people—by effecting their redemption in a way that was true to his own standards of justice. The resurrection, as Paul speaks of it here, was an expression of the satisfaction of a just God that Jesus had paid justly for the guilt of human sin when he "was delivered over to death for our sins." It was more, however; it was an expression of the Father's delight in the Son as a person in all of his obedience, a sign of the Father's delight in his offering up a sacrifice of infinite worth in his life and on the cross.

In his great sermon on the day of Pentecost in Acts 2, Peter refers to the divine vindication of Jesus through the resurrection event three times: "But God raised him from the dead" (v. 24); "God has raised this Jesus to life" (v. 32); and "God has made this Jesus, whom you crucified, both Lord and Messiah" (v. 36). The emphasis in each case is that *God* raised him. There are occasions in the New Testament in which the subject of the resurrection act is Jesus himself. Those passages stress the reality that he rose again by virtue of his own divine power and authority. For example, in John 10:17, Jesus says, "The reason my Father loves me is that I lay down my life—only to take it up again." In John 11:25, Jesus boldly declares, "I am the resurrection and the life." Resurrection is a capacity the Son of God possesses. But in Romans 4:25, the emphasis is on *God's* action as a declarative and vindicating action that cries out, "Redeemed humanity has been justified, and it has been done justly!" The One who justifies and the just One are the same redeeming God (Rom. 3:26). The resurrection says that God has been righteous in fulfilling his covenant promises to Abraham and his seed. The resurrection says that God has redeemed them in a righteous way; he has provided the reconciliation and redemption needed for them to be in covenant relationship with him. An expression of that unconditional covenant that God undertook is found in Jeremiah 31:34: "For I will forgive their wickedness and will remember their sins no more."

The mystery, of course, is that Jesus himself is God and that since the triune God is the subject of this act of resurrection, Jesus as the Son of God is himself acting in his own resurrection moment. Just as Jesus on the cross in the enactment of atonement is called both the Judge and the Judged,[1] here in resurrection he is both the Raiser and the Raised, the Exalter and the Exalted. But Peter's emphasis in Acts 2, and that of Paul in Romans 4:25, is

---

1. This is the helpful way in which Karl Barth expressed the mystery of the cross, in which the Son was judged for humanity and yet also, as God, participated in the act of judgment upon humanity's sin. Although clearly Jesus was the sin bearer at the cross and experienced the judgment of God for us, as expressed in the cry of dereliction, we must not make the mistake of saying that the Godhead broke up on the cross, for it is impossible for the Trinity to disintegrate. Significantly, the cry was "My God, my God, why have you forsaken me?" and not "My Father, my Father . . ." The entire Trinity was in operation on the cross, making space for humanity and our guilt and sin, and doing away with it justly in the Son. For more on this, see Hastings, *Total Atonement*.

on the divine action carried out upon the Son, who became human to stand in our place, who suffered death and judgment for us. He was vindicated, and humanity in union with him was vindicated, and above all the covenant faithfulness and justice of God were vindicated.

The same inference that the resurrection signaled a complete atonement is made in the first chapter of the book of Hebrews: "After he had provided purification for sins, he sat down at the right hand of the Majesty in heaven" (1:3). The language of the Epistle to the Hebrews may be different from Paul's, perhaps more priestly and definitely more cryptic. It tends to conflate the resurrection and the ascension into one event, for example. The intent is the same, however: a work of atonement has been effected, a sacrifice has been made, and Jesus has risen and is exalted because his sacrifice was all-sufficient, because it was pleasing to God. Another passage in Hebrews emphatically makes the same point that the resurrection/exaltation of Jesus signals the completion and acceptance of the sacrificial atonement of Jesus: "Nor did he enter heaven to offer himself again and again, the way the high priest enters the Most Holy Place every year with blood that is not his own. Otherwise Christ would have had to suffer many times since the creation of the world. But he has appeared once for all at the culmination of the ages to do away with sin by the sacrifice of himself" (Heb. 9:25–26). Paul's Christ-hymn in Philippians 2 has the same trajectory: Jesus "humbled himself by becoming obedient to death—even death on a cross! Therefore, God exalted him to the highest place" (Phil. 2:8–9).

Does resurrection matter? If the justification of sinful humans and a fallen creation matters, then the resurrection matters. If the covenant commitment of God to humanity matters, then the resurrection matters. In a word, the resurrection was God's yes spoken over the Son, and because the Son became one with humanity at the incarnation, the same yes has been pronounced over humanity and the creation that the Son represented. The resurrection speaks the reality of the justification of humanity because Christ, the last Adam and the representative of humanity, participated in our humanity and stood in our place. All who enter into life in Christ by faith and are therefore in union with Christ receive assurance that they are personally justified. All of this we may speak of as the *forensic* aspect of our salvation.

There has been a tendency in recent evangelical theology to downplay the idea of justification as imputed righteousness, despite its roots in the Reformation. For Martin Luther and the Lutherans, the doctrine of justification was the "first and chief article,"[2] and indeed, Luther spoke of it as the "ruler and

---

2. *The Smalcald Articles* 2.1, in Tappert, *The Book of Concord*, 292.

judge over all other Christian doctrines."[3] Justification was entirely the work
of God, and a clear distinction was kept between justification and sanctification, between faith and works. Faith was not thought of as a condition on
which justification was decided, as if human faith could add to what Christ
had accomplished. Rather, faith was considered to be receptive, contributing
no merit at all. In fact, even as something that was merely instrumental in
receiving the gift of justification, faith was itself considered to be a gift from
God given by the regenerating Holy Spirit. John Calvin also kept justification
distinct from sanctification; but more than Luther, he insisted that sanctification came along with justification. They were inseparable—both grounded
in union with Christ, yet distinct from one another.

Over against this, some theologians in the evangelical tradition have made
the move toward conflating justification and sanctification. This is under-
standable, given that the church fathers, even including Augustine, as well as
both the Eastern Orthodox and Roman Catholic traditions, seem to have used
these terms interchangeably. They thought of sanctification as the evidence
of justification, but the sentence of righteousness awaited the final judgment
to be pronounced. There are definitely exceptions to this view among the
Orthodox, and, indeed, since Vatican II there has been a definite recognition
by the Catholic Church of justification by grace through faith. This recognition even led in 1999, after much ecumenical dialogue, to a "Joint Declaration
on the Doctrine of Justification" by the Lutheran World Federation and the
Catholic Church.[4] Some nuanced differences still remain with respect to the
nature of faith and works, and assurance, but much progress has been made
in this ecumenical dialogue toward recovery of justification as a divine declaration of righteousness over those who believe.

There were, in fact, some differences even in how various theologians in the
Reformation and after viewed justification and its relationship to sanctification. What united them is the belief that faith and faith alone is the instrument
by which union with Christ occurs, and that the two graces of justification
and sanctification are given within that union. The distinction between justification and sanctification was also held in common. However, as much as
both Luther and Calvin kept these graces distinct yet inseparable, it is likely
that Calvin was correcting Luther's delight in justification and his perceived
neglect of sanctification when he chose to write about sanctification before
justification in his *Institutes*.

---

3. *Luther's Works*, 2:32.
4. See "Joint Declaration on the Doctrine of Justification" by the Lutheran World Federation and the Catholic Church, 1999, https://www.lutheranworld.org/sites/default/files/Joint
%20Declaration%20on%20the%20Doctrine%20of%20Justification.pdf.

Jonathan Edwards, the New England sage, stressed union with Christ as the prime category in salvation, as Calvin did, but in so doing he almost certainly emphasized sanctification—especially the affections and actions of the believer—as assurance of justification, and at the expense of justification. The matter of the believer's assurance of justification became complicated,[5] especially given Edwards's strong commitment to particularistic election—that is, the election of some to justification and the election of others to damnation.

Karl Barth is in many ways *the* theologian of justification in the Reformed tradition. His answer to the inward turn for assurance that theologians such as Edwards had taken before him (though Barth shows no awareness of Edwards or English-speaking theologians in general), and that Schleiermacher had taken in his time, was to point to Christ, who rose again for our justification. In fact, the point of departure for Barth's entire theology as it is expressed in his *Church Dogmatics* is, as Joseph Mangina has suggested, "the presence of the resurrected [Jesus], the bearer of God's new creation."[6] Not that Barth in any way minimized the importance and the efficacy of the theology of the cross and its implications for our salvation and our suffering as the people of God. But there was for Barth a yes from God that in its finality would drown out the no of human sin and its consequences in creation. This yes was the resurrection and the justification it proclaimed, not just of humanity but of the entire cosmos.

Marvelous commentaries on Barth's doctrine of justification have been offered elsewhere.[7] As Trevor Hart has observed, discussion of creation and covenant is the road in for Barth's discussion of justification.[8] In Barth, the critical article of the church is "not justification as such, but its basis and culmination: the confession of Jesus Christ . . . the knowledge of his being and activity for us and to us and with us."[9] It is by means of the concept of *homoousios* and incarnational theology that Barth links all humanity to Christ and by means of which an objective and real justification is actualized concretely for all humans. The essential meaning of the word *homoousios* (the nominative form of the noun; *homoousion* is the accusative form) is the sharing of substance or essence. God the Son has shared eternally in the same divine essence as the Father and the Spirit. But by means of the incarnation, the Son of God became *homoousios* with humanity—that is, he shared also in

5. For more on this, see Hastings, *Jonathan Edwards and the Life of God*.
6. Mangina, "Mediating Theologies," 436.
7. See, for example, Hart, *Regarding Karl Barth*, 48–73; and McCormack, "*Justitia Aliena*."
8. Hart, *Regarding Karl Barth*, 51. Here Hart cites para. 61 in Barth, *Church Dogmatics*, III/1, 369–70.
9. Barth, *Church Dogmatics*, IV/1, 527.

our humanity. As a result of this sharing in our humanity, all that he was and all that he did as a human person he did vicariously for humanity. He could legitimately stand in our place. His life and death and resurrection were legitimately vicarious for us. Grounding justification in the *homoousios* concept means that who Christ *is*, is our justification. God's yes over humanity—and indeed, over creation—was pronounced in the person of Christ. What transpired in his death and resurrection affects not just our forensic status; it is a reality transition, a new ground for being. In other words, it is ontological. Our justification is a matter of human being. It does entail also the notion of covenant. The first Adam was brought into covenant relationship with God, and neither he nor the nation of Israel to which he gave rise could fulfill that covenant. But God, in the last Adam, provided for himself his own human covenant partner. In Christ, a new humanity is brought about, one that benefits from the new covenant ratified unconditionally in the risen Christ.

In sum, it is the primacy of the incarnate Christ in uniting creation and covenant that paves the way for the Barthian doctrine of justification. The pronunciation of God over creation, "It is good," is deemed by Barth not to refer to aesthetics (as it might in Edwards's thought, for example) nor even to its consonance with some divine blueprint. Rather, Barth maintains that the creation is declared "right" "insofar as it is *capax infiniti*, able to be taken up by God in the incarnation and brought concretely to its *telos* in fulfilment of the covenant."[10] This divine assessment of creation and the new humanity in Christ thus anticipates the ontological aspect of justification that for Barth then determines the forensic aspect—that is, justification as it relates to law, sin, and justice. God, as Creator and Lord of the covenant, has a "right" over his creatures and covenant partners, and in Christ, the elect Man, God establishes the right of humans to existence by putting to death that which contradicts God's purpose in creation, replacing it with the new creation.

Justification is thus a declaration of righteousness not simply with respect to the law but, more fundamentally, with respect to God's purpose for us as creatures, as human beings, and as covenant partners. Sin is an ontological condition primarily, and God judges that condition in Christ on the cross and reveals his sentence on humans by the resurrection so that, just as sin is ontological, so justification is ontological too, resulting in the establishment of new creatures and faithful covenant partners who can truly be assessed as "good." It is common for the triumphant word of Christ as he died, "It is finished" (Greek *tetelestai*), to be interpreted in a juridical way. The work of making atonement for the guilt of our sin was over. While not negating

---

10. Hart, *Regarding Karl Barth*, 51.

this, it is possible to see it first as a declaration that the old humanity was finished with.[11] A new humanity would begin in the resurrected Christ. That ontological reality is the grounding of the forensic one. The key issue is that the existence of this new humanity as good is not one of "potential," or "as if," but one of actualities.[12] Barth's point is that justification, as ontological, means that we are not merely treated as if we were just; we actually *are* just in God's eyes.

Central in Barth's theology of ontological justification is the location of this justification in the history of the incarnate Son of God, Jesus Christ, and then secondarily in the histories of individual men and women. Barth develops this thought in his consideration of the doctrine of election. According to Barth's accounting, in the eternal counsels of God, the Son is the person in the Godhead elected to become human. In the incarnation, he who had been for all eternity *incarnandus*—that is, oriented toward becoming human—actually becomes incarnate. He is the elect Man in whom our being is entwined and through whom God's purposes for humanity are focused.[13] Christ is representative of humanity in an authentic sense, since he has become fully human, sharing in human nature in the reality of the *homoousios*. Christ, the one Man for all humanity, is identified as the One in whom all things were created in the beginning and in whom all things continue to live and move and have their being.[14] Thus we have our existence only in relation to him. This relationship is deepened by the fact that the Creator takes on flesh, becomes a human person, and fulfills his own creative and covenantal purposes. Thus, our identity and being are no longer determined solely by our relationship to God. They are also determined by our relationship to this Man, *Deus incarnatus*, in such a way that "his particular history is the pre-history and post-history of all our individual lives."[15] This is why the source of our assurance of salvation is not ultimately how *our* souls are doing, how *our* affections are ordered or disordered, how *our* actions are ethical, or generally how we are feeling. These things have their place, but our source of assurance that we are righteous in God's sight is the risen, righteous Christ, in whom all has been made right. Over all who are in Christ, God has said yes.

This makes all pursuit of godliness in the process of sanctification evangelical (that is, of the gospel) and not legal. This means that the ordering of our

---

11. John Behr, public lecture, Regent College, Vancouver, BC, May 31, 2021.
12. Barth, *Church Dogmatics*, IV/1, 542–45.
13. Barth, *Church Dogmatics*, II/2, 77–194.
14. Barth, *Church Dogmatics*, III/1, 29–31.
15. Hart, *Regarding Karl Barth*, 59. The quotation is from Barth, *Church Dogmatics*, III/1, 27.

affections and the purifying of our actions is not an ongoing performance to secure the yes of God, his approval. We live in that approval. We bask in his complacent delight in Christ, and therefore in us.

Resurrection and the Filial Grounding of Justification

It has already become clear that the forensic aspect of our salvation is grounded in another aspect of what the atonement and the resurrection mean. The *act* of atonement Christ accomplished cannot be separated from who Christ is as a person—that is, from the *being* of Christ. Separating Christ's work and his person is in fact an old heresy called the Latin heresy. What happens within the *being* of Christ is referred to as the ontological aspect of his death and resurrection (again, "ontological" describes what has to do with being). We may also refer to this as its *filial* aspect. Filial has to do with persons, with family, with parental realities. It is very important to assert that what Christ did for us is dependent on *who he is*, on what took place within his person; and given that he became one with us, this then determined *who he is for us*. The history of his being (*ordo historia*, the order of the history of Jesus) becomes the history of our being (*ordo salutis*, the order of salvation entered into by faith). Whatever was "transacted" happened within his own being and affects our being (because of the *homoousios*) since he became one with us.

The Atonement in the Person of Jesus in Hebrews

Another way to look at this is to say that Christ's body was the temple in which atonement happened. The writer of Hebrews makes this point eloquently when he says, "We have confidence to enter the Most Holy Place by the blood of Jesus, by a new and living way opened for us through the curtain, that is, *his body*" (10:19–20, emphasis added). What this writer has in mind is that the real physical body of Christ is the fulfillment of the tent or tabernacle of the Old Testament where sacrifices were made. His body is the Most Holy Place, for in that body is the very presence of deity, the communion of the triune Godhead.

The sacrifices made on the Day of Atonement are often in the mind of the author of Hebrews. On that day the high priest could enter the Most Holy Place with blood, which he sprinkled seven times before the ark of the covenant and once on the mercy seat over the ark. The word "mercy seat" is the word "propitiation" in the New Testament. For one day a year, one person could pass through the veil and access the presence of God. The message of Hebrews is that now, since Jesus came, every Christian may access the presence of God at any time because in the body of Jesus the atoning sacrifice has been offered to God and in that body satisfaction has been made. That body, since it is the portal of ongoing access to God, must therefore be raised from the dead. In fact, without the resurrection there is no ascension, and if there is no ascension, there is no access to the Father for us. In this sense, Christ's resurrection in a body is *part of* the atonement as well as being the *seal* of what happened at the cross. This is suggested in Romans 4:25, where there is a cadence: "He was delivered over to death *for our* sins and was raised to life *for our* justification."

It is also suggested by the emphasis the writer of Hebrews places on the unending nature of the life of Christ for our salvation. In 7:24–25 he states, "But because Jesus lives forever, he has a permanent priesthood. Therefore he is able to save completely those who come to God through him, because he always lives to intercede for them." Earlier, in verse 16, the writer explains that the efficacy and the power of the high priestly ministry to save are based on "the power of an indestructible life." Clearly salvation—our justification and sanctification—is based on *both* the deep, mysterious work of atonement, in which Jesus offered up the sacrifice of his own life as substitute and satisfaction, *and* the risen, indestructible life of Jesus at the Father's right hand. The former has been completed forever. The latter is ongoing, for in heaven "he always lives to intercede for them" (v. 25).

Hebrews 9:23–28 makes the same connection. This passage actually speaks of three "appearings" that are crucial to our salvation. The first appearing, chronologically speaking, is referenced in verses 25–28: "Nor did he enter heaven to offer himself again and again, the way the high priest enters the Most Holy Place every year with blood that is not his own. . . . But he has appeared once for all at the culmination of the ages to do away with sin by the sacrifice of himself. Just as people are destined to die once, and after that to face judgment, so Christ was sacrificed once to take away the sins of many." On the basis of these statements, there can be no doubt about the completed nature of what transpired on the cross. Notice the implications of the phrase "nor did he enter heaven to offer himself again and again." We think of the cross where Christ offered himself up to God as being on earth, and it was. But the writer of Hebrews speaks of Christ's death on the cross as being an appearing in heaven. For the writer of Hebrews, all is sacred space. Jesus was crucified on earth, but his offering up of himself to God was most definitely an event in heaven, where the triune God enacted the great and complete atonement of our sin and guilt.

But the passage actually begins with a reference to Christ's appearance in God's presence now. This began when he entered heaven itself after his resurrection, at the ascension, and he continues "now to appear for us in God's presence" (Heb. 9:24). This aspect of our salvation, Jesus's ongoing intercession for the people of God, sustaining and restoring and making them holy (10:14), depends absolutely on the resurrection of Jesus from the dead and on the fact that his life is utterly indestructible. He will appear there for us until he comes again, as 9:28 indicates: "He will appear a second time, not to bear sin, but to bring salvation to those who are waiting for him." This is the third appearing. Of course, this appearing, in which our salvation will be perfected, depends also on the resurrection of Jesus!

The Atonement in the Person of Jesus in Peter and Paul

To come back to Peter's Pentecost sermon, the three declarations that God raised Jesus are in fact all meant as a vindication of the *identity* of Jesus as the One he claimed to be: conqueror of death, Lord of life, Lord and Christ. That is, they emphasize his being: who he is, and therefore who he is for us. They emphasize that what happened in his body had ontological significance: death was taken up by Jesus, and it was defeated. Salvation, then, as accomplished by the resurrection, is not just salvation from the penalty of sin (forensic); it is also victory over death (ontological). What Christ does *for us* is ontological in that sense. We are persons taken out of spiritual death and made alive in Christ: "But God raised him from the dead, freeing him from the agony of death, because it was impossible for death to keep its hold on him" (Acts 2:24); "God has raised this Jesus to life, and we are all witnesses of it" (v. 32); "Therefore let all Israel be assured of this: God has made this Jesus, whom you crucified, both Lord and Messiah" (v. 36). In the estimation of sinful human beings, Jesus was fit to be crucified for his high claims. God's estimation of him is seen in his resurrection and exaltation. He truly is the Son of God and the last Adam, destined to rule the cosmos. And all that is true of him is true of us. As a result of the incarnation, his saving history becomes our salvation history. Again, the *ordo historia* becomes the *ordo salutis*.

This ontological nature of the resurrection is in one sense only the culmination of what happened at the incarnation. The story goes that when Karl Barth was asked when he was "saved," he responded by pointing to the day Christ died. But his protégé, T. F. Torrance, went farther back still. He said that he was "born again when Jesus Christ was born of the Virgin Mary." He then added that he "rose again from the virgin tomb, the first-born of the dead."[16] The incarnation and the resurrection are vitally linked. It is not that

16. T. F. Torrance, *The Mediation of Christ*, 86.

Torrance did not believe in the crucial importance of the death of Christ. He was simply pointing to the irreducible ground of the work of the cross in the person of Christ. At the incarnation, the Son of God took on a human nature that was corrupt and sinful. In his taking on that sinful nature, he cleansed it. Some theologians, like John Calvin, believe this happened immediately at the moment of the incarnation by the power of the Holy Spirit. Others, like John Owen and Torrance, believe this happened throughout Jesus's life and was completed at the cross. Irrespective, all could agree with Torrance that Jesus "took my corrupt humanity in his Incarnation, sanctified, cleansed and redeemed it, giving it new birth in his death and resurrection." Torrance goes on to say that "our new birth, our regeneration, our conversion, are what has taken place in Jesus Christ himself, so that when we speak of our conversion or our regeneration we are referring to our sharing in the conversion or regeneration of our humanity brought about by Jesus in and through himself for our sake."[17] The resurrection is therefore the culmination of what began in the incarnation. Jesus's resurrection does not merely justify us in a forensic sense. It is a witness to the fact that human nature has been cleansed and is now made new. This is the core meaning of Paul's opening paragraph in Romans 8:

> Therefore, there is now no condemnation for those who are in Christ Jesus, because through Christ Jesus the law of the Spirit who gives life has set you free from the law of sin and death. For what the law was powerless to do because it was weakened by the flesh, God did by sending his own Son in the likeness of sinful flesh to be a sin offering. And so he condemned sin in the flesh, in order that the righteous requirement of the law might be fully met in us, who do not live according to the flesh but according to the Spirit. (Rom. 8:1–4)

The verdict in this passage of "no condemnation" for those in Christ is not the forensic atoning work of the cross, as in Romans 3:22–26. Here it is an internal work in the very being of the believer. The principle of sin, not its penalty, is Paul's concern here—the power of sin, not its guilt. And how has this reality been accomplished? It has been accomplished in the Son, who took on our fallen nature and cleansed it vicariously for us. This is not to say that Jesus in his own person was sinful, as we will soon clarify. Yet the phrase "in the likeness [Greek *en homoiōmati*] of sinful flesh" should not be misunderstood, as if the flesh Christ assumed at the incarnation was a mere apparition of sinful flesh. That would be the heresy of Docetism, which argued against the notion that Christ had a real human body. This phrase

---

17. T. F. Torrance, *The Mediation of Christ*, 86.

has a parallel in Hebrews 2:17–18: "For this reason he had to be made like [Greek *homoiōthēnai*] them, fully human in every way, in order that he might become a merciful and faithful high priest in service to God, and that he might make atonement for the sins of the people. Because he himself suffered when he was tempted, he is able to help those who are being tempted." As in Romans 8, the author of Hebrews does not have in mind an appearance that isn't real. Rather, it means what the explanatory phrase in Hebrews 2:17 says it means: "fully human in every way." Philippians 2:8 contains a parallel idea: "And being found in appearance [Greek *en homoiōmati*] as a man . . ." We do not assume from this text that Jesus was only in the appearance of a man and not really a man, just as we do not assume that Jesus was merely in the appearance of sinful flesh and not really.

Gregory of Nazianzus, the great Cappadocian theologian, once said with regard to the fallen nature of the humanity of Christ, "That which he has not assumed he has not healed; but that which is united to his Godhead is also saved."[18] God is able to sanctify our humanity by his grace, making it like Christ's, because God has first cleansed and healed human nature in the hypostatic union of the Word made flesh. This is the language of the great exchange that describes our salvation. It is precisely what Paul is expressing in Romans 8:3–4: "For what the law was powerless to do because it was weakened by the flesh, God did by sending his own Son in the likeness of sinful flesh to be a sin offering. And so he condemned sin in the flesh, in order that the righteous requirement of the law might be fully met in us, who do not live according to the flesh but according to the Spirit."

Naturally, an objection arises to this idea. Does this mean that Christ himself as a person was sinful? This is an abhorrent notion to the faithful Christian, and of course it is contradicted many times in the New Testament. Jesus as a person in himself was completely holy, and only a completely holy offering could accomplish our atonement. Hebrews 7:26 speaks categorically to this issue: "Such a high priest truly meets our need—one who is holy, blameless, pure, set apart from sinners, exalted above the heavens." So what does Paul mean in Romans 8:3 by "in the likeness of sinful flesh to be a sin offering"? We are to understand this in a vicarious way. He carried sinful human nature upon himself, not within himself. Theologians call this an anhypostatic as opposed to an enhypostatic relation between sinful nature and the person of Christ. Sin could never penetrate his own unique holy person (enhypostatic),

---

18. Gregory of Nazianzus, *Epistle* 101, "To Cledonius the Priest against Apollinarius," http://biblehub.com/library/cyril/select_letters_of_saint_gregory_nazianzen/to_cledonius_the _priest_against.htm.

and he remained sinless despite carrying our sinful nature upon him. And having purified that sinful nature, either in conception at the incarnation event (as per Calvin, my own preference) or during his life and ultimately in death (Owen, Barth), he was then able to offer up a sin offering for us.

Notice that Paul refers to a "sin offering" here—a "sin offering," as in Leviticus 4:1–5:13, and not a "guilt offering," as in Leviticus 5:14–6:7. In the Old Testament, burnt, grain, and peace offerings brought satisfaction to God as an "aroma pleasing to the Lord" (Lev. 1:9) and have been called "sweet savour" offerings;[19] by contrast, the sin offerings and the guilt offerings together were categorized as "sin offerings." They dealt more directly with the appeasing of divine judgment for sin. The sin offering, however, as opposed to the guilt offering, seems to have been offered when sin was unintentional and acknowledged the innate sinfulness and corruption of humans who sin, sometimes even unintentionally, because they are sinners. Paul, I suspect, chooses "sin offering" to refer to what Jesus did by cleansing us from the principle and power of sin. Elsewhere, he definitely speaks of the death of Christ in a more forensic way, such as in Romans 3:22–26. Here he wishes to emphasize that the vicarious life and death of Jesus changes *persons*. Persons, and not just their legal status before God, are transformed through his person. The resurrection is the sign and seal of both.

The truth of union or participation is absolutely foundational to both of these aspects of our great salvation. The great exchange—Jesus's righteousness for our guilt, his purity for our corruption—depends on two great unions of the Christian gospel. The first is that God the Son became human, fully and truly human. He became one with us, one of us. That union with our humanity is the reason that all that he became, all that he is, and all that he did are *for us*. This incarnational or christological union is the first critical reality that makes our salvation real. It is of course dependent on the reality that Christ, as the Son of God, the Second Person of the Trinity, was in complete eternal union with the Father and the Spirit. His being as the Son was of the same essence as the Father and the Spirit and was eternally in perfect communion with the Father and the Spirit. The historic term in the working out of the doctrine of the Trinity in the fourth-century deliberations of the Nicene church fathers was *homoousios*, which means "of the same essence" and for the Nicene fathers specifically referred to the divine essence. When the Son became human, that reality of *homoousios* did not change. However, as we have noted, a new *homoousios* reality became true when the Son as a

19. This term arises from the King James Version rendering of "aroma pleasing" as "sweet savour."

person assumed our human nature. He was now *homoousios* with humanity, of the same essence and communion with humanity. This is the reason why the purifying of that nature by Jesus became a reality for us humans, and why the resurrection of Christ made real our justification and our cleansing and is the ground of our regeneration. Whatever is true of Christ is true of humanity.

This great ontological reality is really real, and, in fact, it is the most really real reality of our human existence. But this explanation could make it sound like everyone is saved, that universalism is the consequence of Jesus's life and death and resurrection for humanity as an ontological unity. The desire of God *is* for all to be saved (1 Tim. 2:3–6), but the Scriptures also make it abundantly clear in many places that only those who believe may know that they are saved. This presses us to describe another great union that the New Testament reflects. The most important prepositional phrase of the New Testament is "in Christ." Christ's union with humanity is real, but it is only rendered effectual by the work of the Third Person of the Trinity, the Holy Spirit, who makes the church and each believing person one with Christ. The Spirit regenerates us, enabling us to have faith and joining us to Christ, and in this union we become aware of the realities of justification and sanctification. They become real for us. Once in union with Christ—that is, "in Christ"—we enter into what the death and resurrection of Christ have accomplished for us. Calvin summarized this by referring to union with Christ (*unio cum Christo*) and its two main consequences, the twin graces (*duplex gratia*) of justification and sanctification.[20] All of this happens simultaneously—the regeneration by which we are made alive, our union with Christ, the declaration of imputed righteousness or justification, and the impartation of the righteousness of Christ within us, which is sanctification. But the union is the key category in our salvation. J. Todd Billings expresses it this way: "Although the righteousness that the believers come to possess is formally external to themselves, Calvin uses the images of union, adoption, engrafting, and participation to describe this 'wondrous exchange' so that the imputation is not from 'a distance' but from union with Christ."[21]

20. Calvin, *Institutes of the Christian Religion* 3.1.3. See Garcia, *Life in Christ*, 3–21; and Muller, *The Unaccommodated Calvin*, 140–42, for an explanation of the need to keep the two graces connected to union with Christ.

21. Billings, *Calvin, Participation, and the Gift*, 106–7. Hans Boersma comments, "The tension in Calvin's thought seems palpable at this point. After all, for Calvin, God's acceptance of us in justification 'consists in the remission of sins and the imputation of Christ's righteousness' (*Inst*. 3.11.2). It is not clear to me how this external justifying righteousness fits with Calvin's robust theology of union and participation" (Boersma, "Justification within Recapitulation," 190n109). It seems to me that some form of representative headship makes sense of this. We

The resurrection of Jesus is vital in all of this. We can be brought into union only with someone who is alive. All that he accomplished in his death forensically becomes effectual for us in his risen person, and the satisfaction of God with his atoning work, expressed in the resurrection, is vicariously ascribed to us. The undergirding reality that makes the forensic effectual and the satisfaction transferrable is the ontological reality that the Son of God participated in and became one with our humanity at the incarnation and rose again for us three days after he died. *Everything* about him was therefore vicarious for us: his incarnation; his obedient and worshipful life; his death, in which we died; and his resurrection, in which we too rose again spiritually with him and will one day be raised bodily with him.

Discussion Questions

1. Explain the *forensic* (or legal or juridical) consequences of the resurrection of Jesus and how they are grounded in what is *filial* (or ontological) about the Jesus of the resurrection.

2. The phrase "wondrous exchange" beautifully describes the essence of salvation. Our salvation is grounded in our filial union with Christ. He became one with us through the incarnation, and we become one with him by faith through the work of the Spirit. What exactly is exchanged as a result? What does he take from us, and what does he give to us?

3. What does it mean to practice resurrection in light of this chapter? What graces or virtues may be formed in us as the reality of justification through Christ's resurrection settles in our consciousness? See Romans 5:1–11, for example.

---

cannot be represented by Christ and accrue his benefits if we are not one with him by the incarnation (*unio hypostatica*) and by the Spirit (*unio cum Christo*).

3

The Resurrection as the Substance of the Atonement

As we enter the blessed Sabbath, the Lord now rests from all his
works in the tomb before us.
It is finished—it is completed: Behold the man, the true human
being,
the one who loved us till the end,
even if I do not know him, and cannot comprehend him.

—John Behr[1]

The emphasis in this chapter shifts from resurrection as a sign of a completed atonement, forensically speaking, to reflection on the possibility that the resurrection is in itself an atoning act. This possibility arises from the reality that the work of the atonement was accomplished within the *person* of Christ. The atonement is ontological before it is forensic or juridical, logically speaking. The reality of who Christ is, including in his death and resurrection, must always be linked with who we are. He became one with us by the incarnation. He, the divine Second Person of the Trinity, of the same essence (*homoousios*) with the Father and the Spirit, entered into union or

1. John Behr, "It Is Finished!," St. John the Wonderworker (blog), April 10, 2015, https://www.saintjohnwonderworker.org/blog-articles-news/it-is-finished-by-fr-john-behr.

participation with our humanity, sharing the same essence (*homoousios*) with humanity. This oneness with our humanity means that whatever is true of his history becomes true of our history by grace. His history involved death and resurrection. Our history is a participation in his death and resurrection. By his death he died *for our sin*, and by his death he *put sin to death* in himself. Therefore, since he died *for our sin* as our vicarious substitute, we have been freed from sin's guilt. And since he died *to sin*, we have been freed from sin's power. These realities were shared in the previous chapter.

But what of the reality that Christ rose from the dead in glorious triumph and that he did so vicariously for us? If the history of Jesus is our history, what does our participation in his resurrection mean? A resurrection is something radically ontological. His resurrection therefore means our spiritual resurrection, what the New Testament calls regeneration; and in a day to come it will mean our bodily resurrection. Paul speaks clearly about the first of these realities, our regeneration, in Ephesians 2 in a participatory context. At the end of chapter 1, he speaks of the death and resurrection of Jesus, the Head of the church: "That power is the same as the mighty strength he exerted when he raised Christ from the dead and seated him at his right hand in the heavenly realms" (Eph. 1:19–20). And then in chapter 2 he links what happened to Jesus to what happens to those who believe in him: "As for you, you were dead in your transgressions and sins. . . . But because of his great love for us, God, who is rich in mercy, made us alive with Christ even when we were dead in transgressions—it is by grace you have been saved. And God raised us up with Christ and seated us with him in the heavenly realms in Christ Jesus" (Eph. 2:1, 4–6). Paul's answer to the wrath of God that is expressed against sin in Romans 3 is to speak of the propitiating death of Christ for us, but here in Ephesians 2, his approach is ontological rather than juridical. The second reality that Christ's resurrection secures is our bodily resurrection at the second coming of Christ, a topic we will postpone until chapter 6.

The point of this chapter is that the resurrection of Jesus included within it the defeat of death in his humanity and therefore the defeat of death for our humanity. In that sense, the resurrection was atoning because inherent within Christ's resurrection was the defeat of death—that is, the defeat of spiritual and eternal death for us also. In other words, the resurrection is crucial to the ontological nature of the atonement; it is not just a sign of the accomplishment of the juridical aspect of the atonement.

When Jesus rose again and showed himself to his disciples, his being was of a new order. He was unmistakably still the same Jesus. The fact that Thomas could place his finger in the wounds in Jesus's hands and side (John 20:24–28) is evidence of the *continuity* of personhood between the pre- and the post-resurrection Jesus. But there is also *discontinuity*. Now Jesus has a body that can pass through walls and ascend into heaven. Now his body is more spiritual in orientation, as 1 Corinthians 15:44 suggests, although it is still clearly a body and not a spirit. Spirits do not have scars, and spirits do not cook fish (John 21:9–14). Even today Jesus is a man, and he has a body, at the right hand of the Father as our Great High Priest. When he returns at the second coming, as Luke assures us, he will come literally and personally and bodily (Acts 1:11). And when he comes, all of redeemed humanity will also be resurrected in him, in real bodies. We are alive in him.

It becomes very clear as the New Testament unfolds that Jesus, as an embodied human person, was more than a mere individual person. Certainly, he was an irreducibly unique and idiosyncratic person like every other person, a person located in a particular place and culture and time (his enhypostatic nature). But he was also a representative or communal person who represented all humanity (his anhypostatic nature). His resurrection affected the entire human race, ontologically speaking.[2] Paul speaks of Jesus as "the last Adam," and both by inference and explicitly he contrasts the last Adam with "the first Adam." These persons were both collective or communal persons in such a way that what they did affected all humanity. In 1 Corinthians 15:20–23, Paul explains the corporate nature and effect of the last Adam in bringing life to all humanity through his conquest of death in resurrection: "But Christ has indeed been raised from the dead, the firstfruits of those who have fallen asleep. For since death came through a man, the resurrection of the dead comes also through a man. For as in Adam all die, so in Christ all will be made alive. But each in turn: Christ, the firstfruits; then, when he comes, those who belong to him." It becomes abundantly clear that because of Jesus's union with all humanity, which became a reality at the incarnation, and because, therefore, of his representative nature as the new Head of humanity, and by virtue of the fact that the resurrection spells victory over death, the resurrection of Jesus is in fact atoning.

There are three important theological themes inherent in this great passage: participation in humanity, recapitulation, and the *Christus Victor* aspect of the atonement.

2. Oliver D. Crisp has discussed the way in which "Adam's posterity are somehow metaphysically one entity with Adam such that Adam's sin just is the sin of the whole of humanity," and, by implication, how Christ's obedience and resurrection are in fact the obedience and resurrection of humanity, in "Federalism vs. Realism," 55. See also Crisp, "On Behalf of Augustinian Realism."

Participation in Humanity

The idea that Christ represents the new humanity is, as already suggested, a consequence of his *participation* in humanity. He can act representatively for all humanity because he is one with it. However, he can do so because from all eternity, as the Son, he was destined to become incarnate. He was predestined to be the one true human for humanity. Although the first Adam is important in the unfolding of the drama of redemption, there can be no doubt that Jesus, as the last Adam, was God's first thought in connection with humanity. Jesus was not a plan B, not an emergency rescuer of an initial plan gone wrong. Texts such as Acts 2:23 ("This man was handed over to you by God's deliberate plan and foreknowledge; and you, with the help of wicked men, put him to death by nailing him to the cross") and Revelation 13:8 ("the Lamb who was slain from the creation of the world") confirm this. The words "the last Adam" may be translated "the *eschatos* Adam," "the Adam of the eschaton," "the Adam of the fulfillment of the ages," or "the Adam on whom the redeeming purpose of God was always focused." Jonathan Edwards once expressed the idea that what God reveals last he often intended first.[3] For example, Edwards states his belief that the covenant of God with the second Adam, though only revealed after the breaking of the covenant with the first Adam, was "entered into first in order of time" only between God as lawgiver and the Son as man's surety and representative. Thus he concludes, "The covenant of redemption was the covenant in which God the Father made over an eternal reward to Christ mystical, and therefore was made only with Christ the head of the body."[4]

In sum, then, Christ's participation in humanity helps us to understand how his resurrection becomes our resurrection. This is accentuated by an understanding that this is what God intended within his premundane, eternal councils, when God determined to be *for* the humanity he would create and when he determined to become human for us in Christ.

Recapitulation

There is another way of seeing this representative nature of Christ for us in his saving history, including the resurrection. The apostle Paul, in his Letter to the Ephesians, speaks of the reconciling history of Jesus as having the aim

3. Edwards, *Dissertation I*, 405.
4. Edwards, "Observations concerning the Scripture Oeconomy of the Trinity and the Covenant of Redemption," 93.

"to bring unity to all things in heaven and on earth under Christ" (Eph. 1:10). The word for "to bring unity" is *anakephalaioō* in Greek, or *recapitulare* in Latin. God's purpose in uniting all things in heaven and on earth in the headship of the incarnate Christ once more accentuates the primacy of the last Adam within God's eternal purpose. This passage led to the development of the important doctrine of recapitulation, especially in the theology of Irenaeus (AD 130–202), a very influential church father from Lyons in France. Hans Boersma has made the comment that Irenaeus's "theology of recapitulation (objectively speaking) and our participation in God through Christ (subjectively speaking) . . . together form the proper framework within which to understand Irenaeus's doctrine of justification."[5] Irenaeus served the church well in his defense of the faith against Gnosticism, which devalued matter and the human body, and Marcionism, which discounted the Old Testament as divine revelation. Whereas the Gnostics spoke of Jesus as merely "the vessel of Christ" and denied that the Son of God ever really became the Son of Man, "Irenaeus counters with a ringing affirmation that all created things are united (or, are recapitulated) in the incarnation, in Jesus Christ."[6] As Irenaeus stated,

> There is, therefore, as we have shown, one God the Father and one Christ Jesus our Lord, who comes through every economy and *recapitulates in Himself all things*. Now, man too, God's handiwork, is contained in this "all." So He also recapitulated in Himself humanity; the invisible becoming visible; the incomprehensible, comprehensible; the impassible, passible; the Word, man. Thus He *recapitulated in Himself all things*.[7]

This, for Irenaeus, means that humanity, all of it, has been ontologically recapitulated in Christ and is therefore "justified," though personal appropriation of recapitulation is necessary for this to be effectual. The role of the resurrection in this "justification" is important. Since all human beings share the human nature of Jesus Christ, by his resurrection all human nature has been restored. There is a link between the resurrection and the adoption of humans to become the children of God, a link that is suggested in passages such as Galatians 4:4–6; Romans 1:3–4; and 8:14–17.

However, the only complication is that the content of the term "justified," for Irenaeus, is not in any manner forensic. The term's meaning is *solely* ontological. It means that humanity has been adopted, regenerated,

5. Boersma, "Justification within Recapitulation," 170.
6. Boersma, "Justification within Recapitulation," 171.
7. Irenaeus of Lyons, *Against the Heresies* 3.16.6 (trans. Unger, 82 [emphasis original]).

deified, and made holy in order one day to see the beatific vision and be glorified. It does not mean to be imputed with an alien righteousness. The resurrection is crucial in Irenaeus's recapitulation theology. However, the "great exchange" phrase so central in historical soteriology, for Irenaeus, does not include juridical or imputed righteousness. It means the exchange of life for death, of adoption for alienation, of maturity for immaturity. The human nature has been made new through the resurrection of the risen Head. Irenaeus would insist that although this has been accomplished for all humanity, it is only efficacious for those who believe, who participate through faith in what has been accomplished. It is that faith that is imputed and imparted to the convert, not righteousness of a forensic kind. Faith is the gift.

As Boersma sums it up, "Justification is a subset of our deifying union with God in and through the recapitulation of humanity in Christ."[8] Clearly, however, this "justification" is not that which Luther espoused and delighted in. Could these two concepts be compatible—that is, the concept of ontological change from death to life, from alienation to adoption, and the concept of juridical justification? Interestingly, Boersma seems to view the ontological nature of recapitulation and salvation as being over against the juridical, as if it were an either/or issue. Yet the ontological does not, it seems to me, eliminate the juridical. It is freely acknowledged that the ontological comes first, from a logical perspective, and in this chapter we are celebrating the ontological and salvific nature of the resurrection. But surely these concepts are not antithetical or contradictory? Is this not Calvin's point? Union *of* Christ with humanity first, so that his history is our history. Union *with* Christ first, logically, and then righteousness imputed and sanctification. Irenaeus is right in his assertion that justification comes within recapitulation and that it works because of participation. But it seems to me that missing the forensic altogether is a failure on Irenaeus's part to be faithful to Paul at various important points (Rom. 3:22–26; 5:1, for example).[9]

It is possible to delight in the ontological reality of what the resurrection has done for humanity—our regeneration, our adoption, our assurance of future resurrection, the power for spiritual transformation—and to enter these

---

8. Boersma, "Justification within Recapitulation," 190.

9. Irenaeus's viewpoint is a consequence of an interpretation of the fall as indicating immaturity rather than grave sin and guilt. It is also a consequence of how he viewed the law, a matter that Boersma explains very well. The difficulty in Irenaeus's view, or at least with this interpretation of Irenaeus, is its internal contradiction. Remission and justification are spoken of as "juridical" categories, serving to get "the initial project of 'Christification' back on track" (Boersma, "Justification within Recapitulation," 178), but then the juridical nature of these terms is denied.

realities by faith, knowing that the risen Christ, who has received the yes of God, has also atoned for our sins. Hebrews 10:14 speaks precisely of both of these aspects of what has been transacted and effected in the lives of believers in Christ: "For by one sacrifice he has *made perfect forever* those who are *being made holy*" (emphasis added).

Christus Victor

There is another facet to the ontological change that Christ brought about by his death and especially his resurrection. The notion that the Son participated in humanity, and is the recapitulated Head of humanity, contains within it a view of the atonement that has for centuries been called the *Christus Victor* (Christ the Victor) model. It is my conviction that the principal *theory* of the atonement that undergirds the various rich motifs and *models* of the atonement is participation—that is, the participation of the Son in our humanity.[10] In the last chapter, the primary models inferred or spoken of relate to the juridical or forensic aspect of the atonement. These are the *substitutionary* (Aquinas, Luther, Calvin) and the *satisfaction* (Anselm) models, both of which are sacrificial in their nature. Together they could be called the *Christus Vicarious* (Christ the Substitute) models. These models are absolutely necessary for the expiation and propitiation of guilt and of sin. They rely completely on the ontological reality that the Son became one with us so that our sin may be taken away, that righteousness may be imputed to us, and that we might become one with him.

The *Christus Victor* model stresses the cross and the resurrection as a victory over sin and Satan and death. This model does not contradict the vicarious models. In fact, it seems to me that they are interdependent. For example, in an important text for this model, the writer of Hebrews, after belaboring the importance of the incarnation for the atonement of Christ, states, "Since the children have flesh and blood, he too shared in their humanity so that by his death he might break the power of him who holds the power of death—that is, the devil—and free those who all their lives were held in slavery by their fear of death" (Heb. 2:14–15). What is celebrated is the breaking of the power of the devil and therefore of death. But implicit in this is the core nature of the devil; he is the accuser (Rev. 12:10). He cannot accuse humans anymore because Christ has died for their sins. In the wider context of this epistle, it becomes clear that it is the once-for-all efficacious

10. I have contended for this in *Total Atonement*, and also for the fact that there are many models and only one theory.

sacrifice of Christ that atoned for sin, and it is this that left the devil bereft of accusations and no longer holding the power of death. The writer of Hebrews conflates the death and the resurrection and the ascension of Christ into one great atoning act of God in Christ, and the consequence is that, yes, the ontological is true—Christ has become one with us, and by his resurrection we need fear death no longer; and yes, the juridical is also true because of the ontological—"We have been made holy through the sacrifice of the body of Jesus Christ once for all" (Heb. 10:10).

Colossians 2:13–15, that other great passage on the *Christus Victor* nature of the atonement, further illustrates the interdependence of this model with the substitutionary and satisfaction models: "When you were dead in your sins and in the uncircumcision of your flesh, God made you alive with Christ. He forgave us all our sins, having canceled the charge of our legal indebtedness, which stood against us and condemned us; he has taken it away, nailing it to the cross. And having disarmed the powers and authorities, he made a public spectacle of them, triumphing over them by the cross." The statements of victory and of ontological change ("made you alive," "disarmed the powers and authorities" [vv. 13 and 15]) form a sandwich around the central statements, which are most definitely of a juridical nature: "He forgave us all our sins, having canceled the charge of our legal indebtedness, which stood against us and condemned us."

We therefore celebrate the victory of the cross and the resurrection, but we need not do so at the expense of the great reality that our sins have been removed from the memory of God, and that all the satisfaction the Son offered up to the Father is the satisfaction with which he views us now. But let us not, on the other hand, hold back in celebrating what the ontological participation of God in humanity, which made the juridical possible, means for us. The resurrection makes us new creatures. It makes us the sons and daughters of God. It removes the specter of death from us in an ultimate sense. In addition to leading to celebration, however, a robust ontological perspective leads us to understand that even in the part we have to play to appropriate all this, we owe everything to Christ. In this vein, T. F. Torrance said the following:

> In a profound and proper sense, therefore, we must speak of Jesus Christ as constituting in himself the very substance of our conversion, so that we must think of him as taking our place even in our acts of repentance and personal decision, for without him all so-called repentance and conversion are empty. Since a conversion in that truly evangelical sense is a turning away from ourselves to Christ, it calls for a conversion from our in-turned

notions of conversion to one which is grounded and sustained in Christ Jesus himself.[11]

This is a timely word for our age of individualism and anthropocentrism.

Ordo Historia and Ordo Salutis

An appropriate place to end this chapter is to remember that the participation of the church and the personal believer in the history of Jesus Christ, the *ordo historia*—his death, resurrection, ascension, and session—is that which enables the *ordo salutis* (the order of salvation). But even our participation in his history is engraced and is a small echo of his great participation in our humanity for us. The good news of the gospel is that his history is also our history, but his history is paramount. As an individual discovers the reality of the resurrection of Jesus and humanity's resurrection, and that they are already justified in Christ, they are not merely in a "state" but rather are plunged into a reality transition. They are called to live in the awareness that true reality is the supreme reality of what has taken place in the history of Jesus.

Justification, as Karl Barth viewed it, is therefore an alien history to our own but *which we discover to be our own*, and "which projects us into the crisis of eschatological transition, living out the Kingdom of God in the midst of the world, living by faith in that reality *which lies beyond our experience*, but which stands over against us as our reality nevertheless."[12] As Trevor Hart has stated, "Precisely what we must not do . . . is simply to ask after our own intrinsic or natural state, what we *are* considered in and of ourselves apart from Jesus Christ, since reality proper, the 'really real,' is not to be found here."[13] Some self-examination of the authenticity of our faith and of our inner life and state is biblical and necessary. But the obsession ought not to be ourselves but Christ, who stood in our place and is for us. If this is true, even someone as great as Jonathan Edwards seems to veer a little off-center in his approach to justification and conversion, which too greatly stresses our human self-examination to ensure that we are really of the faith.

Edwards's assumptions and those of Barth concerning reality differ, and this difference goes back to the critical issue of the determining hermeneutic. For Barth, reality is christologically understood: it is our ontological related-ness to Jesus Christ, whose history—death and resurrection—is ours. This

---

11. T. F. Torrance, *The Mediation of Christ*, 86.
12. Hart, *Regarding Karl Barth*, 62 (emphasis added).
13. Hart, *Regarding Karl Barth*, 60. See also Webster, "'The Firmest Grasp of the Real.'"

would explain the joy of the disciples in John 20 when they saw their risen Lord with nail-scarred hands!

Discussion Questions

1. What does it mean to say that the *ordo historia* of Jesus becomes the *ordo salutis* of the believer?

2. There is a tension in this chapter between the realization that our justification in the risen being of the victorious and recapitulated Christ "lies beyond our experience" (because it is a matter of being—his, and ours in his) and the fact that those who enter into union with the living Christ do indeed experience and indeed must experience the signs of regeneration. How does a focus on Christ and who he is for us contribute to our assurance of salvation? How does our faith and what we experience of sanctification contribute to our assurance?

3. What does it mean to nurture our life in the risen Christ in both the contemplative way of looking away to Christ and in the self-examining or introspective way? What spiritual practices, ecclesial and personal, might foster these ways of being?

4

The Resurrection as the Ground of Participation in the Life of God

Before long, the world will not see me anymore, but you will see me. Because I live, you also will live. On that day you will realize that I am in my Father, and you are in me, and I am in you.

—John 14:19–20

On the basis that the Son of God was made one with humanity at his incarnation, we have established that his death and resurrection event is efficacious in bringing about our regeneration and establishing our justification. The great exchange that is at the heart of the gospel involves our reception of life in place of death and righteousness in place of guilt. We have also established that although Christ's atoning and reconciling work is sufficient for all humanity, there is a need to appropriate it by faith. We may think of this as the participation of believing humans in the risen Christ (*unio cum Christo*). This is a relational participation that is effected by the Holy Spirit, who awakens us from spiritual death, enabling us to have faith and uniting us to Christ. As established earlier, this union with Christ has two immediate consequences, the twin graces (*duplex gratia*) of justification and sanctification: being imputed with righteousness (justification) and being actually *made* righteous in our beings (sanctification), which is the focus of this chapter.

The word "sanctification" is sometimes used in the New Testament in a fully completed sense that makes it, in these usages, very close in meaning to justification. The emphasis in these passages is on our having been declared "holy" (*positional* sanctification) from the moment of conversion, in addition to our having been declared "righteous" (justification). For example, in 1 Corinthians 6, after indicating a number of sins that used to characterize the converts in libertine Corinth, Paul says in verse 11, "And that is what some of you were. But you were washed, you were sanctified, you were justified in the name of the Lord Jesus Christ and by the Spirit of our God." Both realities are true instantaneously and contemporaneously for believers: they are sanctified wholly and justified fully. That act of God by which he sets apart believers for himself in this way—"set apart" is the root meaning of the word "sanctified"—is the ground on which God then continues to act to actually make them holy in their lives. This is their *progressive* sanctification. This involves their minds, their affections, their bodies, their sexuality, their all. In this chapter we ask the pertinent question, What does the resurrection have to do with our actual transformation as persons—that is, our progressive sanctification?

The relationship between justification and sanctification has been considered in various ways in the Christian tradition. Together they are spoken of as *theosis*, or deification, a term that refers to the transformation of believers by grace into the divine fullness in a way that preserves the Creator-creature distinction. It has to do with becoming like God in character as a result of being in union and communion with Christ. This is sometimes referred to as our Christification, our becoming like Christ. Although justification has sometimes been conflated with progressive sanctification in the Orthodox and Catholic traditions, I believe that John Calvin had it right when he kept these two graces distinct in their character yet inseparable, in that they are both derived from our union with Christ. Revisiting Hebrews 10:14, "For by one sacrifice he has made perfect forever those who are being made holy," where "made perfect forever" in the perfect tense (an action in the past with ongoing consequences) describes justification, and "being made holy" in the continuous present tense describes sanctification,[1] our focus in this chapter

---

1. I am aware of a different interpretation of Heb. 10:14 offered by respected New Testament scholars such as F. F. Bruce and George H. Guthrie, who suggest that the phrase "being made holy" in Hebrews refers frequently to "cleansing from sin" by the atoning work of Christ (2:11; 9:13–14; 10:10, 29; 13:12), so that the sense is that we are "made righteous," grounded upon his cleansing sacrifice. The phrase in the present passive participle then has the sense of the "timeless" cleansing of God's people from sin. See Guthrie, *Hebrews*, 357, 421; and Bruce, *The Epistle to the Hebrews*, 360. This is not the unanimous judgment of scholars of Hebrews, however. William Lane, for example, speaks of this phrase as implying the "definite

is the latter: how we are made holy, and what the resurrection of Jesus in particular has to do with this.

Following the *ordo historia–ordo salutis* pattern, sanctification as the second of the twin graces must be considered in light of the union of believers in Christ and, in particular, their participation in his death and resurrection. Although our focus in this chapter is sanctification in light of the resurrection of Christ, we cannot isolate his resurrection from his death. A number of New Testament passages that speak about sanctification are patterned after our union with Christ in death and resurrection. They call us into a mortification/vivification pattern that is shaped around the history of Jesus in death and resurrection (e.g., Rom. 6; Eph. 4:20–32; Phil. 3:10–11; Col. 3). Therefore, the most important dynamic in sanctification is the baptismal pattern of union with Christ in death and resurrection.

There are actually three dynamics that make the pursuit of transformation a pursuit that is in accordance with the good news of the gospel—that is, evangelical rather than legal, joyful rather than a futile and grim grind. These are justification, active communion with Christ, and contemplation of the risen Christ.

Justification

The first dynamic is the first of the two graces that result from Christ's union with humanity and our union with Christ—that is, justification: the reality that is already God's reality, that we are in Christ already righteous, that God's yes is already upon us, that we are not striving for justification but pursuing holiness *from* it. There is a real striving, a real effort to be made in putting off the old patterns and behaviors of our lives and cultivating the graces of Christ by the power of the Holy Spirit. But it is not a striving for a holy grail of the acceptance of God. We have that already, if we have truly believed and are showing signs of divine life, a hunger for God and for righteousness, a hatred of sin. It is a striving from the great first reality of the gospel that

---

consecration" of the new covenant people of God. This involves character and "consecration to the service of God." The saints both have been "decisively purged" and are now being made holy by Christ (Lane, *Hebrews*, 136). My own thought is that it would not be surprising if the structure of this verse is an echo of the new covenant as it is recited in Heb. 8, which involves both decisive forgiveness ("I will forgive their wickedness and will remember their sins no more" [v. 12]) and inward transformation ("I will put my laws in their minds and write them on their hearts. . . . They will all know me" [vv. 10–11]). Even if Bruce and Guthrie are right about this interpretation, the truth of the twin graces is present elsewhere in the book of Hebrews and certainly in the entire New Testament.

in Christ we have already been declared righteous. Nothing can assail that position. It has been secured by the resurrection of Jesus for us. It is true that we still sin, but sin in our lives as Christians does not change our being, our standing before God. It changes our *state*, our enjoyment of fellowship with the Father, and when we confess that sin, our fellowship with God, not our standing before God, is restored (1 John 1:7–2:2).

The way in which Paul expresses this already justified but not yet fully sanctified tension in Colossians 3 is helpful. He begins with the declaration of a fait accompli: "Since, then, *you have been raised with Christ*, set your hearts on things above, where Christ is, seated at the right hand of God. Set your minds on things above, not on earthly things. For *you died, and your life is now hidden with Christ in God*. When Christ, who is your life, appears, then you also will appear with him in glory" (Col. 3:1–4, emphasis added). We live the Christian life *from* the reality that in Christ we have already been raised and that our lives are now hidden with Christ in the very life of the triune God. What we really are as justified people—who are destined, therefore, to be glorified people—is not apparent to others down here on earth. We look like ordinary people, but who we are really, the true us, is hidden in the presence of God in the person of our Great High Priest, who is in turn with the Father and the Spirit in perfect communion.

Active Communion with Christ

This leads us to the second great dynamic that keeps the pursuit of holiness evangelical and hope-filled. It is the dynamic of active communion with Christ in his death and resurrection such that the power of the resurrection is accessed. This communion with Christ allows us to access what is true because we are in union with him, in his death and resurrection. This communion is enabled by the power of the Holy Spirit, the same Holy Spirit whose power was unleashed in the bodily resurrection of Jesus. Following the logic of Colossians 3:1–4, the next section exhorts the people of God to actually and actively live out on earth the life of communion with Christ in heaven. The life that is hidden with Christ in God shows up in practices that correspond to the death and resurrection of Christ. Paul says in verse 5, "*Put to death*, therefore, whatever belongs to your earthly nature: sexual immorality, impurity, lust, evil desires and greed, which is idolatry" (emphasis added). This is an exhortation that may be called *mortification* of vices. If we are one with Christ, and he has died to sin, then we too have died to all forms of sin. Therefore, we must actively mortify, or put to death, all sinful tendencies and actions, as Paul describes in verses 6–9.

But then Paul moves in verse 10 to the theme of the risenness of Christ and our risenness in him, reminding us that we have "put on the new self, which is being renewed in knowledge in the image of its Creator." Our communion with the risen Christ, in whom our lives are hidden in God, shows up in the cultivation of virtues, in what God intended for humans made in his image, humans becoming fully human. These virtues are described in verses 12–14: "Therefore, as God's chosen people, holy and dearly loved, clothe yourselves with compassion, kindness, humility, gentleness and patience. Bear with each other and forgive one another if any of you has a grievance against someone. Forgive as the Lord forgave you. And over all these virtues put on love, which binds them all together in perfect unity."

Notice a few important aspects of this pursuit of the sanctified life in communion with Christ.

1. Its *pattern* conforms to the saving history of Jesus. Since we are in union with him and his history, we commune with him in both his death, mortifying the deeds of the flesh, and his resurrection, vivifying the graces of the Spirit.

2. Although this is first and foremost God's work in us, there is *real human agency*. The verbs Paul uses here are all active, which corresponds very well with what Paul expresses in Philippians 2:12–13: "Therefore, my dear friends, as you have always obeyed—not only in my presence, but now much more in my absence—*continue to work out your salvation* with fear and trembling, for *it is God who works in you* to will and to act in order to fulfill his good purpose" (emphasis added). The mode of sanctification is responsive to God's work in us, but it is active: God's work in us needs to be worked out by us. The compatibility of the work of God and the work of believers here is one that may be described as asymmetric concursus: God works, and we work in his working. It is mysterious but real. Sanctification therefore involves our action; it is consciously dependent on the risen Christ and the Holy Spirit, but it is action nevertheless. It is not graceless action but engraced action, a living out of the reality of union with Christ through communion with him by the Spirit in the life of the church and in personal devotion. A biblical and Reformation-based understanding of sanctification is one that may thus be described as Augustinian activism, over against other views of sanctification that involve a passive or quietist approach. This view says that there will always be hard work to do, given the depth and strength of sin in human lives. It says that the embodied spiritual practices that involve mortification and vivification will be needed all the way until we see Jesus.

3. The *core* of resurrection life—or sanctification, or the virtues that are to be pursued or "put on"—is love. This makes the context of resurrection life unavoidably communal and specifically ecclesial, as we shall see below.

Paul spells this out with various synonyms in Colossians 3:12–14: "Clothe yourselves with compassion, kindness, humility, gentleness and patience. Bear with each other and forgive one another if any of you has a grievance against someone. Forgive as the Lord forgave you. And over all these virtues put on love, which binds them all together in perfect unity." This is very much in keeping with what Jesus taught when he was asked about what he considered to be the greatest commandment. His answer was to love our God and to love our neighbor (Matt. 22:37–39). This was a summation of the Ten Commandments and served to bring continuity between the old and new covenant communities of the people of God. Justification from the curse of a broken law was accomplished by Christ for both communities, and the goal of their ethical life was in both cases love guided by the Ten Commandments.

The primacy of love as a virtue is also expressed a number of times in the Epistles. For example, when Paul lists the virtues of the Spirit, the "fruit" of life in the Spirit, the first one is love, and it is highly possible that the rest are simply a description of the life of love (Gal. 5:22–23). Similarly, Peter, in his second epistle, which begins precisely with a description of the Christian life as "[participation] in the divine nature" (2 Pet. 1:4) and assurance therefore that "his divine power has given us everything we need for a godly life through our knowledge of him" (1:3), offers a list of virtues that moves toward a climax, which is love: "For this very reason, make every effort to add to your faith goodness; and to goodness, knowledge; and to knowledge, self-control; and to self-control, perseverance; and to perseverance, godliness; and to godliness, mutual affection; and to mutual affection, love" (1:5–7).

4. The *goal* of resurrection life, or sanctification, is to recover our identity as those made in the image of the Creator God. Paul says this in Colossians 3:10: "Put on the new self, which is being renewed in knowledge in the image of its Creator." What does this mean? The theology of the image of God is important. This epistle makes it abundantly clear that the ultimate image of God on earth is the man Christ Jesus, "the image of the invisible God" (Col. 1:15). The first Adam was made in the image of God, but that image became seriously marred by his sin. The image was not erased, however, because even post-fall, God points to his having made humans in his image as the basis of his ethical appeal for humans to treat human life as sacred, an appeal against the killing of our fellow humans (Gen. 9:4–6). On this basis we may say that the image of God is shared by every human being in a non-degreed[2] way such that every human life is to be treated as sacred.

---

2. The image of God can for regenerated persons be considered as "degreed" in that they progressively recover the fullness of the image in Christ (2 Cor. 3:18). Yet there is a fundamental

The concept of the image given to the first Adam involved three basic aspects. First, it involved relationality between God and humans—after all, God was imaging himself in us so that we might be in covenantal relationship with him, and with each other as male and female (Gen. 1:27). Second, and in the service of the relational, the image meant something ontological, at minimum the mental and moral capacity of humans to be in relationship with God. And third, also in the service of the relational, it meant something functional: these image bearers of God were representing him on earth and continuing the work of creation by caring for the earth through work and by populating it through marriage and rearing families (Gen. 1:28–2:25).

Recovering the image of God in Christ as his new humanity means entering afresh into all these aspects of the image. On the one hand, it is clear that the intended telos or goal of our resurrection life, our sanctification, is to become more like Christ, who is the image. We do this through communion with him, by participating in his image. This has sometimes been called our Christification. But we should not think of this as somehow making us something more than human. Being like Christ, recovering the image of God by increasing our knowledge of him, makes us fully human—not superhuman, not transhuman, but human. The end goal of our resurrection life in Christ, which will come to fruition when we see Christ face-to-face (1 John 3:2), is to be morally conformed to his image, and even perhaps to have a resurrection body like his, which is oriented toward a heaven-come-to-earth existence. The end goal is not to be an angel or anything other than a human being.

There were stretches in my Christian life, especially when I was younger, when somehow I was taught, or maybe I just imagined, that progress in the Christian life meant avoiding all that is human. Study my Bible all day long. Go to church services three times on a Sunday and once during the week. Meditate all week on the Scriptures so that I will have something to share in the Lord's Supper gathering on Sunday. Never go out on a Saturday night, but instead prepare my heart and mind for Sunday's gathering. Avoid all contact with unbelieving people who might tempt me away from the "spiritual and separated" life I was living. Attend Bible conferences with four sermons, each an hour long, on New Year's Day and Easter. Avoid the dirty work of cultivating a garden and rush through kitchen chores as quickly as possible in order to get to the real work of God in my Bible study. Avoid any "worldly" music and any demonstrations of human culture in movies or theaters. Play sports

non-degreed understanding of the image that is a result of God's creation of every human person. Despite the fall, all humans are in relatedness to the Creator even if they are not in relationship with him, and their lives are therefore sacred. For more on this, see Hastings, *Theological Ethics*, 45, 115. See also McKirland, "Sexual Difference in Christian Theology."

excellently, but be very careful they don't become an idol. Go fishing, but be careful not to get hooked on it! And do my work in the classroom, but get it done as quickly as possible so that I can do the real work of God, studying the Bible and preaching in the church.

This kind of frenetic and zealous life might look like a very virtuous life. However, although there are good elements in it, including good resurrection practices, this is *not* a human life. It is a heady life, a Gnostic life, but not a Christified human life. A sanctified life, a life of resurrection, means embracing all that is fully human: the goodness of work as a participation in the new creation; the goodness of science as giving creation a voice; the goodness of working with our hands; the beauty of good culture in art and good films and programs; the delight in fishing and catching beautiful fish, like Jesus's followers did; the carrying out of spiritual practices that are embodied—eating bread and drinking wine such that we not only remember Christ with our minds but also feed on him viscerally, participating in his death, resurrection, and ascension week by week; giving food to the poor and not just praying for them; experiencing ourselves as sexual beings without necessarily engaging in sex; practicing sabbath as part of the rhythm of death and resurrection.

5. The *context* for resurrection life, for sanctification, for the cultivation of virtues is the community of Christ, in which there are no racial or ethnic or cultural barriers. Paul makes a comment about this right in the middle of his exhortation about resurrection practices and virtues: "Here there is no Gentile or Jew, circumcised or uncircumcised, barbarian, Scythian, slave or free, but Christ is all, and is in all" (Col. 3:11). Paul is, on the one hand, saying that every single human person is invited into this resurrection life because Jesus took on humanity and by his resurrection reaffirmed all humanity. This is a good word in such a time as this, when racial tensions abound. Sadly, the church has not always modeled this racial and ethnic unity and harmony but has bowed to the pressure of racist societies, such as in the southern states of the United States, in South Africa, and in Nazi Germany. In fact, beyond these occurrences—which could be perceived by some to be mere anomalies—racism of many different kinds continues to be pervasive in society and in the church, which often mimics the culture rather than living into the one new humanity in Christ. Deep repentance and the implementation of discerning structural correctives that lead to nondiscriminatory policies are needed in the church and in Christian organizations.

But I suspect that Paul is also making another vital point about how we practice resurrection: we do so in community, and particularly in ecclesial community. There is no sanctification apart from life together in the church in variegated communities where mutual understanding is required. There is no resurrection life and transformation apart from the practices of Eucharist, or the Lord's Supper, of hearing the Word of God expounded, and of confession and absolution. Dallas Willard very skillfully put together a description of personal spiritual practices that correspond to the death and resurrection pattern, to mortification and vivification, spelling out among others the disciplines of fasting, silence, solitude, and chastity in the first category, and the disciplines of community, worship, Bible reading, and prayer in the second.[3] These are very valuable, but the *most* important practices for the resurrection people of God are those they engage in as the church, as people in life together.

Contemplation of the Risen Christ

The third dynamic that keeps the pursuit of holiness evangelical and hope-filled is contemplation of the risen Christ. From a place of imputed righteousness, of being hidden with Christ in God, we pursue active communion with God. It is in our fellowship with Christ and his people that we practice resurrection and are progressively transformed. However, this fellowship is not one in which we are on equal terms with Jesus. He is our Lord. He deigns to commune with us, but our part in that communion is to look away from ourselves and our progress in sanctification and toward the One to whom we owe it all. The practice of contemplating Christ is the most crucial dynamic in our communion with him. Looking into ourselves and doing the hard work of self-examination and practicing repentance as a lifestyle are all very well. But I believe we need to heed the advice of Robert Murray McCheyne, who said, "For every look at yourself, take ten looks at Christ."[4]

There is no better description of this contemplation of Christ in the Epistles than what Paul says in 2 Corinthians 3:17–18: "Now the Lord is the Spirit, and where the Spirit of the Lord is, there is freedom. And we all, who with unveiled faces contemplate the Lord's glory, are being transformed into his image with ever-increasing glory, which comes from the Lord, who is the Spirit." The people of God under the old covenant required Moses, whose face shone with reflected glory, to cover his face so they wouldn't see it fading. But under the era of the risen Christ and the Spirit outpoured, every believer can with unveiled face contemplate the glory of Christ. His glory is not reflected glory; it is iridescent glory, glory that radiates from the face of he who is the risen One, who is very God of very God. We have freedom in the Spirit to do this. Contemplation of the risen Christ is not a well-known

3. Willard, *The Spirit of the Disciplines.*
4. McCheyne, *Memoir and Remains of the Rev. Robert Murray McCheyne*, 293.

practice in our times. It requires prayerful meditation until the presence of Christ is sensed, and then a worshipful contemplation that brings about incredible joy and a transformation that, like Moses's, may be imperceptible on our part but may be noticed by others. Notice that this transformation is progressive, not once for all. With ever-increasing glory! And notice that if the object of contemplation is the risen Christ, the agent is the Spirit, whose deity is asserted unmistakably: "The Lord is the Spirit" (2 Cor. 3:17). The Spirit is the Gift given by the risen Christ. The Spirit is the Giving Gift,[5] who gives us transformation, among other gifts.

There is no better example in the Gospels of this practice of contemplation than that of Mary, who "sat at the Lord's feet listening to what he said" (Luke 10:39). No wonder she discerned so much about what would happen to Jesus. We don't have Jesus in an earthly, bodily way, as Mary did. So how do we sit at his feet and listen to him and contemplate his glory? The practice of listening to him speak and then contemplating him through *lectio divina* is a well-known and ancient practice. I do wish there was more time in the services of churches, and especially around the taking of the Lord's Supper, for such contemplation. I am sounding like an old man, but in my youth I did more contemplating in unhurried church services than I seem to be able to do now. Spiritual impoverishment is the result of the paucity of this practice. Resurrection transformation beckons us as we learn to meditate on Christ's glory and then contemplate it. Isaiah 6 might be a good place to begin.

Discussion Questions

1. "Sanctification" is a troubling word and concept for many Christians. What about the resurrection of Jesus gives us hope that we can be "made holy"?

2. What keeps the pursuit of sanctification evangelical and joyful rather than legal and miserable?

3. Take one passage that presents a picture of the risen Christ, either in the Old Testament or the New, and practice *lectio divina*—that is, read and reread the passage (*lectio*), attentive to what the Spirit of God is drawing your attention to; then meditate (*meditatio*) on those texts and truths that you have noticed; then find yourself in the

---

5. This is how Thomas A. Smail speaks of the Spirit in *The Giving Gift*.

presence of the risen Christ and gazing on his glory (*contemplatio*); and finally, express your adoration to him through prayer (*oratio*). Make this a practice in your daily reading of Scripture. Bring the richness of your communion with Christ into the life of your small group and church.

The Resurrection as the Ground of Vocation and Mission

Mission is God's own going forth—truly an *ekstasis* of God. He is Sender, Sent and Sending (John 17:18; cf. 16:5–16; 20:21–22).

—Paul Stevens[1]

In this chapter, we look for an answer to the question, What does the resurrection of Jesus have to do with our vocation and mission as humans, as Christians in the church in general, and as specific individual Christians? "Vocation," as we are using this term, refers to what all human persons are called to do, in the broadest sense, by the divine Caller. Of course this includes the uniqueness of personal vocations, which enable each human person in their own particular way to fulfill the calling given to all humans. The common vocation of all humans is expressed in various ways in the biblical text. At the broadest possible level, all humans are called to glorify God and enjoy him forever. This may be broken down into three aspects: it is the calling to be human, to fulfill the cultural mandate of Genesis 1–2, which involves our work and our being in communities; it is the calling to love God and love neighbor, the two great commandments given by Jesus in Matthew 22:37–40, summing

---

1. Stevens, *The Other Six Days*, 194. This Sender, Sent, and Sending paradigm reflects the same pattern as Barth's construal of the Trinity as Revealer, Revelation, and Revealedness and Augustine's Lover, Loved, and Love.

up all the ethical commands of Scripture; and it is the Great Commission given by Jesus in Matthew 28 to make disciples of all nations. These can be viewed as concentric circles. The first and widest circle is the vocation to be human, the second is the calling to be holy, and the third is the calling to participate with Christ in his mission to the world in order that persons might be holy and might become more fully human in all aspects of their lives, including in their work and in their family and communal lives.

It is appropriate to refer to all three aspects of the vocation of humanity as *mission*, although some might prefer to restrict the word "mission" to the Great Commission. The advantage of the first option is that evangelism and discipleship are never isolated from their context and purpose as expressed by the cultural mandate and the two great commandments. The purpose of reconciliation to God through Christ is not just for persons to have a right status before God (justification) in a juridical way but to affect their being. It is to begin the process of sanctification and in so doing to reconstitute and re-form them as fully human persons. In this sense, vocation and mission are the same thing and may be used interchangeably at times. However, since "vocation" has a wide range of meaning that includes personal vocations given and discerned by the Holy Spirit, there is not a complete overlap. For example, a person with a vocation to teach chemistry is fulfilling the divine cultural mandate to work, and her work will itself be a fulfillment of the vocation or mission expressed in the cultural mandate. Such a person is "missional" in the sense of the cultural mandate, even if she does not witness to Jesus. Her work matters and is pleasing to God. However, what complicates things is that we would probably say that her *vocation* is to teach chemistry, within the wider vocation of the human to work for the glory of God. We would probably *not* say that her *mission* is to teach chemistry, even if it is in fact a fulfillment of the mission of God for her. In sum, there is a wide semantic overlap between the words "vocation" and "mission," but there are also some distinctions.

The immediate question at hand is this: What does the history of Jesus— that he was raised again in a literal body—mean for our history as embodied and called people? Specifically, since Jesus's resurrection declared his identity as the Lord of creation and the last Adam and thereby signaled God's reaffirmation of humanity and creation, what does this mean for our vocation as human persons united to him? And since our human vocation, or calledness in response to the Caller, is really synonymous with our mission as the new community of the risen One, the church, what is the mission of the church? What missional character is given to the church by the missional Christ, the Sent One who becomes the Sending One who continues to be sent through his sent church? And how does that mission reflect his relationship to creation as the risen Lord and his relationship to the church as the risen Head? In light of who Jesus is as resurrected in a body and as the last Adam, and who he is as having formed a mystical body, the church, as the risen Head, we hope to gain a sense of how creation and redemption come together to give integral depth and width to what mission really is, including the role that our everyday work plays.

The Resurrection Reaffirms Creation and the Cultural Mandate

It is very apparent that the preaching of the gospel by Christ's resurrection community in the book of the Acts of the Apostles is very much focused on the resurrection. Relatively little is said about Jesus's death. Of course, the Epistles balance our understanding of the gospel by expounding the deep atoning, reconciling, redeeming significance of Christ's death for us. Nevertheless, in the earliest records of the preaching of the gospel by the church, the resurrection is central. Why is this? Part of the answer is that the apostles' preaching centered on the identity of Jesus, which was vindicated by the resurrection. The *kerygma*, or core good news, is that Jesus Christ is Lord. He is Messiah. "Therefore let all Israel be assured of this: God has made this Jesus, whom you crucified, both Lord and Messiah" is the climax and core of Peter's sermon on the day of Pentecost (Acts 2:36). What Paul says in Romans 1:4 is a good summation of apostolic preaching in Acts: ". . . who through the Spirit of holiness was appointed the Son of God in power by his resurrection from the dead: Jesus Christ our Lord." The faith-filled realization and affirmation that "Jesus is Lord," enabled by the Holy Spirit, indicated that a convert had been made (1 Cor. 12:3).

The apostles and the church formed under their preaching probably worked backward from the resurrection to articulate their theology of who Christ was. From the resurrection, which revealed both his messiahship and his deity and humanity, they worked backward to form a theology first of the atonement and then of the vicarious and inspirational significance of Christ's life. Then they went all the way back to form a theology of the incarnation, affirming Jesus's true deity and true humanity in one person. They would have done this by seeing the Old Testament in a new light. The earliest audiences who heard the gospel were Jewish people familiar with the Old Testament Scriptures, and therefore they likely knew not only that Jesus was being recognized as Yahweh but also what a resurrected man might mean in light of the creation story they knew. What Paul affirms in 1 Corinthians 15 (vv. 22, 45–49) and Romans 5 (vv. 12–21)—that Jesus was the new and final Adam and that a new humanity had been birthed in him—would not have been difficult for Jewish converts to grasp. They would also have easily seen that what the first Adam was created to be (an image bearer) and to do, by way of vocation (be in community, raise families, work and steward the creation with care), would now be fully fulfilled in the last Adam (*the* image of the invisible God) and the community he birthed, the church. The Hebrew-Christian view of vocation was earthy, not dualistic. Greek converts may have needed to be cured of Platonic dualism and told sternly to value their bodies and to live out a good work ethic (Eph. 4:28; 6:5–9; 1 Thess. 4:11–12), but not the Hebrew Christians.

The point is this: understanding the gospel of the resurrection within the full revelation of the story of God's work in the world—of creation, fall, redemption, and consummation, from Genesis to Revelation—necessitates that we keep creation and redemption together. The fact that redemption through Christ was accomplished by the resurrection of Jesus in a body means that it is redemption *of* creation. This means that Christians are not redeemed to be taken out of creation, to be other-worldly, but to be earthy, fully human, embodied persons in community. Christians are to be people who delight in their union with the risen Christ in heaven and yet who seek to bring heaven to earth every day. As Jesus taught us to pray, "Your kingdom come, your will be done, on earth as it is in heaven" (Matt. 6:10). Keeping creation and redemption together in light of the resurrection of Jesus means that Christians understand that all aspects of the cultural mandate given to the first Adam are part of the vocation of the new humanity in and under the last Adam. Christ followers therefore delight in their everyday work as the continuation of the command given to the first Adam, knowing realistically that the fall has complicated their work (Gen. 3) and that there is always a need for Christ's risen, redemptive influence in their work. Our commitment to work (and to sabbath) will always be inspired by the last Adam, who finished the work the Father gave him to do and was raised up in glory as an expression of the Father's delight.

The Resurrection and the Mission of the Church

An important aspect of the preaching of the early church is that although its central substance was the resurrection, on many occasions the sermon was an explanation of the church community that the risen Christ had formed. The preaching of the *kerygma* was the resurrected Christ, but the opportunity to preach arose from the miracle of the resurrection: *koinōnia*. There was no resurrection evangelism apart from resurrection communities. What was it that impressed people enough for them to ask what was going on in these communities? It was the fact that the members lived out the vocation given to them.

In Acts, it is quite clear that evangelism was not complete until converts were "added to the church" (Acts 2:41, 47). It was impossible to become a Christian and not be in the church. Baptism in the New Testament was a sign and sacrament not only that converts were now in union with Christ in death and resurrection but also that they were one with everyone else who was in Christ. The notion that you could be either an "unbaptized believer" or an "unchurched believer" would have been preposterous to the early church. The point is simply this: when people come into union with Christ, they become part of a local church, which is an expression of the universal church, and in doing so they recover the vocation given to the new humanity in the last Adam. Persons in Christ are profoundly communal and therefore also profoundly missional. The personhood, the life, the way of being of a Christian mirrors the triune God, in that just as the persons of the Trinity are communal persons—persons-in-communion—so every Christian is a person-in-community. We are, in the risen Christ, participants in the life of the Trinity and participants in the life of the church, which is the image or icon of the Trinity.[2]

The most basic insight regarding what the vocation of the church and of each believer might be is the fact that the risen Christ is the constituting center of the church and that every one of his followers is in union with him. That we share in Christ's vocation is made clear graphically by an occasion when the freshly risen Jesus stood among his dispirited disciples, revealed himself as the constituting center of the church, and then commissioned it in a striking way. I am referring to John 20:19–23, where Jesus said, "As the Father has sent me, I am sending you" (v. 21). This is the core of vocation. It is drawn from deep within the life of the Trinity. The "sentness" of the disciples was an extension of and in union with the sentness of the Son by the Father. Our mission as churches today is an extension of and a participation in the sentness or mission the Father gave the Son. This is profoundly organic.[3] Our sentness as a participation in Christ's sending by means of the Spirit is so important to our being in Christ that it is not surprising that Karl Barth called vocation (which he refers to as our mission) the third grace that

2. It is not that we are exactly or univocally persons in communion, as God is. The persons of the Trinity are mutually internal to one another, for example, and we cannot be quite that. We can be interdependent with others, and this is an image or analogy of the Trinity.

3. For a detailed exposition of the church's mission in light of Christ's trinitarian commission in John 20:19–23, see Hastings, *Missional God, Missional Church*.

flows from union with Christ.[4] That is, union with Christ means justification, sanctification, and vocation.

Mission in Barth's ecclesiology is actually spoken of as vocation.[5] This is extrapolated for the individual Christian as the church "scattered." As Kimlyn Bender states, "In Barth's understanding, the vocation of the church is complemented by the vocation of the individual Christian: both the community and the Christian are commissioned and sent to bear witness to God's reconciliation of the world in Jesus Christ (*CD* IV/3.2, 681–3)."[6] This is why Barth himself stated, "Remember: every Christian is a missionary, a recruiting officer for new witnesses! If our congregations do not recognize this, and act accordingly, they cannot be missionary congregations, and, therefore, they cannot be truly Christian."[7] Barth's great emphasis is that the identity of the church, and therefore of the Christian, is profoundly missional because the church is in union with the missional God in Christ and is therefore ensconced in the great work of the divine reconciliation of the world to God. Barth's massive exposition of this doctrine is beyond our scope here, but suffice it to say that the third of its three movements, vocation (justification and sanctification being the first two), is crucially defined as the mission of the church and the Christian. Barth did not understand vocation (German *Berufung*) as the particular callings of individual Christians. As John Flett indicates, Barth's understanding was broader. It intended to convey that "calling, active participation in service to Jesus Christ's prophetic office, is the nature of Christian existence." Similarly, the term "service" (German *Dienst*) meant, for Barth, "the missionary nature of the Christian community."[8]

What a privilege and what a relief it is to know that the church's mission and our own personal callings within it are not to *do* God's mission. This is our identity, not a program. Our vocation is to participate in what Christ is

---

4. Barth, *Church Dogmatics*, IV/1, 128. See also IV/3.2, 1–2, 31–32.

5. Barth's three concepts of the church as the fellowship of the Spirit, the body of Christ, and the people of God in world occurrence are expressed analogously to the incarnation of Christ. One aspect of this is that just as there is a union of the fully divine and fully human natures of Christ that is asymmetric—that is, the divine person of the Son took on a human nature—so also by analogy there is a reciprocal but asymmetric relation between the church and the world. This leads Barth to express a theology of history in which ecclesial history takes precedence in world history. As creation is grounded in covenant in Barth, so general history is the basis and context for the particular history of Jesus Christ, and as his own history includes with it the history of his community, so the history of the world exists so that the particular history of Christ and his church can exist. This is a reason for further expression of hope with respect to the mission of the church in this and every age, no matter how things may appear on the surface.

6. Bender, *Karl Barth's Christological Ecclesiology*, 225–26.

7. Barth, *Church Dogmatics*, III/4, 505.

8. Flett, *The Witness of God*, xi.

already doing. John 20 is not just a commission, therefore; it is a co-mission with the triune God, from the Father, in union with the Son, indwelt and empowered by the Holy Spirit. The risen Lord breathed the Holy Spirit symbolically on the disciples in John 20:22, in anticipation of the day of Pentecost, and then he breathed the Spirit *actually* into them in Acts 2, and the church was on its kingdom way to turning the world upside down.

The particular circumstances surrounding that occasion in John 20 help to inform us of the full depth and width of the vocation of the church. The most obvious conclusion one could perhaps reach on reading John 20 is that, by sending his disciples, Jesus was saying the same thing he said in Matthew 28:19–20: "Therefore go and make disciples of all nations, baptizing them in the name of the Father and of the Son and of the Holy Spirit, and teaching them to obey everything I have commanded you." We call this the Great Commission. Certainly this would be included in Jesus's Johannine commission. In addition, what we call the great commandment, to love God and neighbor, would have been included, since this was the core of Jesus's teaching and would come under the description "everything I have commanded you" in Matthew's commission. But there is something far more rudimentary here in the risen Sender's sending of his disciples. Our vocation as the church must be understood in light of the new-creation context of John 20:19–23. This has profound relevance to the creational and holistic dimensions of Christian mission.

The Resurrection and the New Creation

This new-creation context of the Johannine commission is inferred first by the fact that it occurs, as N. T. Wright has indicated, on the "evening of the new creation's first day." Wright draws an interesting parallel between the initial creation of God and what Christ accomplished by his death and resurrection. With reference to the "first day of the week" (John 20:19), he states, "Jesus had accomplished the defeat of death, and has begun the work of new creation."[9] Wright suggests that the theme of new creation runs deep in this passage. On the day of the creation of the humanity of the first Adam, Adam and Eve "heard the sound of him at the time of the evening breeze." "Now," notes Wright, "on the evening of the new creation's first day, a different wind sweeps through the room." Observing the sameness of the words for "wind," "breath," and "Spirit" in both Hebrew and Greek, he concludes, "This wind is

---

9. Wright, *John for Everyone, Part 2*, 149.

the healing breath of God's spirit, come to undo the long effects of primal rebellion." An additional echo of the creation account in this Johannine passage relates to the parallel between this passage and Genesis 2:7,[10] the moment of the creation of the old humanity itself, when Yahweh breathed into human nostrils the breath of life. "Now, in the new creation," Wright continues, "the restoring life of God is breathed out through Jesus, making new people of the disciples, and, through them, offering this new life to the world."[11] A parallel between the first Adam and the last Adam is made evident in this breathing act. Whereas the first Adam was the recipient of the breath of God in Genesis 2, the last Adam actually is the breather himself, breathing the Spirit into those who are becoming the new humanity in him.[12]

What are we to conclude from this creation–new creation context? That the vocation being passed on by the last Adam had to include the basic commands of God given to the first humanity, which we call the cultural mandate. It means that there was a reaffirmation by Jesus of the vocation to be human, to be image bearers, to work, to raise children in families, to work in the creation and to care for it. It means that the goal of the Great Commission is, yes, to bring people alienated from God into reconciliation in Christ through faith and repentance, and, yes, to baptize and make disciples of people from all nations by teaching them spirituality (love of God) and ethics (love of neighbor). But all of this happens in order that persons might be restored to being fully human persons and, as such, persons in community in the life of the church. This means that mission must be holistic. It must reach the whole person with a view to rehumanizing people, not just evangelizing them. To do the first without the second is the social gospel devoid of spiritual power, justice-seeking without the grace of the gospel. To do the second without the first is dualistic and runs the risk of being manipulative.

What is the vocation (from the Latin *vocare*) of every Christian and every church? It is to model Christian life in church community. (Lesslie Newbigin once said that Jesus called his disciples to be fishers of men but that he did so by "forming a community.")[13] It is to proclaim the gospel of the resurrection, of justification and sanctification and vocation. It is to affirm the gospel to those we seek to reach with deeds of justice and compassion that indicate a

10. There may also be an echo of the double peace benediction of Ps. 122 in this passage.

11. Wright, *John for Everyone, Part 2*, 150. That the Spirit's impartation by the breath of Jesus seems to echo Gen. 2:7 is confirmed also by Bruce, *The Gospel and Epistles of John*, 391.

12. Paul may be referring to this event when he makes this comparison explicit in 1 Cor. 15:45: "So it is written: 'The first man Adam became a living being'; the last Adam, a life-giving spirit." This new-creation context is referred to in more detail in Hastings, *Missional God, Missional Church*, 30–31.

13. Newbigin, *The Gospel in a Pluralist Society*, 227.

love of neighbor no matter what. It is to restore the dignity of humanity, of the image of God, in converts. It is to bring healing and wholeness to marriages and friendships and families and workplaces and industrial conflicts. It is to bring reconciliation to communities and nations torn by racial and ethnic tensions.

Although we rightly stress the creational nature of the mission of the church—that is, that resurrection reaffirms creation—we must also stress that the resurrection was the first day of the *new* creation! The intrigue of John 20:19–23 is that the disciples in that room on resurrection day were in a mist concerning their past and in a fog concerning their future vocation. Wright graphically describes that moment when Jesus, in risen power, "came forward out of the fog to meet" them![14] They began to see that his resurrection meant a new community of humanity and a new kingdom age. The eschaton was upon them. The mission of the church was not just creational but a participation in a new creation. Another way we may express this is to say that the mission of the people of the resurrection was going to be both incarnational *and* resurrectional. It was a mission of bringing hope to the world.

The resurrection body of Christ revealed to the disciples in John 20 signaled this new-creation reality. It had, as we have said, a spiritual and heavenly orientation, with a continuity with his preresurrection earthly body, reflected in his wounds and in the fact that they recognized him, and a discontinuity related to the new creation, as indicated by his miraculous entrance.[15] That his resurrected (and now ascended) body had capacities his kenotic body did not is hinted at elsewhere in the postresurrection narratives. This new capacity, in the opinion of some scholars of Christology, was a consequence of an exchange between the properties of divinity and humanity in Christ's newly risen and soon-to-be-ascended state (sometimes called the *communicatio idiomatum*). It is argued that in Jesus's humble incarnate state prior to the resurrection, his deity, though real, was not visible, except on occasions like the Transfiguration. He was the divine incognito. This was his kenotic state. Now in his risen state, theologians like Luther have argued, his deity has become visible. More likely, in my own opinion, following Zwingli and Calvin, there was never a confusion of Jesus's divine and human natures, even after the resurrection, and Jesus, truly divine and truly human, remains human and

---

14. Wright, *Surprised by Hope*, xiii–xiv.

15. William Hendricksen records antisupernaturalist opinions on how Jesus entered (*New Testament Commentary: Exposition of the Gospel according to John*, 458). For most conservative scholars, there are two main opinions: that he entered miraculously because his resurrection body had the capacity to pass through matter, having a spiritual orientation or even ubiquity, or that he passed through the door by miraculously unlocking it.

located within his humanity. What was evident, therefore, was not so much the deity of Christ but his new humanity in the new creation. The immediate point for us is that the incarnate body of Jesus was still extant but now in a resurrected, "new creation" form. *That resurrected body signifies the trajectory of the gospel for humanity*, which is resurrectional transformation beginning in the "now" through new birth and sanctification and vocation, which affect all of life, to be fully fulfilled through bodily resurrection when Christ returns in the kingdom to come, the new creation.

Mission That Is Resurrectional and Incarnational

The challenge is to know how the church can be both incarnational and resurrectional in its missional engagement. In light of the resurrection of Jesus as the last Adam, how does mission become not just creational but new-creational?[16] Orlando Costas was a missiologist who grappled with this question. He once stated that "incarnation without resurrection is only half a mission."[17] Mission therefore had to be more than mere solidarity with humanity. It needed also to "impart the hope of the resurrection through personal, vocational and communal transformation encountered in the now and fully in the 'not yet' of the kingdom."[18] It would then be more than just half a mission.

In other words, the "mission of the Christian church is to be undergirded by the telos of God for humanity, that is, what he intended when he created humans in the image of God and more particularly when he sent the last Adam to be its fulfillment and archetype."[19] To borrow from Irenaeus, "this incarnation-resurrection dynamic shapes mission to be a participation in God's work, which has as its goal the forming of human persons 'fully alive,' that is, in his image and likeness as recapitulated in Jesus."[20] Mission is not escaping from our humanity or encouraging others to do so. Rather, it has the aim of empowering humans to become fully human persons-in-relation, alive to God, the neighbor, and the creation. The gospel is much more than

---

16. This question is addressed more fully in Hastings, *Missional God, Missional Church*, 148–50.

17. Cited in Moffett, review of *Christ outside the Gate*, by Orlando Costas.

18. Hastings, *Missional God, Missional Church*, 148.

19. Hastings, *Missional God, Missional Church*, 149.

20. Hastings, *Missional God, Missional Church*, 150. "For the glory of God is a living man; and the life of man consists in beholding God. For if the manifestation of God which is made by means of the creation, affords life to all living in the earth, much more does that revelation of the Father which comes through the Word, give life to those who see God" (Irenaeus, *Against Heresies* 4.20.7, https://www.newadvent.org/fathers/0103420.htm).

just a return to Eden or recovering the innocence and constitution of Adam and Eve. On the other hand, the gospel of the resurrection does not make us God; we stay human even after our resurrection. It does, however, make us more fully human, human like Christ in character, sharing in his life. It makes us aware of the amazing grace that has rescued and regenerated us, to know that though in this life we are characterized by much failure, we live in hope of seeing the risen Christ and being transformed into his likeness (1 John 3:2).

As with sanctification, though, vocation has an incompleteness to it in this era of human history. Speaking again of Barth's reference to the three graces associated with union with Christ, we note that he viewed these in a trinitarian fashion. If the verdict of the Father is justification and the direction of the Son is sanctification, then vocation (a reality in Jesus Christ like the other two) is the telos granted to us by the Spirit. Vocation is the telos of justification and sanctification: "The being of man in Jesus Christ is a being not merely in possession and action, but also in expectation."[21] The person in the risen Christ is directed forward as "an eschatological being." Vocation is lived out in hope. We are to seize the future even in the present. What is the role of the Spirit? By the Spirit's power, we respond in faith, hope, and love. The prime sins for Barth are pride and sloth. By the Spirit's power, we begin to overcome the pride that prevents us from seeing our desperate need to die to our sins with Christ; by the Spirit, we overcome the sloth that causes us not to accept God's righteous verdict of us and his pleasure in us as those who are in Christ the risen One. This "now but not yet" reality of vocation provides realism as we seek to find vocation and pursue it. This is particularly relevant to the imperfections of the church and its vocation, and also to the struggles that we as persons go through in seeking to discern our vocations and to find occupations that correspond to those vocations.

The Resurrection and Personal Vocation

The matter of *personal* vocation needs to be seen within the wider context of Christian calling and the three aspects of mission mentioned above: the cultural mandate, the great commandment, and the Great Commission. If it is not, it can become an obsession of self-focused, individualistic moderns who are bourgeois enough to have options. The concept that undergirds the search for calling is the notion of a Caller. We are called by God and to God in obedience. We are called, along with all people, to be human, to seek the

21. Barth, *Church Dogmatics*, IV/1, 128.

obedience that brings shalom, to strive for healthy and holy relationships. This is our *human* calling. As Christians we are also called, along with all the redeemed people of God, to fulfill our *Christian* calling to live according to who we are in Christ (Eph. 4:1), communally and personally. Paul defines the calling of God that is the responsibility of every Christian: "It is God's will that you should be sanctified" (1 Thess. 4:3).

There isn't much to wonder or fret about. Fulfilling the human and Christian callings will take up most of our time and energy. Yet there is a personal calling upon every person's life. Actually, it seems to me that in the normal course of events, when a person is following the revealed will of God faithfully, their personal calling becomes apparent. There are, of course, many exceptions to that. In a fallen world with imperfect relationships, many people, including this writer, can struggle deeply with vocational ambivalence. Sometimes personal calling is very obvious; as Frederick Buechner once wrote with timeless wisdom, "If you want to know who you are, watch your feet. Because where your feet take you, that is who you are."[22] What is in you by way of vocational passion and desire will show in what you end up doing. The same author expressed elsewhere that the confluence of our desires and the needs we see helps to define our calling: "The place God calls you to is the place where your deep gladness and the world's deep hunger meet."[23] This sounds straightforward. However, sometimes when people have many gifts and many possibilities, or when people have struggled to find the confidence to make decisions, perhaps because they were not warmly affirmed by their parents, things are not so clear. The pursuit is worth the work, however, for as Paul Stevens aptly says, a sense of calling overcomes aimless consumerism and "gives our lives direction and purpose because our Creator summons us into a personal relationship with God and into a wonderful purpose that will outlast the world."[24] A calling to participate with the risen Christ in his work in the world is a marvelous thing.

How a calling is discerned is the work of the Spirit of the risen Christ, who gives gifts and abilities to his people generously and works to confirm those gifts through the resurrection community of the church and close friends within it. The calling to be a pastor in Christ's church is not the only calling. It is a high calling, but no higher than other callings. The idea that only the callings of the church matter and that other callings, such as those of a plumber and an executive and a teacher, are lesser callings is an unfortunate

22. Buechner, *The Alphabet of Grace*, 25.
23. Buechner, *Wishful Thinking*, 95.
24. Stevens, *Doing God's Business*, 20.

dualism that hurts the mission of the church significantly. The calling of a pastor does help to elucidate all other callings. In 1 Timothy 3, Paul speaks of or infers four aspects of a pastor's calling: a desire born of right motive (v. 1); a character of integrity and growth in godliness (vv. 2–7); charismatic giftings of teaching, shepherding, and managing (vv. 2, 4); and the recognition of the church community that the first three are true. This last aspect is implied by the fact that Paul is laying out a blueprint by which the church can recognize its pastors.

It is self-evident that if a person thinks they are a teacher but nobody wants to listen to them, or if a person thinks they are a leader and they turn around to find that nobody is following them, they are probably not called to be a pastor. The same general principles apply to all vocations. When a person is walking closely with the risen Christ, they may assume that their vocational desires are God's desires and that God's desires are their desires. We should do what fulfills our desires, what brings joy. We should find occupations that are largely in keeping with our primary giftings. Working outside of our giftings causes great stress. We should look to close friends for confirmation, for they can often clearly see what we can't. We need one another.

In sum, personal vocation is about becoming aware of your passions—what you dream of, what you long to do, and who you long to do it for. It is about being aware of your particular abilities—your spiritual and natural abilities. It is about knowing your personality traits—whether you are an introvert, an extrovert, or somewhere in between, whether you sense things or intuit them, whether you are a thinker or a feeler. In other words, it's somewhat about which of the sixteen types of the Myers-Briggs inventory you fit into. There are many of these kinds of inventories available today, and they can be useful if they provide some self-understanding—but please beware the possibility of becoming self-seeking in the process, of seeking the perfect match for your abilities. Heed the words of Margaret Hebblethwaite:

> One of the greatest pitfalls for people who go in for spirituality, is to waft around in a spiritual zone seeking peace, fulfilment and inner harmony, and leaving the world to rot. Centres of spirituality flourish, master's degrees are taken in prayer, meditation becomes a boom industry, and meanwhile the hungry go on being hungry, the naked go on being naked, the sick and imprisoned have no one to visit them, and the sinful structures of the world continue unchallenged. . . . For someone in the third world, a spirituality movement can be bad news. The theologians of liberation draw attention to the implicitly conservative nature of most of these movements when they are found in Latin America—like the Cursillo retreat movement, and the Charismatic renewal: by turning attention

away from the bitter reality of the way people live, they leave everything the way it was.[25]

So don't become demobilized by the search for the perfect occupation in which you can fulfill your vocation. The words of Maxie Dunnam, church planter, pastor, and former president of Asbury Theological Seminary, live on in their prophetic relevance for us:

> The way most of us serve keeps us in control. We choose whom, when, where and how we will serve. We stay in charge. Jesus is calling for something else. He is calling us to be servants. When we make this choice, we give up the right to be in charge. The amazing thing is that when we make this choice we experience great freedom. We become available and vulnerable, and we lose our fear of being stepped on, or manipulated, or taken advantage of. Are not these our basic fears? We do not want to be in a position of weakness.[26]

Our stumbling around on the matter of vocation reminds us that the resurrection kingdom community has not yet fully come and that we are not yet fully raised from the dead. There are two great realities that sustain us and keep us serving with all our imperfections and lack of clarity about where and how we might serve. The first is the reality that Christ, the One in whom we are risen, the One who lived out his vocation perfectly for us as our Great High Priest, offers up our deeds and words to the Father on our behalf. An aspect of the Eucharist gives us a picture of this every week: the elements offered are not wheat and grapes but bread and wine that require human work to be formed. When bread and wine are offered, we are offering up our labors week by week in response to the completed work of Christ on our behalf, and they are offered up by the ascended Christ to the Father. But there is a second reality that encourages us in our vocations. It is awareness that the Father who sees us, the Father before whom the Son presents our work, is a loving Father. This is expressed well in a prayer Thomas Merton wrote in his journal during a time of deep depression:

> My Lord God, I have no idea where I am going. I do not see the road ahead of me. I cannot know for certain where it will end. Nor do I really know myself. And the fact that I think I am following Your will does not mean that I am actually doing so. But I believe, dear Father, that the desire to please You does in fact please You, and I hope that I have that desire in all that I am doing. I hope that I will never do anything apart from that desire. And so I believe that

25. Hebblethwaite, *The Way of St. Ignatius*, 201.
26. Dunnam, *Alive in Christ*, 150.

if I do this, You will lead me by the right road, though I may know nothing about it. Therefore, I will trust You always; though I may seem to be lost in the shadow of death, I will not fear, for You are with me and You will never leave me to face my peril alone.[27]

The Difference the Resurrection Makes

What real and tangible difference does the resurrection of Jesus make to us? In the appropriate somber reflections of Good Friday, we often look ahead to Easter Sunday and say, "It's Friday, but Sunday's comin'." Well, what about Monday? Monday is always comin' too. And Monday after Monday. How has your vocational life changed since you discovered that Jesus rose again for you? A good place to begin to answer that question is to ask what difference the resurrection made for the disciples of Jesus. Watching the transformation of the disciples as they were experiencing the sporadic postresurrection appearances of Jesus, a transformation from aimless, fearful people into the empowered and communal missional people of God, gives us hope as we seek to live into our resurrection vocations. I think their experience is a parable for how we can be transformed as the awareness of a truly risen Christ dawns on our consciousness. Their experiences are suggestive of what might become "vocational resurrection disciplines" for us.

Take a woman like *Mary Magdalene*, who is deeply grieving until the risen Jesus appears to her. When he reveals to her the reality of the Fatherhood of God for all who are in his family, she is overjoyed, and Matthew describes how she and the other women "hurried away from the tomb, afraid yet filled with joy, and ran to tell his disciples" (Matt. 28:8). She ran to become the apostle to the apostles, the first proclaimer of the resurrection. Notice her abandon!

Then take *the disciples as a whole*. After the resurrection, but in the period when they were not yet conscious of it, their condition is described this way: they "were together, with the doors locked for fear of the Jewish leaders" (John 20:19). After Jesus meets with them and shows them his hands and feet and speaks "peace" to them, the text says, "The disciples were overjoyed when they saw the Lord" (20:20). Note when the change happened—when they saw him in resurrection glory. This is the key to their transformation. Although reticent at first, they were all, after a few encounters, filled with that same joy, abounding in freedom and passionately committed to the kingdom community. But it all began with seeing Jesus. Jesus was alive! Death had not destroyed the community. And that community would last forever because its

27. Quoted in Claypool, *The Light within You*, 159.

members too would outlast death. After the ascension of Jesus and the descent of his Spirit to fill them, bound, timid disciples who hid behind locked doors came out of the upper room in Spirit-freedom and boldness to openly declare the good news no matter the consequences. They became people "clothed with power," just as Jesus anticipated (Luke 24:49). They became powerful witnesses, participating in his unshakable kingdom. Their experience speaks first of a resurrection practice of seeing the risen Lord, contemplating him daily that we might live in his contagious joy, and finding the freedom to fulfill our work enthusiastically for the day, conscious that it is his work. Practicing resurrection is the passionate pursuit of the calling God has given us, fixing our eyes on Jesus and having an orientation to the other, to the kingdom community, and to all humanity in its need; working as unto the Lord to meet the needs of our family and those in need; and serving in the work world and in the church with equal vigor.

But it is *Peter* in particular whose story fascinates me the most—Peter, who has seen the Lord once with the others but who, I suspect, could hardly bring himself to look Jesus in the eye when he did see him. The last time Jesus had looked him in the eye was right at the fireside when Peter had disowned him. Then Peter had gone away and wept bitterly. He had blown it by denying his Master. He is a guilt-ridden, remorseful soul. He cannot forgive himself. So in John 21, when Jesus had not made an appearance for a few days, Peter decides he is going fishing. Some think this was just a temporary relief from the pain of not seeing Jesus. It might have been that he and his disciple friends were short of a good meal. But I think there's more to it than meets the eye. This is Peter saying, "I'll never make an apostle now. I denied my Lord. I couldn't stand the heat, so I may as well get out of the kitchen. That thing Jesus said about me being rock-like—some rock! How can I ever be his church builder? I may as well get back to my old profession, the thing I used to do before I met him." Note the individualism in Peter's statement—not "Let's go fishing, chaps" but "I'm going out to fish" (John 21:3). The tone as I read it is "I don't really care whether you want to or not, but that's what I'm going to do. You guys probably still have a future with Jesus because you didn't deny the Master. I did, so I'm off. I better get those old angling and net skills down again." Then they all say, "We'll go with you."

It is quite clear that Peter believes in the resurrection as a historical fact at this point. He still had questions when he first saw the graveclothes in the tomb. Luke 24:12 says he went away "wondering to himself what had happened." But after the appearance Jesus made in John 20:19, Peter, like all the others, was convinced and indeed overjoyed. However, it is one thing to know his Master is risen and to rejoice in what that means theologically and missionally for the world. It is another thing altogether to personally know him intimately in his risenness. At this point, Peter has a strain in his relationship with his Lord—some unfinished business, you could say. Before he can be released into the kingdom ministry Jesus had predicted for him, he is going to need to "see" Jesus again. Peter, in his resurrection transformation journey, has a step or two to go.

Vocational Resurrection Disciplines

What made the difference in Peter? And how did it show? The story of this restorative encounter of Peter with the Master is touchingly poignant. It is rich with experiences that can become our disciplines in our return to the vocations to which we have been called.

First, Peter encountered Jesus and knew him intimately in restoration by means of the risen Christ's repeated fishing miracle. This was not just any miracle done to convince the disciples in general that he was risen. It was to convince Peter that Christ's intentions for him as a "fisher of people" were left unaltered by his failure in denying him. We have to read this story alongside that in Luke 5, where Jesus first commissioned the disciples, and Peter in particular. In Luke 5, Jesus performed the same miracle. The only difference is that the nets broke in Luke 5; and that may have its own significance, perhaps indicating the disciples were not yet ready to be fishers of people. By contrast, John 21:11 seems to emphasize that "even with so many [fish] the net was not torn." It might be that this depicts the fact that only after the resurrection of Christ, and with the risen power of Christ in the disciples through the Holy Spirit, could the disciples manage the catch.

On the occasion in Luke 5, right away Peter fell at Jesus's feet and said, "'Go away from me, Lord; I am a sinful man.' . . . Then Jesus said to Simon, 'Don't be afraid; from now on you will fish for people.' So they pulled their boats up on shore, left everything and followed him" (Luke 5:8, 10–11). Note that this was a commissioning miracle. Fast-forward to John 21, and it is clear that, for Peter, déjà vu is written all over this. And Jesus is not just performing this miracle again for the fun of it. It's a recommissioning miracle for Peter. It's a miracle signifying Peter's forgiveness, and it's a miracle by means of which Jesus is saying, "My decision about your future vocation in my kingdom as a human fisherman and leader is unchanged by your failure in denying me." Isn't that amazing grace? Let's watch what Peter does when he sees the catch and it dawns on him that he's seeing the risen Lord. The text says, "As soon as Simon Peter heard [John] say, 'It is the Lord,' he wrapped his outer garment around him (for he had taken it off) and jumped into the water" (John 21:7). No wonder I like the way Frederick Buechner describes this: "Peter hurled himself into the water like a whale and somehow swam and scrambled his way to shore ahead of everybody else."[28] The consequence of resurrection "seeing" for Peter is that he is filled with great joy, an abandoned, reckless joy! This is our *first vocational resurrection discipline*, the contemplation of the risen Jesus, as we noted above.

But there's more. I don't think Peter missed the symbolism. But in case he did, Jesus makes the message crystal clear. This comes in the form of a second sign: on top of the miracle of the déjà vu fishing lesson there is the breakfast of bread and fish. This recalls the miracle of the feeding of the five thousand with five loaves and two fish. In John 6 it seems clear that this was another commissioning miracle. Jesus had broken the loaves symbolizing his broken body and then distributed the bread to the disciples to feed the five thousand, symbolizing their sharing of the good news of salvation through his body given for humankind. Notice the parallel in John 21:13: "Jesus came, took the bread and gave it to them, and did the same with the fish." Déjà vu again! So there is further reassurance for Peter of his forgiveness and reinstatement.

There is more in this story, though. Jesus is about to ask Peter three times to feed his sheep. But before he asks Peter to feed his sheep, Jesus wants to make sure that Peter is fed by him. Here is a symbolic lesson for Peter that must become a *second vocational resurrection discipline* for us if we are to live in resurrection power in our vocations in a sustained way, whether in the academy, the marketplace, or the church. We must feed on Christ, from Christ—first, as a priority—if we are to feed others. Buechner describes this beautifully in "The Great Dance," a chapter of his book *Longing for Home*:

> "Feed my sheep," Jesus said to Peter as the first rays of the sun went fanning out across the sky, but, before that, he said something else. The six other men had beached the boat by then and had come up to the charcoal fire knowing that it was Jesus who was standing there and yet not quite knowing, not quite brave enough to ask him if he was the one they were all but certain he was. He told them to bring him some of the fish they had just hauled in, and then he said something that, if I had to guess, was what brought tears to their eyes if anything did. The Lamb of God. The Prince of Peace. The Dayspring from on High. Instead of all the extraordinary words we might imagine on his lips, what he said was, "Come and have breakfast." I believe he says it to all of us: to feed his sheep, his lambs, to be sure, but first to let him feed us—to let him

28. Buechner, *Wishful Thinking*, 130.

feed us with something of himself. In the sip of wine and crumb of bread. In the dance of sun and water and sky.[29]

But Peter's vocationally transformative resurrection encounter wasn't left only to symbolic actions. It involved a conversation with Jesus. In addition to the déjà vu signs, there is the message of a thrice-repeated confession of love and a thrice-repeated commissioning.

Breakfast is over. The plates are washed. And Jesus turns his eyes on Peter. Then three times he asks him, "Simon, son of John, do you love me?" The three times of asking and the three times of commissioning him are of course a threefold opportunity for Peter to renounce his threefold denial. This is grace. This is part of Peter's path to freedom. The challenge Jesus gives the first time—"Do you love me *more than these?*"—will remind Peter of how he'd said that "even if all fall away, I will not" (Mark 14:29). His arrogant self-reliance is being exposed. The fact that Jesus changes the "love" verb the third time from *agapaō* to the less demanding *phileō* is another sign of grace, though Peter is upset that perhaps Jesus didn't trust even his lesser love profession. Each time Jesus had used *agapaō*, and each time Peter had replied with the less confident *phileō*. What Jesus is effectively telling Peter by using Peter's word the third time is that if that is all he can offer at this point, that is fine with him. If he is lacking the confidence to profess the higher form of covenant, stick-to-it love at this point, then that's okay with Jesus for now. But the main point is this: the charge to Peter in this postresurrection encounter with Jesus that transforms him personally and vocationally forever is a charge to look away from himself to see Christ's sheep, to be committed to an "other" orientation. Verse 18 also spells out how this controller Peter is not going to be in control of his destiny anymore.

This story is so significant for us. Even when we lose sight of who Jesus is and even when we have not been very good at following him, the Lord Jesus values our professions of love, no matter how tentative and lacking in confidence they may be. And his response to us is the same as that which he gave to Peter: "Feed my lambs," "Take care of my sheep," and "Feed my sheep." In other words, show your love for me by feeding those who belong to me. Stop being obsessed with your own self and your own failures and start feeding others. This is the *third vocational resurrection discipline* to which we are called in order to fulfill our vocation as humans, as a church, as persons. The fact that Jesus rose again means that his people will rise again. We are therefore part of an eternal community that we are responsible to feed. And

29. Buechner, *Longing for Home*, 131–32.

we are to call others into that community by feeding them. Our joy is based on Christ and also depends on our being oriented toward others, feeding others around us with words and acts of kindness.

After his restorative encounter with the risen Christ, Peter becomes a guilt-free apostle who takes delight in reflecting on the glories of his Lord and writes about them eloquently in his epistles. He is transformed from a fear-filled people-pleaser into a fearless preacher and spiritual feeder of sheep who ultimately cares so little about what people think of him, and yet so deeply about people, that in feeding them he is willing to give his own life in martyrdom for his Lord by being crucified upside down in Rome. Peter becomes totally, purposefully, passionately kingdom-community committed. He starts to feed others. That's resurrection relevance. These are the vocational resurrection disciplines in a nutshell. See Christ. Feed on Christ. Feed Christ's people and those on the way to being his.

The resurrection was a sign that the kingdom of God Jesus had spoken of before he died was not over. His ascension as the risen King emphatically declared it. As Dallas Willard has written,

> The resurrection was a cosmic event only because it validated the reality and the indestructibility of what Jesus had preached and exemplified *before* His death—the enduring reality and openness of God's Kingdom. It meant that the Kingdom, with the communal form his disciples had come to know and hope in, would go on. . . . That, and the fact that Jesus was not dead after all—and that when *we* die, we won't stay dead—is what made the resurrection earthshaking, transforming good news.[30]

The transformation in the disciples of Jesus as a result of the resurrection is radical and stark. It is an amazing phenomenon. Here is what characterized that change most notably: freedom instead of guilt and fear, unrestrained joy instead of despair, passionate commitment to Christ's kingdom community instead of purposeless inactivity or futile, frenetic activity. I am convinced that most evangelical Christians, despite the fact that they would die for the belief that Jesus Christ arose literally and bodily from the dead, and despite the fact that they believe notionally in the fact that the resurrection was God's guarantee that we are justified and forgiven of all our sins, know very little about resurrection living—that is, guilt-free, joyful, and passionately missional, other-oriented Christianity: Christ's *life* expressed in their work, in their play, in their relationships, in their care for the creation of which God

---

30. Willard, *The Spirit of the Disciplines*, 37.

has made us stewards, in their pursuit of justice and compassion for the poor, in their affirmation and proclamation of the gospel in their words and deeds.

A closing benediction: Jesus died for your sins, so be forgiven. You are loved by the Father, so be healed of your self-despising. You are accompanied everywhere by the Holy Spirit, so be helped and guided and empowered to live beyond yourself, above yourself, for the greater glory of God. Amen.

Discussion Questions

1. If vocation belongs along with justification and sanctification as a third grace that flows to every Christian by their being in union with the risen Christ, what does this mean for every Christian?

2. How should the fact that our mission (cultural mandate, great commandment, and Great Commission) is grounded in union with the missional, risen Christ guide our thinking and practices regarding the depth and width of the missional church?

3. What are some steps to living a life of prayer in order that mission would be an outflow of our identity and life in God rather than something "extra" we feel guilted into doing?

6

The Resurrection as the Ground of the Bodily Resurrection

Dear friends, now we are children of God, and what we will be has not yet been made known. But we know that when Christ appears, we shall be like him, for we shall see him as he is.

—1 John 3:2

In this chapter we move on from consideration of what the resurrection means for us in the kingdom that has come to ask this question: What does the resurrection mean for the kingdom *when it is fully come*? This leads to questions such as, What is the future of Christians after they die, or when Christ returns? John Owen, an English Puritan of the seventeenth century, wrote, "Nor do the effects of the death of Christ rest here. They do not leave us until we are settled in heaven, in glory and immortality forever."[1] But what is meant by the glorification of the believer and bodily resurrection? What do we know about resurrected bodies in light of the nature of Jesus's postresurrection body? We begin by seeking to understand why there is a time lapse between the resurrection of Christ, the last Adam, and his people.

1. Owen, *The Death of Death in the Death of Christ*, 14.

An Eschatological Question: Why the Gap between Christ's Resurrection and Ours?

There is certainly a time gap between Christ's triumph over death in his death and resurrection and the end of death for the rest of humans at the final resurrection. A tension exists in the New Testament. On the one hand, the writer to the Hebrews tells us triumphantly that the death of Jesus is the death of death for humanity: "Since the children have flesh and blood, he too shared in their humanity so that by his death he might break the power of him who holds the power of death—that is, the devil—and free those who all their lives were held in slavery by their fear of death" (Heb. 2:14–15). This passage clearly indicates that the death (and resurrection) of Jesus in a human body and on behalf of humanity means the end of death. It does acknowledge implicitly that there is still death now, even if it is not to be feared by those in Christ. But the primary intent of the author is to say that death is no more! Yet in 1 Corinthians 15:26, Paul expresses the reality that death is the last enemy still to be destroyed. How can death be both destroyed and waiting to be destroyed?

One popular way to explain this is to say that by the cross and resurrection event, the decisive battle was won by Christ over death, but the mopping-up operations of the war will continue until the moment when the Victor reappears. This moment is depicted in Revelation 21. It is the moment when Christ comes back again, this time in great glory and power and authority, when the resurrection of the dead has occurred, the judgment of all has been enacted, the new heavens and the new earth have begun, and the new Jerusalem has descended to earth. Then John says,

> And I heard a loud voice from the throne saying, "Look! God's dwelling place is now among the people, and he will dwell with them. They will be his people, and God himself will be with them and be their God. 'He will wipe every tear from their eyes. *There will be no more death*' or mourning or crying or pain, for the old order of things has passed away." (Rev. 21:3–4, emphasis added)

T. F. Torrance spoke eloquently about the resurrection of Jesus and its significance. He asserted its historicity by saying it is "an event datable in history,"[2] and he insisted that "any 'resurrection' that is not bodily is surely a contradiction in terms."[3] But Torrance also had a good way of explaining the time gap between Christ's victory over death and the time when death will

2. T. F. Torrance, *Space, Time and Resurrection*, 87.
3. T. F. Torrance, *Space, Time and Resurrection*, 82.

actually be no more. Ever since the resurrection and ascension of the Savior, our lives take place "in the eschatological reserve created by the ascension."[4] "Because of the ascension," he said, "there has been introduced, as we have seen, into the midst of the one whole *parousia* of Christ, an eschatological pause, so that in all our relations with Christ, there is an eschatological reserve or eschatological time-lag."[5]

Torrance thought of Christ's appearing, or parousia, at his first and second comings as one great event. The New Testament certainly speaks of the last days or the end or the eschaton as having been brought about by Jesus's first coming (Acts 2:17; Gal. 4:4; Heb. 1:2). In Jesus's first coming we have what is sometimes referred to as *inaugurated* eschatology. In that sense the last days are already with us. What happens when Christ returns to bring about futurist eschatology is simply the extension or final fulfillment of what has been inaugurated and is working itself out now. Salvation has been accomplished by his first coming, and the second coming, because it is connected to the first, in Torrance's view, "will be more of an apocalypse or unveiling of the perfected reality of what Christ has done than the consummating of what till then is an incomplete reality." As such, it will be the "unveiling of the finished work of Christ." The work of judgment and the bringing in of the new creation will happen, but these are not works in addition "to his finished work on the cross or in the resurrection." The events of the second coming, on this account, are more like "the gathering together of what the cross and resurrection have already worked throughout the whole of creation and the unveiling of it for all to see, and therefore an unfolding and actualization of it from our point of view."[6]

In the meantime, since the ascension of the risen Christ, "his eschatological operations are veiled from our sight, by the fact that we live with the time-form of this world, and communicate with the new creation only through the Spirit in Word and Sacrament."[7] There is a sensory veil between us and where Christ is at the right hand of the Father. The church participates in what Christ is doing now by the indwelling of the Holy Spirit, who works in us and through us. The eschatological "gap" is what enables the ingathering of many people into union with the risen Christ by the Spirit through the mission of Christ through his church. Through the Spirit we already partake of the new creation in the risen Christ; by the Spirit we are united to the ascended Christ and therefore to his future when he comes again; and by the Spirit, we

4. T. F. Torrance, *Space, Time and Resurrection*, 152, 156, 157.
5. T. F. Torrance, *Space, Time and Resurrection*, 152.
6. T. F. Torrance, *Space, Time and Resurrection*, 152.
7. T. F. Torrance, *Space, Time and Resurrection*, 152.

continue the sending of Christ into the world in mission, as indicated in the previous chapter. This does not mean there is nothing entirely new at the final end, but the end will largely reflect the process already at work in and through the church. In this New Testament way of expressing things, eschatology is "the act of the eternal within the temporal, by the acts of God, within our world of space and time," and as such, these acts "are teleological as well as eschatological. . . . They are acts that gather up time in the fulfilling of the divine purpose."[8] It is for this reason that we may sometimes speak of realized eschatology and future eschatology as one thing, inaugurated eschatology worked out in two stages that are nevertheless overlapping rather than distinct realities. They are "woven together all the time *in Christ*."[9]

For Torrance, in sum, the eschatological is a description of the "final Act of God," yet one that is "still in arrears so far as our experience and understanding of it are concerned."[10] But most crucially, eschatology for Torrance is not so much about the *eschaton* as it is about the *Eschatos*—that is, Christ, the One who is both the *Protos* (the First) and the *Eschatos* (the Last), "the One who is the Last because he is the First." He who has already "come and accomplished his work of salvation in our midst will bring it to its final manifestation and consummation at his coming again."[11]

The "now but not yet fully" nature of the kingdom and of our resurrection has some important lessons for us as people living the Christian life. On the one hand, the "now" creates an expectancy regarding our pursuit of holiness and healing, since death and the devil have been defeated. Yet on the other hand, the "not yet fully" aspect of things points toward a humility and away from triumphalism about the Christian life and what is possible in sanctification and in ministry. Paul Molnar explains that the eschatological gap "means that our work for the Kingdom is always our fallible work that takes place from a center in Christ and looks forward to his ultimate renewal of all things. It can never claim to be more than an ambiguous work within history because history is not yet fully redeemed."[12] This holding together of ascension and parousia keeps us from triumphalism, while it nevertheless encourages a proper sense of triumph, even in suffering in mission, as we live

8. T. F. Torrance, *Space, Time and Resurrection*, 151.

9. T. F. Torrance, *Space, Time and Resurrection*, 154 (emphasis original).

10. T. F. Torrance, *Space, Time and Resurrection*, 151.

11. T. F. Torrance, *Space, Time and Resurrection*, 151–52. Torrance exposes the mistake of speaking of a "delayed parousia" in Acts or the New Testament in general. It is only when we fail to hold the elements of realized and future eschatology together in Christ, the beginning and the end, and in his one act, that we then project back onto early Christianity this notion that the "arrival of the end has been delayed" (154).

12. Molnar, *Thomas F. Torrance*, 246.

into the blessed hope before us. It is the way in which suffering and resurrection go together that forms us in sanctification through union with Christ's death and resurrection. The power of his resurrection and the fellowship of his sufferings can never be pried apart. In this economy of suffering and resurrection, our greatest brokennesses become our greatest ministries. Karl Barth once said that "only on the lips of a person who is themselves affected, seized and committed, controlled and nourished, unsettled and settled, comforted and alarmed by it, can the intrinsically true witness of the act and revelation of God in Jesus Christ have the ring and authority of truth which applies to other humans."[13] Keeping suffering and resurrection together preserves us from triumphalism, on the one hand, and despair, on the other. There can be no *theologia gloriae* without the *theologia crucis*, and vice versa—in our lives, and in the life and worship of the church.

A Teleological Question: What Is the End Goal of the Christian Journey?

In approaching the matter of what it will mean for Christians when the second coming of Christ finally does occur, we may summarize this as the *glorification* of the believer. The seeds of this are already here within our union with Christ. It is perhaps surprising that neither John Calvin nor Karl Barth spoke of glorification as the third grace (in Calvin's case) or the fourth (in Barth's case). Both do speak of glorification, but not as one of the distinct graces given to us "in Christ." No doubt Calvin would have thought of it as the extension of sanctification, and Barth as the end goal of sanctification and vocation. The reason their views are surprising is that Paul does speak of these great salvific realities together. For example, in Romans 8:29–30, Paul states, "For those God foreknew he also predestined to be conformed to the image of his Son, that he might be the firstborn among many brothers and sisters. And those he predestined, he also called; those he called, he also justified; those he justified, he also glorified." Here precisely we see evidence of what Torrance refers to as the coalescing of the saving act of Christ in the first and second advents of Christ. Justification and glorification are brought together as one, glorification is spoken of as already a fait accompli, and all these acts of grace are sourced in the predestining work of God in eternity. To be in Christ is to be justified and also already glorified. Though not yet glorified in terms of human time, in the purposes of God we already are.

13. Barth, *Church Dogmatics*, IV/3, 657.

So being glorified is the end goal of the journey of every believer in Christ. But what does that mean? The obvious answer might be to say that when Christ returns, when Christians who were dead and those who are living "meet the Lord" at his second coming in order to be forever "with the Lord" (1 Thess. 4:17), "we will all be changed" (1 Cor. 15:51–52). This means that Christians will be resurrected to have imperishable and immortal bodies (1 Thess. 4:16; 1 Cor. 15:50–55) and that they will contemporaneously *receive glory*. Paul says this in 1 Corinthians 15:43–44: "It is sown in dishonor, it is raised in glory; it is sown in weakness, it is raised in power; it is sown a natural body, it is raised a spiritual body." Most crucially, Paul grounds this glorification above all in who Christ is for us: "And just as we have borne the image of the earthly man, so shall we bear the image of the heavenly man" (1 Cor. 15:49).

Glory is an attribute of God. In God's case, glory is radiant or iridescent. It comes from within his being. It is actually more like a summation of all his attributes in their beautiful proportions. Glory as an attribute of God is especially the outshining of his inward excellence that is derived from his trinitarian nature. He is three persons in perfect communion and as such is, as Jonathan Edwards described him, the supreme Harmony of all.[14] As an attribute of God, glory is one of those attributes that he shares with his creatures by grace. But unlike his glory, which is radiant glory like that which shone from within the person of Jesus on the Mount of Transfiguration (Matt. 17:2; Mark 9:2–4; 2 Pet. 1:16–17), the glory we humans receive now (2 Cor. 3:18) and will receive when we see Jesus is a *reflected* glory.

Going back to Romans 8, Paul already in verse 29 signals what our glorification looks like. Our intended telos as glorified people is in accordance with our having been "predestined to be conformed to the image of his Son, that he might be the firstborn among many brothers and sisters." Our telos is to be like Christ—glorification is specifically Christification. Our telos is also to be united with the whole community of the family that God the Father has given his beloved Son. Like justification and sanctification and vocation, glorification is derived from and consists in our union with Jesus, and it is

---

14. See Edwards, *Religious Affections*, 238, for just one example. As Gerald McDermott claims, Edwards's aesthetic vision "distinguishes him as probably the foremost of Christian theologians who relate God and beauty" (McDermott, review of *The Sermons of Jonathan Edwards*, ed. Kimnach, Minkema, and Sweeney). Robert Jenson sums up his own important study of Edwards in this fashion: "As we have had occasion to note in almost every chapter, the very template of his vision is that God as Triunity is 'the supreme Harmony of all.' . . . Indeed, he did not merely maintain trinitarianism; he renewed it" (Jenson, *America's Theologian*, 91). Jenson is here citing Edwards's own reference to "the supreme Harmony" in *The "Miscellanies,"* no. 182 (*Works of Jonathan Edwards*, 13:329).

defined by likeness to Jesus and his glory. He is, as the writer of Hebrews says, "bringing many sons and daughters to glory" (Heb. 2:10). There can be no doubt that the glory we will receive when we see Christ will be glory reflected from Christ. It is also crystal clear that our glorification does not make us God, as if we are swallowed up into the essence of God. It makes us fully human, just as Christ is fully human. First Corinthians 15:49 informs us that we will "bear the image of the heavenly man." The nature of our glorified state is that of the immortal humanity of the risen, ascended Christ, not that of angels, and not that of God.

It is important to clarify what the theological terms "theosis" and "beatific vision" mean. There has been a tendency for Western and specifically Protestant theologians to critique the term "theosis," or "divinization" or "deification," which has typically been more prominent in Orthodox theology. (The theme is also present in Western Catholic theology and in Lutheran and Protestant theology.) The critique is that there is a blurring of divinity and humanity, an accusation that human persons in Christ are "Godded with God" and that the beatific vision therefore climaxes this process with the transformation of humans into God. This is an unfortunate and crass critique. The reality is that, going all the way back to Athanasius—who said of Christ, "He was made human so that he might make us gods [or God]"[15]—the term "theosis" did not have the metaphysical confusion that we may imagine. Athanasius was so orthodox as to even define orthodoxy in his christological debate with Arius. The Catholic theologian John of the Cross spells out unequivocally that the patristic understanding of theosis did not seek to do away with the fundamental metaphysical difference between God and humanity. He assures us that even after glorification, "it is true that its natural being, though thus transformed, is as distinct from the Being of God as it was before."[16] Our church fathers were trying to emphasize that our salvation, including glorification, has its source not within ourselves but within God, and in particular within our union with Christ, which was brought about by his union with our humanity. Just as in the hypostatic union the divine and human natures are unmixed, or unconfused, so in our union with Christ our personhood and Christ's are unconfused. We become morally like Christ, not metaphysically like him. We are at best reflectors of his glory. We reflect it because we are in relational union with Jesus. And when, as 1 John 3:2 puts it, we see Jesus at the end of our journey of sanctification, we will be like him morally but remain metaphysically still human like he is.

15. Athanasius, *On the Incarnation of the Word* 54.3.
16. John of the Cross, *The Ascent of Mount Carmel* 2.5.7, quoted in Foley, *The Ascent of Mount Carmel*, 38.

The comments above defending the intent of church fathers concerning theosis and the beatific vision should not be taken to mean that all the fathers spoke all the time with clarity and truth. For example, Augustine compares the bodies of the saints to "the ethereal bodies of the stars."[17] T. F. Torrance rightly suggests that this showed the influence of Plato on Augustine more so than the Scriptures. Torrance maintains that the term "spiritual bodies" in the New Testament (1 Cor. 15:44), which refers to our resurrected and glorified state, should not be thought of as something more or less than human. In fact, he says, "To be a spiritual man is to be not less than man but more fully and truly man."[18] The body of Jesus when he was raised is what determines the nature of our bodies, and as Paul Molnar points out, his "was a 'spiritual body' only in the sense that it was raised by the Spirit and healed of all corruption and decay."[19]

John's assertion that when we see Christ we will be like him (1 John 3:2) creates the expectation of what has often in the Christian tradition been called the "beatific vision." In the Eastern Orthodox tradition this is the culmination of theosis, known as *theōria*, which is the vision of the glory of God, and specifically will involve a saving knowledge of God in his triune nature. The term "theosis" can sometimes refer to the whole process of the sanctification of the believer, but sometimes to the end of that process when the beatific vision is seen. There are various versions of the beatific vision in the different traditions, including the Protestant tradition. In some traditions it is the privilege of the very saintly, whereas in the Wesleyan and Reformed traditions it is the grace given to every true believer.

The basic idea is that this is a "vision" and therefore not just mediated knowledge. It is a seeing of God that utterly transforms. We will actually see God in Christ. When we do, salvation, which Christ accomplished and which has been at work in us by the Spirit, will then be fully fulfilled (1 Pet. 1:9), and transformation into the image of Christ will be complete (1 John 3:2). Inexpressible joy will be the immediate result of this vision, hence the term "beatific." Immortality is also communicated to the believer through this encounter. Paul speaks of the grace of God given to every believer before the beginning of time but now "revealed through the appearing of our Savior, Christ Jesus, who has destroyed death and has brought life and immortality to light through the gospel" (2 Tim. 1:10). Notice again that this has been conceived in eternity past, then already accomplished in the first appearing of

17. Augustine, Sermon 241.7, referenced in T. F. Torrance, *Space, Time and Resurrection*, 140.
18. T. F. Torrance, *Space, Time and Resurrection*, 141.
19. Molnar, *Thomas F. Torrance*, 240n99.

Jesus, and yet awaits the final fulfillment at the return of Christ or the going home to be with the Lord of the believer.

The opening passage of 1 Peter actually reflects the concept and hope of the beatific vision without naming it. In fact, it moves toward the notion of the beatific vision as the climax of salvation "when Jesus Christ is revealed at his coming" (1:13). The passage begins with praise to "the God and Father of our Lord Jesus Christ" who "has given us new birth into a living hope through the resurrection of Jesus Christ from the dead" (1:3). Thus the Christian hope is *grounded* in the mercy of God, and it is *inaugurated* by the resurrection of Jesus. Peter then describes the nature of the inheritance that defines the *content* of Christian hope: an imperishable, incorruptible, unfading inheritance that is preserved in heaven even as we are protected until we enter into it (1:4). For how long? Peter says, "Until the coming of the salvation that is ready to be revealed in the last time" (1:5). Here we get confirmation that there will be a culmination of a salvation already accomplished.

Peter then points to this future aspect of salvation with all its inherent benefits to encourage and inspire his readers during the times of their impending trials. This is the *power* of hope. Their purgative and refining purpose to produce faith and all its inherent virtues will bring glory to Jesus when he is revealed (1:7). This indicates that there will be, at the time of seeing Christ, an appraisal and appreciation of virtues, and elsewhere Paul indicates that there will be a reward for faithful service to God (1 Cor. 3:10–15). Then while affirming the joy they have now, Peter, in a backdoor kind of way, seems to anticipate the beatific vision that will occur on that day of the revelation of Jesus: "Though *you have not seen him*, you love him; and even though *you do not see him now*, you believe in him and are filled with an inexpressible and glorious joy, for you are receiving the end result of your faith, the salvation of your souls" (1 Pet. 1:8–9, emphasis added). And then, after reassuring the believers that their salvation is in continuity with and a fulfillment of God's purposes in the Old Testament, Peter reaches the climax of the pericope in verse 13: "Therefore, with minds that are alert and fully sober, set your hope on the grace to be brought to you when Jesus Christ is revealed at his coming." This is the focus and climax of hope that transcends our inheritance and our immortality—the revelation, the unveiling of the person of Jesus Christ. He is the hope and the object of eternal contemplation for the believer.

Charles Wesley, the eighteenth-century hymn-writing theologian, refers to the beatific vision in this hymn: "Spirit of Holiness, let all thy saints adore thy sacred energy, and bless thine heart-renewing power. No angel tongues can tell thy love's ecstatic height, the glorious joy unspeakable, the beatific sight."[20] He appropriately makes the present and the future aspects of eschatology coinhere with each other. Jonathan Edwards, in the Puritan-Reformed tradition, was very much enamored of this vision of the glory of God. His idea of the beatific nature of the vision was rooted in the beatific nature of the very being of God as Trinity. The Father and the Son exist throughout all eternity in beatific delight, and the Spirit hypostasizes that delight, for he is the mutual love of the Father and the Son in the Western conception of the Trinity. Since we have been infused with the Holy Spirit, and since we are in Christ, we participate in the love of the Father for the Son, and we express the love of the Son to the Father. When one day we see Jesus, our beatification will be to be like him and to be drawn into the very love life of the Trinity.

One of the most difficult questions about beatification or glorification concerns the differing states of people when they die or when Christ returns. Is it the case that no matter where we have arrived in our pilgrimage of grace, we will be completely sanctified when we see Jesus and are beatified? Jonathan Edwards had one resolution to this question. He believed that the transformation that will take place when we see Jesus will be completed not instantaneously but in a way that moves ever closer over infinity. Thus, in whatever stage of maturity the believer may be, the glorification does remove their corruption and decay and evil propensities, and in that sense they are immediately made like Christ, but they will spend eternity contemplating his glory and inhabiting the new creation within the communion of the saints, and will gradually mature in all the moral graces of Christ. Other traditions have different answers to this question. The idea of a purgatory in the Roman Catholic tradition offers a solution in this regard.

Another solution is simply to say that, yes, indeed, by God's sovereign grace, we will all be immediately transformed into the perfect moral image of Christ no matter what stage of development we are at when we die. Is this not in keeping with the principle of Jesus's parable of the workers in the vineyard in Matthew 20:1–16, in which no matter what time of day the worker began to work, he received the same pay as the others in the end? After declaring the sovereign right of the owner of the vineyard to pay what he wanted, symbolizing the sovereign right of the Lord to reward as he sees fit, Jesus ended the parable by saying, "So the last will be first, and the first will be last" (20:16). Peter's comment that our virtues will receive praise (1 Pet. 1:7) and Paul's assurance that our works will be rewarded (1 Cor. 3:10–15) do not necessarily contradict the possibility that we will be transformed into Christ's likeness immediately. It seems impossible to square John's assertions that "we shall

---

20. "Maker, in Whom We Live" (1774), lyrics by Charles Wesley (1707–1788).

be like him, for we shall see him as he is" (1 John 3:2) with the possibility that only some believers will have that experience and that being "like him" somehow means different levels for different people. In any case, this is ultimately about Christ, about Christ being glorified in the glorification of his people, about Christ with his bride—a bride who reflects the Bridegroom's glory. Psalm 45 forms that picture of the Bridegroom arrayed in beauty and glory, and Hebrews 1 confirms that Christ is being portrayed in that psalm. But then a picture of the bride is described. Hers is reflected glory, and even the beauty she does have is oriented toward the Bridegroom. The focus of her beauty is him: "Let the king be enthralled by your beauty; honor him, for he is your lord" (Ps. 45:11). This is the focus of the beatific vision: his beauty, then ours, and then ours glorifying his!

An Ontological Question: What Is the Nature of Christ's Resurrection Body and Ours?

Having established that our glorification is one of derived and reflected glory, and that we stay human when we are glorified, we are still left with these questions: Even if we are still human, what will our resurrected bodies be like? Will we be recognizable as the persons of irreducible identity that we are now, with unique DNA and unique life histories?

The resurrection of believers is referred to in a concentrated way in 1 Corinthians 15, 1 Thessalonians 4, and John 11. A theology of the resurrection involves the future, holistic resurrection of all humans in Christ. And according to Paul, Christ's resurrection is the firstfruits and prototype of ours (1 Cor. 15:20–23). Therefore, the nature of Jesus's body when he encountered the disciples in John 20 surely tells us something about the resurrection state. He is identifiable as Jesus, and he is touchable. Thus there is a clear sense of continuity between his pre- and postresurrection bodies. There are differences, however. He can pass through locked doors and walls. Caesarius of Arles asks, "You ask me and say, If he entered through closed doors, where is the bulk of his body? And I reply, If he walked on the sea, where was the weight of his body?"[21] Postresurrection, the nature of the body has changed. Jerome concluded, with respect to the resurrection body of Jesus in John 20, that the "substance of our resurrection bodies will certainly be the same as now, though of higher glory."[22] He no doubt did so on the basis of Pauline insights: "So will it be with the resurrection of the dead. The body that is

21. Caesarius of Arles, Sermon 175.2, quoted in Elowsky, *John 11–21*, 356–57.
22. Jerome, *Against Jovinianus* 1.36, quoted in Elowsky, *John 11–21*, 358.

sown is perishable, it is raised imperishable; it is sown in dishonor, it is raised in glory; it is sown in weakness, it is raised in power; it is sown a natural body, it is raised a spiritual body" (1 Cor. 15:42–44).

Augustine asserts what he knows with certainty—that resurrection bodies "will be spiritual in the resurrection of the faithful and righteous" and that "there will be no corruption in them, and for this reason they will not then need this corruptible food that they now need. They will, nonetheless, be able to take and really consume such food, not out of need." "Otherwise," he reasons, "the Lord would not have taken food after his resurrection." However, as to the exact nature of these spiritual resurrection bodies, Augustine professes much less clarity: "But I do not know the character of a spiritual body, unknown as it is to us, can be either comprehended or taught. He manifested himself as both incorruptible and touchable to show us that his body after his resurrection was of the same nature as ours but of a different sort of glory."[23]

Pastoral Questions: How Is Human Personal Identity Maintained after Death, and Where Does the Person "Go" at Death?

With this awareness of what we can and cannot know for sure, we may well ask two questions. First, how does God maintain the continuity of human personal identity when death brings dissolution of the substance of the body, so that when resurrection occurs, the continuity continues (as well as the discontinuity, illustrated by the nature of Jesus's postresurrection body and expressed concretely in Paul's words "a spiritual body," in contrast with a "physical/natural" body [1 Cor. 15:35–50])? Given that even the DNA breaks down when a body decays or is burned, this is a real question. Or is it? Is it any more a question than how Jesus was raised from the dead? John Polkinghorne suggests that the soul is the *information-bearing pattern* of the body. He has invoked the ancient concept spoken of by Aristotle and Aquinas, who believed that the soul is the form (or pattern of the body), but with the very significant adaptation that he is speaking of a soul-body unity, not a dualistic "soul in a body" entity. Polkinghorne's concept does not rule out but rather includes our genome or genetic code of the body, which is crucial to the body-soul unity that humans are. But Polkinghorne wants especially to insist that this must include our "web of relationships that play so significant a part in the character of my personhood," as well as all the experiences that have shaped our identity.[24]

23. Augustine, Letter 95.7, quoted in Elowsky, *John 11–21*, 356.
24. Polkinghorne, *Science and the Trinity*, 162.

Thus, the soul possesses no inherent immortality. When someone dies, the information-bearing pattern of the soul-body unity dissolves with the decaying process. However, Polkinghorne crucially adds—and this is a *however* of divine faithfulness, not of naturalistic expectation—"It seems to me to be a perfectly coherent hope to believe that the pattern that is me will be preserved by God at my death and *held in the divine memory* until God's great eschatological act of resurrection, when that pattern will be re-embodied in the 'matter' of the new creation." He then adds, "A credible Christian hope centers on death and resurrection, and not on spiritual survival."[25]

This naturally leads to a second tough question: Where does the person "go" when he or she dies and the soul-body unity decays in the ground or as ashes? While I wish to affirm the broad strokes of Polkinghorne's thesis, I also want to challenge the now popular notion that soul-body integrated unity must mean that there is no hope that departed loved ones are in some sense in heaven now. I agree absolutely with the sentiments of N. T. Wright when he emphasizes that resurrection on a new earth is our destiny when we die, that "going to heaven" is not the ultimate, and that the intermediate state is less important and in fact a temporary state on the way to the resurrection state.[26] However, Wright does not in fact negate the possibility that departed saints are with Christ in heaven now. I wish to argue on the basis of the straightforward witness of Scripture that when believers die, their spirit—or the immaterial aspect of their being—goes to be with Christ immediately. I say this despite the risk of appearing to harbor Platonic notions of anthropology.

When Jesus himself died, he said, "Father, into your hands I commit my spirit" (Luke 23:46). His words of comfort to the penitent thief were "Today you will be with me in paradise" (23:43). In Philippians 1:21–24, Paul's line of argument that to depart from this life is "gain" (1:21) and "better by far" (1:23) is explicable only in light of the fact that he understood that death was "to depart and be with Christ, which is better by far" (1:23). Similarly, in 2 Corinthians 5:1–10, Paul again asserts that if the choice was just personal, he "would prefer to be away from the body and at home with the Lord" (v. 8). Death for the Christian means to be at home with the Lord. That much is clear. Earlier in this pericope, Paul seems to recognize that the disembodied nature of the intermediate state is anomalous for human existence. It is a naked state rather than one clothed with a resurrection body: "For while we are in this tent, we groan and are burdened, because we do not wish to be unclothed but to be clothed instead with our heavenly dwelling, so that what

25. Polkinghorne, *Science and the Trinity*, 163 (emphasis added).
26. Wright, *Surprised by Hope*, 190, 246.

is mortal may be swallowed up by life" (2 Cor. 5:4). Although the so-called intermediate state is a wonderful state, it is nevertheless a penultimate one that looks forward to the resurrection, when the inner being is again embodied, this time with a heavenly resurrection body.

If the idea of a body-soul distinction stretches the integrated anthropology that is rightly defended over against a Platonic view in which body and soul are separated, then perhaps some stretching should be done. An integrated anthropology merely says that body-soul integrity is the normal state for a human being. It seems possible and even necessary—given the biblical data above, particularly that Jesus committed his spirit to his Father as his body died and promised the penitent thief that he would be with Jesus in paradise that day of his death—that the body and the soul or spirit or consciousness are very closely linked yet are capable of being separated. There are various opinions about whether human consciousness is emitted by the brain, transmitted from it, or merely compatible with or permitted by it. The first is the materialist position, which does not seem to correspond with biblical language about the soul or consciousness. I do not think that this defines the body-soul integrated viewpoint. The "transmit" viewpoint is a participational view—that is, what the brain does and what consciousness is are mutually interconnected, yet each is distinct. It is conceivable that consciousness could therefore be separated off when a person dies and be sustained by the power of God. The last view, which says that consciousness is merely compatible with or permitted by the brain, involves a slightly greater degree of separation of soul and body—that is, the norm is togetherness, but separation is possible. My conclusion is that one must ground one's theology of the intermediate state in the plain sense of Scripture and allow some modifications to a rigid theological anthropology.

So it is clear that the most important thing about our future in the risen Christ is not that we "go to heaven and are there forever" but that heaven comes down to earth (Rev. 21:1–4) and humans are embodied in resurrection bodies. The trajectory of human history is creation as embodied beings, "animated bodies," then the fall, then redemption, and finally consummation in a new creation in which humans are embodied, not spirit beings or angels. The cultural mandate will be fulfilled in resurrected humanity in the last Adam. We will reign as co-creators with Christ in a renewed and reconciled creation. We will work in union with Christ on the new earth to which heaven will have come down. The bodies we have then will have continuity with who we are now, as well as significant discontinuity. They will be spatially limited yet will have a spiritual and heavenly orientation.

What characterizes us above all in this new earth is a metaphysical likeness to Christ's risen body and a moral likeness to him as a result of having seen the beatific vision (1 John 3:1–2). And we will reign with him as persons-in-relation, with the triune God, as members of the new humanity in the last Adam. And all will be glorious and for the glory of God.

A Third Pastoral Question: Is There a Resurrection of Unbelieving People and to What End?

In Acts 24:15 Paul certainly appears to indicate that "there will be a resurrection of both the righteous and the wicked." His belief is no doubt founded upon the expression of this idea in the Old Testament, specifically in the prophecy of Daniel: "Multitudes who sleep in the dust of the earth will awake: some to everlasting life, others to shame and everlasting contempt. Those who are wise will shine like the brightness of the heavens, and those who lead many to righteousness, like the stars for ever and ever" (Dan. 12:2–3). In Matthew 25:46, Jesus speaks of a judgment that naturally must follow the resurrection of all, with the result that some "go away to eternal punishment, but the righteous to eternal life." In John 5:28–29, Jesus unequivocally speaks of the resurrection and of his judgment of all people: "Do not be amazed at this, for a time is coming when all who are in their graves will hear his voice and come out—those who have done what is good will rise to live, and those who have done what is evil will rise to be condemned." The purpose of the resurrection of unbelieving humanity thus seems to be the receiving of judgment, leading to condemnation. In Revelation 20:12–15, John depicts the scene of the final Great White Throne judgment of all humanity in clear, graphic terms:

> And I saw the dead, great and small, standing before the throne, and books were opened. Another book was opened, which is the book of life. The dead were judged according to what they had done as recorded in the books. The sea gave up the dead that were in it, and death and Hades gave up the dead that were in them, and each person was judged according to what they had done. Then death and Hades were thrown into the lake of fire. The lake of fire is the second death. Anyone whose name was not found written in the book of life was thrown into the lake of fire.

Believers—that is, those whose names are in the book of life—will hear of the judgment on their deeds and will be acquitted and granted eternal life. The basis of the judgment of the unbeliever will be "according to what they had done," and they will be assigned to the second death, from which there is no resurrection but only a "lake of fire." Does this mean conscious torment forever and ever? Or is this a metaphor for the "nothingness" of evil, the absence of the presence of God, suggesting the possibility of annihilation? Even though apocalyptic literature is hard to interpret and conclusions must be tentative, if God takes the trouble to raise unbelievers and condemn them, it would seem difficult to hold the position that when they die they are simply annihilated into nothingness. It would seem pointless to resurrect people and then put them through a detailed judgment from the record of their lives in God's books if the sentence were annihilation. There is a passage in Jesus's teaching when he speaks about degrees of punishment, suggesting that the sentence is not the same for everybody: "Truly I tell you, it will be more bearable for Sodom and Gomorrah on the day of judgment than for that town" (Matt. 10:15). God knows not only the deeds of human persons but also how much revelation it would take for them to convert: "Woe to you, Chorazin! Woe to you, Bethsaida! For if the miracles that were performed in you had been performed in Tyre and Sidon, they would have repented long ago in sackcloth and ashes" (Matt. 11:21).

Another possibility for assessing this sober issue is to assume that there is conscious punishment for all who refuse to believe but then to bring this reality of Revelation 20 into conversation with passages that seem to suggest that all humanity will one day be redeemed. The destruction of death itself in the lake of fire seems to point in the direction of a purgation. One such passage that the church father Origen made much of was Hebrews 2:9: "But we do see Jesus, who was made lower than the angels for a little while, now crowned with glory and honor because he suffered death, so that by the grace of God he might taste death for everyone." On the basis of the assertion that Jesus, in his atoning death and resurrection, tasted death for everyone, Origen and other church fathers expounded a doctrine of *apokatastasis*, meaning restoration of all humanity.[27] One of the great philosophical difficulties with the concept of an eternal lake of fire in which humans and demons suffer forever is reconciling this with the fact that in Christ, by his death and in his resurrection, the whole cosmos has been reconciled (Col. 1:20). How can folks in heaven enjoy their bliss knowing that somewhere else in the universe such awful suffering is occurring? Indeed, if Christ is all in all in a new creation that includes the whole cosmos, how can there still be evil in it in the lake of fire? On the other hand, the great difficulty with universalism of this kind is how much Jesus himself spoke about hell. It seems best to me—given the representative nature of the life, death, and resurrection of Jesus; given that election in the New Testament is invariably christological and communal (that is, for all humanity in Christ); and given Paul's comment that it is the

---

27. See Ramelli, *The Christian Doctrine of* Apokatastasis.

desire of God to save all people (1 Tim. 2:4–6)—to say the following: there is provision of atonement that is sufficient for all, but God will not force those who refuse his grace, and his view of them in light of the risen One, to come into heaven if they don't want to be there.

Discussion Questions

1. How does the resurrection of Jesus lead you to offer hope to people who have lost loved ones to death?

2. What is your conception of the so-called intermediate state, and how is it consonant with hope?

3. In times of adversity, the church has often been adept at living into the blessed hope and the glorious appearing of the risen Christ with songs that reflect this orientation. Is there such a thing as a spiritual practice that cultivates the living hope of the resurrection in our times—one that does not lead to neglect of our mission but rather inspires it? One example to get you going is the Lord's Supper, which should always be taken in anticipation: "until he comes."

PART 2

Christ's Resurrection Has *Ontological* Significance

7

The Resurrection Declares
Jesus's Unrivaled Supremacy

Because of that obedience, God lifted him high and honored him far beyond anyone or anything, ever, so that all created beings in heaven and on
earth—even those long ago dead and buried—will bow in worship before
this Jesus Christ, and call out in praise that he is the Master of all, to the
glorious honor of God the Father.

—Philippians 2:9–11 (The Message)

Theologian Alister McGrath has expressed the opinion that the Christian
doctrine of justification "constitutes the real centre of the theological system
of the Christian Church."[1] Even though justification is very prominent in the
theology of Karl Barth, he insists that the critical article of the church is "not
justification as such, but its basis and culmination: the confession of Jesus
Christ . . . the knowledge of his being and activity for us and to us and with
us."[2] Of course, both who Jesus is as Lord and justification are declared by
the resurrection of Jesus. But in terms of logical precedence, the resurrection
declares, *first*, that Jesus Christ is Lord and then, *second*, that humanity in
Christ has been justified in him. In previous chapters the emphasis was on

1. McGrath, *Iustitia Dei*, 1.
2. Barth, *Church Dogmatics*, IV/1, 527.

the relationship of the resurrection to justification, juridically speaking, and even on the ontological grounding of this in the Son, who became one with humanity and died and lived again vicariously for us. In this chapter, we probe the person of Jesus more deeply.

From considering the saving efficacy of the resurrection, we turn to questions of *being* that are the foundation of that efficacy. In other words, our emphasis now is on questions of an ontological nature, beginning with what the resurrection means for the being, and therefore for the functioning, of the Son of God, Jesus Christ, as Lord. What does the resurrection do with respect to the person of Christ? How is he different after the resurrection, and how is he the same? In other words, what does the doctrine of the resurrection contribute to the doctrine of the person and work of Christ, which is sometimes called Christology? All the questions of our filial and forensic salvation hang on this, as we have noted, but in this chapter, Jesus *himself* is the focus. The focus is on what it was about his person that made resurrection inevitable, on what transpired within his person, on what intratrinitarian dynamics occurred in the resurrection, and on what was accomplished of a declarative nature by it. The emphasis is on the role the resurrection has in the attestation of the person and glory of Christ as Lord, as Messiah, as the Son of God in triumph.

It is impossible to overestimate the importance of the subject of Christology. Christian theology may include many topics, such as creation, humanity, sin, and evil, but the decisive grounding and criterion of all that it says must be the person and work of Jesus Christ. This is true noetically—that is, for how we come to know God—because even theology proper, or the study of God as Trinity, is revealed principally through the self-revelation of God in Jesus Christ. Christ is the revelation of God textured by his embodied humanity among us. As Daniel Migliore says, "Theological reflection on any topic is *Christian* to the extent that it recognizes the centrality of Jesus Christ and the salvation he brings." He goes on to say that it is for good reason that the second article of the Apostles' Creed is by far the longest: "Neither the first article on God the creator nor the third article on the Holy Spirit and the church has any distinctively Christian content apart from its relation to the second article. For Christian faith 'the Father Almighty, maker of Heaven and Earth' is identified as the Father of our Lord Jesus Christ, and 'the Holy Spirit' is primarily defined as the Spirit that empowered Jesus and continues his work in the world." He concludes, "Christology is not the whole of Christian doctrine, but it is the point from which all else is illumined."[3]

---

3. Migliore, *Faith Seeking Understanding*, 139.

I would add that any doctrine that can function without the Lord Jesus Christ as its controlling motif is suspect. A view of election distanced from the election of Christ or distanced from the covenantal and communal nature of Christ is problematic. A theology of the participation of creation in God that does not need the person of Christ, that moves from personal to substantial categories, flirts with pantheism. Ecclesiology that emphasizes the theological constructs of unity, holiness, apostolicity, and catholicity but allows these creedal concepts to be politicized and disconnected from Christ as the practiced center of the church becomes dry and dusty, sectarian and inwardly focused. This chapter cannot cover all aspects of this great and central subject of Christology. The focus is on what the resurrection teaches us about Christ.

It is necessary to say also that expressing the centrality of Christ in divine revelation is not meant in any way to diminish the deity and honor of the Holy Spirit. In fact, the role of the Spirit is tied up in what happens to the Son in resurrection power. Without the subjective revelation of the Holy Spirit within us, the objective revelation of God to us in the Son would be in vain. Even the objective-subjective way of expressing this has limits. The Son's existence as a human person at the incarnation and throughout his life on earth was enabled by the Holy Spirit. Even the offering up of his life at the cross was "through the eternal Spirit" (Heb. 9:14). The Son and the Spirit, although distinct in their irreducible identities as persons, are mutually internal to and interpenetrated by each other in a complete sense. Their works are indivisible. The indwelling of the one within us means the indwelling of the other within us (Rom. 8:9). Corresponding to his eternal, mutual relations with the Father and the Son, the primary work of the Holy Spirit related to us is his initiating us into two central relationships that are summed up in two confessions: "*Abba*, Father" (Rom. 8:15) and "Jesus is Lord" (1 Cor. 12:3). The third article theology (TAT) initiative by some theologians to honor the Third Person of the Trinity is laudable, to be sure. Yet the teaching of Jesus makes it clear that the Holy Spirit delights to point toward and glorify Christ (John 14:26; 16:14). This is evident especially with regard to what we may learn from the resurrection. The Spirit raises Jesus from the dead (Rom. 8:11) yet remains in the background as Jesus is proclaimed Lord in this event.

The meaning of the resurrection for who Jesus Christ is may be summarized as follows: it declared him the victor over death and the devil; it vindicated his essential identity as God the Son and declared that he is Lord, the Christ (Messiah), the Son of God in power, the Kingly High Priest exalted to the right hand of the Father, the Head of the church and the Lord of creation;

its upshot was the outpouring of the Spirit; its confession became the criteria and agent for human conversion.

The Resurrection Says Jesus Is Lord, the Victor over Death and the Devil

The New Testament asserts on a number of occasions that the resurrection of Jesus vanquished death and the sinister spiritual force behind it, thereby making Jesus the Lord. For example, in Romans 14:9, Paul declares that "Christ died and returned to life so that he might be the Lord of both the dead and the living." Since Jesus in his essential deity is God the Son, the eternally existent Second Person of the Trinity, surely he was already the Lord of all the dead and all the living—that is, the Lord of all humanity. Yet even if by divine right he was this, his resurrection as the Son who became a man—indeed, the representative Man, the last Adam—declared this to be true for the humanity he represented. When the Son became a man, he was something he had not been before. God had not taken humanity into himself until the incarnation, and even if the divine and human natures were not confused or mixed, the divine person of the Son entered into union with human nature. It is true that the Son was always destined to become human—that is, he was, as some theologians think, *incarnandus*, or oriented toward becoming human, before he was incarnate. This was even eternally so, some would say. This resolves the challenging issue of the immutability of God. How can God at the incarnation become something he was not before—God become flesh? Some might say that because the eternal determination of God to be God involved the decision that the Son would become incarnate, this was not really new. Interestingly, the conclusion of an increasing number of theologians in our time is that this new phase in the life of God means that God, rather than being timeless, is actually temporal. This does not mean he is temporary. These theologians are not saying that God is not eternal. Rather, the eternal God has some form of time in his existence, a divine time that is different from human time but is time nevertheless. There was in divine "time" a time when he had not yet created and when he had not yet become incarnate, and then a time when he had done both. God also seems even to accommodate himself to human time.

The point is that when God the Son became human and died, and then rose again, he became Lord of all the living and all the dead in a new way, as a man who is God. Death—understood as separation from God, spiritual death—entered human history when the first Adam fell. The intention of God for the first humans crowned as image bearers was that they would not die. It is unlikely that death did not exist in the animal world as it evolved, including in the species that were precursors to the first persons over whom God declared his image. Once humans became human and received the image of God, they were not intended for death. Death for humans came through the sin of the first humans. They were warned that "you must not eat from the tree of the knowledge of good and evil, for when you eat from it you will certainly die" (Gen. 2:17). For this curse to be removed, a new representative human had to be born and die and rise again—that is, conquer death by going right into death, as a human person, and by conquering its perpetrator, Satan, in death and in resurrection. This is expressed in Hebrews 2:14–15: "Since the children have flesh and blood, he too shared in their humanity so that by his death he might break the power of him who holds the power of death—that is, the devil—and free those who all their lives were held in slavery by their fear of death." It is also the crux of Colossians 2:13–15: "When you were dead in your sins and in the uncircumcision of your flesh, God made you alive with Christ. He forgave us all our sins, having canceled the charge of our legal indebtedness, which stood against us and condemned us; he has taken it away, nailing it to the cross. And having disarmed the powers and authorities, he made a public spectacle of them, triumphing over them by the cross."

The Role of the Death of Christ in the Victory

What role did the death of Christ have in the victory? Hebrews 2 and Colossians 2 make it clear that Christ's *death* itself was instrumental in the abolishing of death. In the great treatise by Puritan theologian John Owen, *The Death of Death in the Death of Christ*,[4] Owen's focus is on Christ's death. The death of death is first a part of the reconciliation effected by God's action in Christ on the cross, overcoming the enmity between God and humanity. This results in the justification, sanctification, adoption, and glorification of the people of God. Through Christ's death, therefore, and in Christ, dead human beings are made alive, are made children of God, and are eternally glorified. This is Owen's approach. It is not to reveal some mechanism by which death was killed, as it were, in Christ's dying. Humanity in Christ is raised from death spiritually, holistically, and ultimately so that death has no power over it. In pressing more deeply for a mechanism whereby death loses its power in the death of Christ, we are forced to engage the sinister person who inflicted death, our adversary, the accuser (Job 1:6–12; Rev. 12:10), who "holds the power of death" (Heb. 2:14). Something about the death of Christ

4. Owen, *The Death of Death in the Death of Christ*, 14.

destroyed Satan, and therefore death. This points to the model of the atonement called *Christus Victor*. Christ inflicted death on the one who inflicted death, ironically by dying. But how? It is easy for us to grasp that the resurrection destroyed Satan, since death was overcome in that act of the Savior. But what about the death piece?

I believe this is related to Satan's nature as the accuser and antagonist of humanity. As a result of the propitiating and reconciling work that Christ enacted on the cross, in his own being, in union with the whole triune Godhead, our sin and guilt were atoned for, silencing the accuser forever. This brings together the *Christus Victor* model and the *Christus Vicarious* model. It was because the Son acted vicariously for us from the time of his incarnation all the way to his death at Calvary that God took away our sin and its guilt, and victory over Satan was ensured. If, as Paul says in Romans 3, what Christ did as our propitiation and redemption and reconciliation enabled God to be just in justifying guilty humanity, then Satan is forever silenced. His power to accuse us is gone. The curse of the broken law of God has been removed and all righteousness has been fulfilled in Christ (Gal. 3:13). This legal aspect of salvation is also connected to the disarming of the powers and authorities in Colossians 2:13–15: "He forgave us all our sins, having canceled the charge of our legal indebtedness, which stood against us and condemned us; he has taken it away, nailing it to the cross. And having disarmed the powers and authorities, he made a public spectacle of them, triumphing over them by the cross." If the law of God has been satisfied, then Satan and his emissaries have been nullified. This is the death of death in the destroying of Satan's power over it.

In sum, the agent whom God permitted to hold death's power was destroyed in Christ's death, but this is dependent on an even more important dynamic of the death of Christ, which is what it enacted within the Godhead. Christ's death was both the substitution that enacted the decisive forgiveness or justification of guilty humanity by a just and holy God, and the satisfaction that brought positive righteousness and delight to the Father on our behalf. Both of these realities depend on the vicarious nature of Jesus as the recapitulated Head of humanity, the One who became one with us that we might become one with God. This last Adam, by triumphing in the midst of Satan's ploys in the desert and then ultimately prevailing against Satan's temptations in the garden of Gethsemane, reversed the failure of the first Adam in the garden.

The Role of the Burial of Christ in the Victory

What about the burial of Christ and its role in the victory over Satan and death? An article in the Apostles' Creed affirms that Christ "was crucified, died, and was buried; he descended to hell." Though neither of the creeds that expand on this, the Nicene Creed of AD 325 and the Niceno-Constantinopolitan Creed of 381, includes this clause,[5] there is ample support in the writings of the church fathers. Polycarp, Irenaeus, and Melito of Sardis make reference to it, for example.[6] Indeed, one of the anathema statements from the Council of Constantinople relates to the denial that Christ's soul descended into Hades.[7] One of the most challenging aspects of this doctrine is that some Scripture passages that appear to refer to Christ descending beneath the earth into Hades, the realm of the dead, can in fact be legitimately translated to mean the earth itself. Such a passage is Ephesians 4:9, which in the New International Version (NIV) is expressed as "What does 'he ascended' mean except that he also descended to the lower, earthly regions?" whereas in the King James Version (KJV) it is translated as "Now that he ascended, what is it but that he also descended first into the lower parts of the earth?" In the NIV translation, the text simply says that Jesus came from heaven to earth in his first advent, or even that Jesus's body was placed in the grave. The KJV assumes a body/soul or body/spirit separation and that the soul of Jesus was in a place where conscious spirits await resurrection and final judgment. As I expressed in chapter 6, the Pauline anthropology of the intermediate state seems to involve some measure of separation of the body and its normally integrated soul. Therefore, it seems feasible to assume that when Jesus died, his inner person was present in the spirit realm.

Another challenge to this view is that when Jesus died, he prayed, "Father, into your hands I commit my spirit" (Luke 23:46). While this text seems to offer support for the relative freedom of the soul from the body in death, it brings a locational challenge: Was Christ in heaven or hell? I suppose it is feasible that his spirit ascended to the Father and then took a victory tour into Hades. This anticipates the other great challenge to this doctrine of the descent of the soul of Jesus into hell, which is the difficulty of interpreting the passages in Peter that appear to affirm his descent: "He was put to death in the body but made alive in the Spirit. After being made alive, he went and made proclamation to the imprisoned spirits" (1 Pet. 3:18–19). One of the interpretations of what this means is relevant to the matter of finding a mechanism that accounts for why the burial of Jesus destroyed the power of death. This interpretation suggests that the proclamation Jesus made in hell was his defeat of the devil and death so that spirits in an imprisoned state due to sin might now be set free. It is

5. Holcomb, *Know the Creeds and Councils*, 35, 78.
6. See Alfeyev, *Christ the Conqueror of Hell*, 43, 44.
7. Miller, *Hells and Holy Ghosts*, 25.

not clear whether Peter uses the example of spirits who had been disobedient in Noah's time as a sample of all humanity, or what his aim is. He quickly moves to speaking about the few who were saved in Noah's time and making the water that buoyed the ark a type of the baptism that saves us in our time. He then clarifies what the real source of salvation is: "the resurrection of Jesus Christ, who has gone into heaven and is at God's right hand—with angels, authorities and powers in submission to him" (3:21–22).

The burial of Jesus, if interpreted in this way, provides some answer to the question, Exactly how did Jesus put death to death? As Polycarp, the church father who is the link between John the apostle and Irenaeus, says, Christ rose again "having loosed the pangs of the grave."[8] He appears to have entered the realm of the dead, declaring the victory he had won on the cross, and placed all authorities and powers under his lordship. His having entered that realm and then exited from it on the third day broke the power of the grave. As the hymn writer put it, on resurrection morning "he tore the bars away, Jesus my Lord."[9]

The Role of the Resurrection of Christ in the Victory

These mechanisms are valid and helpful, yet they still feel indirect in the sense that death itself seems to be an elusive thing. How can death become dead? What makes this challenging is that it seems nonsensical, a double negation, since death is not a reality per se but the absence of life. It is a nothingness that God meets with something, life—with Someone, Jesus![10] It is not possible to fully express the defeat of death unless we invoke the resurrection. In light of the crucial importance of the resurrection in the defeat of death, I suspect that even when some of the biblical authors speak of the "death" of Jesus, they are including the entire death-resurrection event. This is probably true for the writer of Hebrews, given his propensity to conflate the historical acts of Jesus. When this writer says that "by his death he might break the power of him who holds the power of death" (2:14), the resurrection is most likely included in the defeat of the devil and death.

In what way does the resurrection defeat death? If the death of Christ answered all the accuser's questioning and broke his power, the resurrection is the

---

8. Alfeyev, *Christ the Conqueror of Hell*, 43.

9. "Low in the Grave He Lay" (1874), lyrics by Robert Lowry (1826–99).

10. Karl Barth is well known for his consideration of sin, evil, and death as "nothingness" in *Church Dogmatics*, III/3, para. 50, 289–368. He illustrates well the primacy of Christ by making the Christocentric doctrine of election the basis for considering matters of theodicy, thereby ultimately replacing "theodicy" with "witness." For Barth, in the person of Jesus, nothingness (death) meets reality in the resurrection of Jesus.

demonstration of Christ's power. His resurrection defeated death precisely by breaking the power of Satan in his own realm, death and the grave; precisely by reversing the death principle at work in creation and mortal humanity with irrepressible, immortal life; precisely by replacing the nothingness of death with the endless, indissoluble reality of Jesus's life; and precisely by replacing the loss and pain in death with victorious freedom, peace, and joy.

Peter, in his Pentecost sermon, captures the essence of this: "But God raised him from the dead, freeing him from the agony of death, because it was impossible for death to keep its hold on him" (Acts 2:24). Later in the sermon Peter speaks of life and of the outpouring of the life-giving Spirit, which Christ's resurrection brings (2:32–33). Paul expresses this also in the triumphant language of 2 Timothy 1:9–10: "He has saved us and called us to a holy life—not because of anything we have done but because of his own purpose and grace. This grace was given us in Christ Jesus before the beginning of time, but it has now been revealed through the appearing of our Savior, Christ Jesus, who has destroyed death and has brought life and immortality to light through the gospel." Paul here includes the entire advent of Jesus in the victory that has destroyed death, but given that his statement also speaks of the destruction of death as a fait accompli, it implies the agency of the resurrection. It is surely the resurrection that "has brought life and immortality to light through the gospel."

In summary, as the old hymn by Thomas Kelly goes:

> Look, ye saints, the sight is glorious:
> see the Man of Sorrows now;
> from the fight returned victorious,
> ev'ry knee to him shall bow.
> Crown him! Crown him!
> Crowns become the Victor's brow.
>
> In the seat of pow'r enthrone him,
> while the vault of heaven rings.
> Crown him! Crown him!
> Crown the Savior King of kings.
>
> Jesus takes the highest station;
> O what joy the sight affords!
> Crown him! Crown him!
> King of kings, and Lord of lords.[11]

11. "Look, Ye Saints, the Sight Is Glorious" (1809), lyrics by Thomas Kelly (1769–1855), music by Joachim Neander (1650–80).

The Resurrection Says Jesus Is Lord: Vindication of Essential Identity, Declaration of Functional Reign

As the above hymn suggests, in addition to defeating death and introducing life (two ontological concepts), the resurrection changes something about Jesus. More accurately, it changes his role or function and titles. We have already noted that something about Jesus's body changes with the resurrection: it is now immortal, whereas before it was mortal. It is now oriented toward both earth and heaven, a body that is still physical yet one that is profoundly spiritual. It is now regal and glorious, whereas before it was a humble, earthly body, subject to limitations, in a state of kenosis (Phil. 2:7)—that is, the state into which he entered when he emptied himself of his preexistent glory and became human at the incarnation. But these changes to his human nature that are now part of the new humanity of Christ are also a signal of a change in his role.

On the one hand, nothing changes about the Son at his resurrection—that is, as far as his essential deity is concerned. In fact, it seems to me that the reason Peter at Pentecost preaches that "God raised him from the dead, freeing him from the agony of death" is because "it was impossible for death to keep its hold on him" (Acts 2:24). A man who is God cannot stay dead. He must break death's power. Another way to say this is that the resurrection proved that Jesus was God, specifically God the Son. In that sense, the resurrection was inevitable. Yet something does change for Jesus, considered as both God and man. As indicated earlier, although certain passages suggest that Jesus rose in his own right as the Son of God who has power over death, the preponderance of passages emphasize that it was God who raised him from the dead. In doing so, God the Father was saying something about his beloved Son, the man for all humanity. He was expressing his approval and pleasure regarding his atoning life and death. But even more so, he was exalting him into a new role.

The climactic statement of Peter's great sermon is this: "God has made this Jesus, whom you crucified, both Lord and Messiah" (Acts 2:36). The grammar is unmistakably saying that now that Jesus has been raised by the Father, he is Lord and Messiah in a way he has not been before. This same nuance is present in the summary description of Jesus with which Paul begins his magisterial Epistle to the Romans. There Paul states that the gospel is "regarding his [God's] Son, who as to his earthly life was a descendant of David, and who through the Spirit of holiness was appointed the Son of God in power by his resurrection from the dead: Jesus Christ our Lord" (1:3–4). What Paul says here does not give fuel to the heresy of Adoptionism, the idea that Jesus the man became God only at the resurrection. Paul's language is not essentialist language. He was "appointed," not begotten, at the resurrection—appointed not to essential sonship but to messianic sonship, a new function as "the Son of God in power." He was always God the Son for all eternity, eternally begotten of the Father. He was God the Son become human at the incarnation. He was still God the Son when he was resurrected. But now he is something he has not been before—he is a risen Man and, as such, the fulfillment of messiahship and the last Adam crowned to reign over the creation as the Son of God, who was the agent in creating and now is its Head, leading a new humanity to care for it.

The title "Son of God" in this context has Old Testament background and specifically relates to the Davidic covenant. In 2 Samuel 7:11–14, Yahweh declares his everlasting covenant with David and his descendants: "The LORD declares to you that the LORD himself will establish a house for you: When your days are over and you rest with your ancestors, I will raise up your offspring to succeed you, your own flesh and blood, and I will establish his kingdom. He is the one who will build a house for my Name, and I will establish the throne of his kingdom forever. *I will be his father, and he will be my son*" (emphasis added). The language used for the relationship between God and David's future son, the Messiah, is one of sonship. Psalm 2:7–9 repeats this same theme concerning a future ruler in a father-son relationship with Yahweh. It emphasizes the reigning of this person over all nations:

I will proclaim the LORD's decree:

>He said to me, "You are my son;
>>today I have become your father.
>Ask me,
>>and I will make the nations your inheritance,
>>the ends of the earth your possession.
>You will break them with a rod of iron;
>>you will dash them to pieces like pottery.

The New Testament declares that this is fulfilled by David's greater son, Jesus, and that the resurrection moment is his entry into this role. Hebrews 1 quotes these very same texts, 2 Samuel 7:14 and Psalm 2:7, as referring unequivocally to Jesus. The point of the writer of Hebrews in this first chapter, it seems to me, is to establish that Jesus is indeed the essential Son of God as someone superior to angels (1:2–4, 8–10). However, this is intertwined with declarations concerning his function as Davidic King and Messiah, which he gained by his resurrection/exaltation when he sat down at the right hand of God (1:3).

What the writer of Hebrews in chapter 1, and Peter in Acts 2, and Paul in Romans 1 are all saying is that in Christ's resurrection moment, the Father signaled that Jesus is David's royal son but that, as such, he is also the Son of Yahweh, as the Davidic covenant had promised. It is a declaration for Israel and the world to see that the Messiah has come and that he is Lord of the entire universe. Matthew's record of the Great Commission contains a similar statement: "Then Jesus came to them and said, 'All authority in heaven and on earth has been given to me. Therefore go and make disciples of all nations'" (Matt. 28:18–19). What the titles "son of the father" (2 Sam. 7:14; Heb. 1:5), "Son of God in power" (Rom. 1:4), and "Lord and Messiah" (Acts 2:36) mean has to do with an office that Jesus stepped into when he was raised and exalted by the Father. It is feasible to say that the Adamic covenant, the Abrahamic covenant, and the Davidic covenant all found their fulfillment in the risen Jesus, who began on resurrection morning to be the Lord of creation, the recapitulated Adam in a new humanity. And as such, he is reigning now at the right hand of the Father with all authority and power, working through his people, who in making disciples of all nations are bringing the reign of Christ to fruition until that day when all his enemies will be a footstool for his feet.

Philippians 2 majestically describes in what appears to be poetic form the change that was made to the office of Christ postresurrection. A full exposition of this majestic passage is not possible here, but two comments on the text will emphasize the change in Jesus while establishing what does not change. The V structure of this passage moves from exaltation to humiliation and then back to exaltation. The first comment relevant to our christological theme relates to the Son's essential deity, which is unchanged throughout the movements of his saving history. In moving from his state of exaltation in eternity to becoming a servant, a human, and then obedient all the way to death on a cross, he was always God. The repetition of the Greek word *morphē* in verses 6 and 7 is noteworthy. It is translated "nature" in verse 6 ("who, being in very nature God"), where it is expressed in the present continuous of his eternal existence, and again in verse 7 ("He made himself nothing by taking the very nature of a servant"), where it refers to his incarnation and servant life on earth. His essence as God is not incompatible with his essence as a servant. He is God the Son whether he is in the glory he had with the Father before the world began (John 17:5), or on earth as Jesus of Nazareth, or back in heaven having been raised and crowned with glory. His deity does not change.

The second comment points to what does change in the upward movement in Philippians 2:9–11: "Therefore God exalted him to the highest place and gave him the name that is above every name, that at the name of Jesus every knee should bow, in heaven and on earth and under the earth, and every tongue acknowledge that Jesus Christ is Lord, to the glory of God the Father." The resurrection, which is implicit but obvious in this text, means that Jesus has something he did not have here on earth in his humiliation or in his preexistent glorious state. He is exalted to the highest place; he is given a name of unrivaled glory and supremacy; he is given universal acclaim. He is also made a priest, a theme we will reserve for the next chapter.

This is mysterious yet wonderful. The Second Person of the Trinity cannot be more God and more iridescent in glory than he is eternally. He is God of very God. Yet in his becoming human and acting as the Human for all humanity, he lives as a servant, dies as a sacrifice for our sin, conquers sin and guilt and death and the devil in his own being, and as a consequence receives more glory, a new name, and universal acclaim. This side of the cross there is the beauty of revealed grace, the glory of a God with us, a God for us. There is glory that is seen by humans and angels not seen before the resurrection of the incarnate Son. Perhaps a way to reconcile these things is to say that what from our perspective is unfolded in our time was always the eternal decree of God in his time, so that although his glory is new from our human perspective, it was always in God, for there is no potentiality in God, only actuality.

A hymn comes to mind that may focus our affections on our risen, glorious King:

Majestic sweetness sits enthroned
upon the Savior's brow;
His head with radiant glories crowned,
His lips with grace o'erflow.

No mortal can with Him compare
among the sons of men;
fairer is He than all the fair
who fill the heavenly train.

To Him I owe my life and breath,
and all the joys I have;
He makes me triumph over death,
and saves me from the grave.

To God, the Father, my abode,
He brings my weary feet;
shows me the glories of my God,
and makes my joys complete.

Since from His bounty I receive
such proofs of love divine,
had I a thousand hearts to give,
Lord, they should all be Thine.[12]

The Resurrection Says Jesus Is Lord: The Outpouring of the Spirit

Another great consequence of the resurrection—one that may reasonably be thought to be placed under the general heading of his exaltation as the Son of God in power—is the outpouring of the Spirit. The texts about this event seem to suggest that Jesus rose and was exalted by the Father, who in delight at his Son's accomplishment gave him the gift of the Spirit so that he in turn might pour out the Spirit upon his people. Peter expresses this succinctly in his Pentecost sermon: "Exalted to the right hand of God, he has received from the Father the promised Holy Spirit and has poured out what you now see and hear" (Acts 2:33). There could be no greater witness that Jesus is truly Lord than the Father's gift to him of the divine Third Person of the Trinity so that the risen Lord can in turn pour out the Spirit upon his church.

This was the great sign of the advent of the Messiah spoken of in Old Testament depictions (Isa. 61:1–3; Ezek. 37:1–14; Joel 2:28–32). It was also the fulfillment of what the forerunner John the Baptist had prophesied concerning Jesus: "I baptize you with water, but he will baptize you with the Holy Spirit" (Mark 1:8). It is this that would spell out the messianic superiority of Jesus as the Son: "After me comes the one more powerful than I, the straps of whose sandals I am not worthy to stoop down and untie" (Mark 1:7). And from the perspective of what was going on in the Trinity in this great event, nothing could be more honoring to the Son than to receive the Father's approbation and to be in communion with the Father as the Spirit was poured out. This signaled a passing of the baton from the Son to the Spirit as the primary agent in God's ongoing mission to the world. Not that the Spirit would be working on his own, for he would be in perichoretic union and communion with the Son and the Father. Yet the Son's work on earth was complete, and the new phase of the Spirit's work on earth was evidence of the Son's exaltation. The Son had become incarnate, dwelling among humans; now the Spirit was coming in order that the Son could dwell in all believing humans as Lord.

12. "Majestic Sweetness" (1787), lyrics by Samuel Stennett (1727–95), music by Thomas Hastings (1784–1872).

The question of who gives the Holy Spirit in the working out of God's economy, and what that corresponds to within the eternal or immanent or ontological Trinity, has been a vexed question in the history of the church. The Eastern Orthodox Church has typically stated that the Holy Spirit proceeds eternally from the Father only and that this corresponds to the fact that in the economy, in accordance with most biblical texts, it is the Father who gives the gift of the Spirit to humanity. The Orthodox reject what is known as the *filioque* clause, which the Western Church added when it opined that the Spirit proceeds from the Father *and from the Son*. History is on the side of the East in this regard. The *filioque* clause was not included in the Niceno-Constantinopolitan Creed of 381. It was added in the late sixth century in some Latin churches and came to be included in liturgical practice in Rome starting in 1014. A possible solution to this impasse is to say that the Holy Spirit proceeds from the Father *through* the Son.[13] The substance of Acts 2:33 supports precisely this arrangement, as do other texts, such as John 14:26 ("But the Advocate, the Holy Spirit, whom the Father will send in my name, will teach you all things and will remind you of everything I have said to you") and John 16:15 ("All that belongs to the Father is mine. That is why I said the Spirit will receive from me what he will make known to you").

The instrumentality of the Son in the giving and in the ministry of the Spirit suggested by the phrase "through the Son," or even "and the Son," does seem to correspond well with the action of the Spirit in the Son's life. From the incarnation onward and throughout Jesus's life, and even in his resurrection, the Spirit was at work in and with the Son. In Romans 1:4 Paul states that it was "through the Spirit of holiness [that Jesus Christ our Lord] was appointed the Son of God in power by his resurrection from the dead." Again, in Romans 8:11 Paul makes it plain that the active agent in Christ's resurrection was the Spirit: "And if the Spirit of him who raised Jesus from the dead is living in you, he who raised Christ from the dead will also give life to your mortal bodies because of his Spirit who lives in you." So if the Son is raised by the Spirit, then there is a mutuality to the outpouring of the

13. This assumes that the Spirit proceeds in a single procession from the Father but receives from the Son also. The Orthodox have nevertheless generally rejected even the "through the Son" possibility. There are many factors to consider. Is this rejection a remnant of subordinationism, which the Orthodox hold on to and which may suggest somehow an access to the Father apart from the revelation and mediation of the Son? The plus side of the *filioque* is that it preserves the idea of the intratrinitarian communion of the Father and the Son. The *filioque* also does justice to the fact that in the economy, the Spirit unites his own mission to the mission of the Son, thereby serving the mission of Christ. This is in keeping with the Gospel witness. The downside of the *filioque* is that it fails to give full hypostatic freedom and personhood to the Spirit, a tendency in Western pneumatology since Augustine.

Spirit by the Son, and, as such, it is a corresponding honoring of the Spirit in his being outpoured. The concept of the outpouring of the Spirit can have the feeling that it slightly devalues the Spirit, as if he is the divine messenger. The opposite is true.

Theologians have been anxious to give honor to the Spirit as divine and as person in this event that glorified Jesus. After all, what greater gift can be given, even to a divine person, than the gift of another divine person. Of course, this mutual donation of the one to the other is what has been going on for all eternity. The economic actions of the one to the other, the Spirit giving life to Jesus at the resurrection and the Son sending the Spirit into his church, simply correspond with the perichoretic interpenetration of the persons and acts of the Trinity in all eternity. Nothing honored the Son more than doing something that reflected the inner life of the Trinity: honoring the Spirit in his new mission.

Thus, regarding the giving of the Spirit by the Father to the Son and by the Son to the church, defending the honor of the Spirit as God and as person simply magnifies the extent to which Jesus is declared Lord in this action. Here is the sheer wonder of this moment. One divine person, the Spirit, is given as a gift to another, the Son. And this divine Gift given by the Father to the Son is the Giving Gift, the Gift who gives out gifts that only God can give: regeneration, adoption, love, joy, peace, hope, the charismata. We often think that the Spirit was given so that what Christ has accomplished could be applied to human persons. This application of what Christ has accomplished is real and marvelous and crucial to our salvation. But *who* that gift is, is far more significant than what he does for us. He is the Giving Gift, the Third Person of the Trinity, God of very God. He is first a gift to the risen, exalted, divine-human Son and then a gift to us. The point is that the value and honor of the gift *purchased* correspond to the *cost*, which was the infinite suffering of Christ, and to the merits of his offering to God on the cross. Yes, the gift of the Spirit was the pinnacle of Jesus's exaltation as Lord!

The Resurrection Says Jesus Is Lord: Confessing This Is Salvation

And ever since the pouring out of the Spirit into human hearts, there has emanated from human tongues the cry "Jesus is Lord!" Jesus has been proclaimed as Lord by millions ever since the day of Pentecost. This confession, when it truly reflects the heart's belief, is the sign of the atonement accomplished by Jesus in his death and resurrection, and the sign of the regeneration of the Spirit. At the outset of his Epistle to the Romans, Paul speaks of the core of the gospel as concerning the Son, who is "Jesus Christ our Lord" (Rom. 1:4). Then in the section where he speaks of how salvation is appropriated by humans, he affirms that confession of Jesus as Lord is critical: "If you declare with your mouth, 'Jesus is Lord,' and believe in your heart that God raised him from the dead, you will be saved. For it is with your heart that you believe and are justified, and it is with your mouth that you profess your faith and are saved. . . . 'Everyone who calls on the name of the Lord will be saved'" (Rom. 10:9–10, 13). Notice the place given to the resurrection in this confession. Saying that Jesus Christ is Lord is almost another way of saying that he has risen from the dead! Later in his epistle Paul says, "Christ died and returned to life so that he might be the Lord of both the dead and the living" (Rom. 14:9). In his First Letter to the Corinthians, he states that the sign that a person is indwelt and gifted by the Spirit is their confession "Jesus is Lord" (1 Cor. 12:3). Peter's words on the day of Pentecost, "God has made this Jesus, whom you crucified, both Lord and Messiah" (Acts 2:36), set off a chorus of glorious confessions that continues to this day. This was in fulfillment of what Jesus had promised his disciples when he spoke to them about the coming of the Spirit. The Spirit's purpose would be to "guide [them] into all the truth" (John 16:13). The primary "truth" he was referring to was no doubt that he is Lord—and it included all the graces and offices and glories that went with that: "He will glorify me because it is from me that he will receive what he will make known to you" (16:14).

It is really important to note that our saving confession concerns *who Jesus is as the risen One*, that he is *Lord*. It is a confession of an objective reality. It is subjectively arrived at by the Spirit's inner working, but the primary emphasis is not actually *us*. It is about him! It is not primarily about our subjective state; it is about his objective reality, his lordship. Now, this is not to say that repentance or confession of our sin is not involved in becoming a Christian. Jesus's parable of the Pharisee and the tax collector who went up to pray in the temple makes it clear that it was the confessing sinner who "went home justified before God" (Luke 18:9–14). We cannot be confronted with who Jesus is as Lord and not be moved to confession. But it is really important to note that confession of sin is *evangelical* (of the gospel), not legal, motivated by the sight of who Christ is. Repentance at its core is first a change of mind about who Jesus is, logically, before it is a change of heart and mind about our sin. These things happen inseparably, and maybe imperceptibly from our perspective, chronologically speaking.

Nor does this diminish the importance of "faith" as that which justifies. Romans 10:9–10 makes it crystal clear that faith in Jesus and confession of

Jesus are inseparable: "If you declare with your mouth, 'Jesus is Lord,' *and* believe in your heart that God raised him from the dead, you will be saved. For it is *with your heart that you believe* and are justified, and it is *with your mouth that you profess your faith* and are saved" (emphasis added). Some of the debates about what justifying faith really means have focused on whether it is the confession of the identity and lordship of Jesus that brings justification, or whether it is awareness of his work on the cross that leads to a trust in Christ for our decisive forgiveness. Scripture knows of no truncation between these, or between faith and repentance. You cannot have half of a Christ when you believe in him and confess him as Lord. He is Savior and he is Lord. How much a person coming to faith knows about the intricacies of the atonement may vary, but they will know enough to know that he has died for them. How much a person knows about all the doctrines of Christology, including his hypostatic union and his Melchizedekan priesthood, will certainly vary, but they will know and confess that Jesus Christ is Lord. Every time a person believes in response to the preaching of the gospel by the Spirit's awakening and regenerating work, that person adds to the chorus that will one day fill the entire cosmos, with "every tongue" acknowledging "that Jesus Christ is Lord, to the glory of God the Father" (Phil. 2:11).

Two implications for the life of the church arise in this context. The first is that confessing Jesus as Lord could not be conceived of in the time of the early church without the baptism of the confessor. Baptism *was* the act of confessing Christ as Lord. Separating the moment of conversion too far from the act of baptism or making baptism an added extra to the act of confessing Christ is unfortunate and dualistic. It says we can confess with our hearts and lives but not with our bodies, as if somehow the body is not part of who we really are. Confessing Christ as Lord in baptism also gives a visible picture of the death and the resurrection of Jesus and of the union of the convert with Christ in death and resurrection. Real things happen, I am convinced!

The second implication of conversion as the confessing of Jesus as Lord is that he continues to be Lord in the converting life of the believer, in all of life, in every aspect of life, forever. The gatherings of the church are for the liturgical, eucharistic, and proclamational expressions of worship of Jesus as Lord. The scattering of the church in mission is with the chief purpose of witnessing through deeds and words that Jesus is Lord. When that mission includes work as a working with and for the Lord, and when it is seen as a caring for the creation Christ made and reaffirmed, Jesus Christ is proclaimed Lord.

Discussion Questions

1. Sum up what this chapter reveals about the objective reality of who the risen Christ is.

2. What does "Jesus is Lord" as a confession mean for you?

3. The singing of psalms, hymns, and spiritual songs is a powerfully transformative practice. The "resurrection as victory" theme and the "identity of Jesus" theme as a consequence of his resurrection are prominent in hymnology. Just one example is "Crown Him with Many Crowns" (Matthew Bridges [1851]), in which verse 2 relates to his resurrection triumph. Consider searching out hymns and songs that focus objectively on who Christ is and not so much on your experience. Sing one a day at the end of your time of Bible reading and prayer.

8

The Resurrection Signals Christ's Entry into His Office as Great High Priest and King

Lord, enthroned in heav'nly splendor,
first-begotten from the dead,
Thou alone, our strong Defender,
liftest up Thy people's head.
Hallelujah! Hallelujah!
Jesus, true and living Bread![1]

One aspect of the lordship of Christ declared in his resurrection that we deferred consideration of in the last chapter is that of his great high priesthood. His identity as the risen Lord certainly includes his priesthood. Hebrews is in large part an exposition of Psalm 110. This psalm speaks of the exaltation of Christ at his enthronement after his resurrection. In Hebrews 7, where Psalm 110:4 is quoted twice ("You are a priest forever, in the order of Melchizedek"), Christ's priesthood is celebrated precisely as a victorious exaltation to the right hand of the Father, and the passage explicitly states that he qualifies for it by virtue of the fact that he has an "indestructible life" (Heb. 7:15–17). It makes sense, therefore, to consider his priesthood as an aspect of his lordship entered into through the resurrection. This is further supported by the fact that

---

1. "Lord, Enthroned in Heavenly Splendor" (1874), lyrics by George Hugh Bourne (1840–1925).

the nature of the priesthood of Jesus, in the "order of Melchizedek," unites the priesthood with *kingship*. The resurrection and Jesus's indestructible, risen life declared him to be a priest (which includes the role of a prophet [Heb. 3:1–6]) who is also a king, as will become evident. How are we to understand this uniting of offices of priest and king in this one risen divine-human person?

To get at this, a little clarification is needed to shed some light on what the priestly-kingly "order of Melchizedek" means in Hebrews. For the writer of Hebrews, it is crucial to explain how Jesus could be both a king in the line of David and also a priest who was not in the line of Aaron or of the tribe of Levi. Hebrews points out that Christ's priesthood was not according to the Old Testament Aaronic order but in accordance with the order of somebody called Melchizedek. Melchizedek is a mysterious character in Genesis who is both a priest and a king. He appears suddenly in the narrative of God's dealings with Abraham, as recorded in Genesis 14. After Abraham had been engaged in a battle to rescue his nephew Lot, he is met and refreshed by this man: "Then Melchizedek king of Salem brought out bread and wine. He was priest of God Most High" (Gen. 14:18). Note that he is both a king and, at the same time, a priest of God Most High.

For a number of reasons, some scholars of Hebrews are convinced that Melchizedek is not just a type, like Aaron and his priestly order. He seems to represent God Most High directly rather than mediately. He blesses Abraham (this assumes he is greater than Abraham), and he is the recipient of tithes (a status normally reserved for God). Even the way in which the writer describes him in Hebrews ("Without father or mother, without genealogy, without beginning of days or end of life, resembling the Son of God, he remains a priest forever" [7:3]) suggests that he is a real person who, just like God, does not have an origin or an ending. So some scholars postulate that he is in fact the preincarnate Son in temporary human form on earth—a Christophany, which is the Son of God making an appearance before he became permanently incarnate.

This seems quite convincing to me, but even if the writer to the Hebrews intends his description of Melchizedek to be metaphorical by building on "the enigmatic nature of Melchizedek's appearance in the narrative,"[2] what he accomplishes is the same. On the one hand, the writer of Hebrews works out his priestly theology on the basis that Jesus is the antitype who fulfills all the typological pictures given to us in the Old Testament concerning the Aaronic order of priesthood. This is true of the priesthood itself, the sacrificial system, and the covenant undergirding God's dealings in the Old and New

2. Longman, *How to Read Genesis*, 172.

Testaments. On the other hand, he informs us that Jesus, in his functioning as a priest, did so according to a different order, that of Melchizedek, either by fulfilling a type described in Genesis or because he is the actual Melchizedek who started that order in Genesis 14 as the preincarnate Son and is now functioning as a priest in that Melchizedekan order. The writer of Hebrews speaks of a real sanctuary in heaven, "the true tabernacle set up by the Lord, not by a mere human being" (Heb. 8:2). This sanctuary is what the earthly sanctuary, the tabernacle or temple, was modeled after. It would seem that there has always been a priest in that sanctuary—one who appears suddenly in preincarnate form in Genesis 14 and then in a permanently incarnate way when Jesus was born.

All of this leads us to celebrate the worthiness of the risen Jesus to receive our trust and our praise and our worship. By virtue of his resurrection and his eternal, risen life, he has been declared to be *the King* who reigns forever over everything in the created cosmos, including over every human life. At the same time, he is *the Priest* who guarantees the eternal security of the salvation of his people, who presents the worship and prayers of his people to the Father, and who constantly intercedes for them, sympathizing with them in all their trials and suffering. Jesus became this King-Priest over and for redeemed humanity, first by becoming human so that he could stand in our place salvifically and stand by our side, sympathizing with us, having suffered himself; and second by being resurrected as a human being and assuming his position on the highest throne, where he represents us to the Father.

Having introduced the resurrection and the risen life of Jesus and their relation to his royal priesthood in a general way, we will now explore some specific connections. What does the resurrection of Jesus have to do with his priesthood? The Epistle to the Hebrews, Romans 8, and John 17 will provide some insights. The conflation of the resurrection and the ascension in the Letter to the Hebrews gives us license to do the same. We will observe that the *act* and the *fruit* of the resurrection are associated with the *sitting down* and the ongoing *intercession* of Jesus. References to his sitting down will be considered first.

The Act of Resurrection and the Seating of the King-Priest

In the rich opening verses of Hebrews, the writer immediately describes the resurrection/ascension "moment" as an installation into Jesus's kingly priesthood: "After he had provided purification for sins, he sat down at the right hand of the Majesty in heaven" (Heb. 1:3). It is a priest who makes purification for sins. It is a king who sits down in the seat of Majesty. This statement comes at the end of six statements about the Son of God as God's full and final revelation to humanity:

> But in these last days he has spoken to us by his Son, whom he appointed heir of all things, and through whom also he made the universe. The Son is the radiance of God's glory and the exact representation of his being, sustaining all things by his powerful word. After he had provided purification for sins, he sat down at the right hand of the Majesty in heaven. (Heb. 1:2–3)

The six statements seem to be in an A-B-C-C′-B′-A′ chiastic structure. Being "appointed heir of all things" (v. 2) answers or is fulfilled by "sat down at the right hand of the Majesty" (v. 3, the explanatory phrase concerning his provision of purification goes with that). The creating of the universe (v. 2) answers to "sustaining all things" (v. 3). The central phrases, "radiance of God's glory" and "exact representation of his being" (v. 3), speak directly to the eternal divine nature of the Son and explain his ability to reveal God as the full and final Prophet. The passage is actually introduced by a reference to the prophetic office of Jesus, who transcends the Old Testament prophets since he is, as Son, in a different category from them.

The offices of Jesus as they are introduced here and reflected throughout Hebrews can be referred to as the *triplex munus*. T. F. Torrance draws attention to the fact that the three offices are not often spoken of together (only three times in the Old Testament: Mic. 3; Jer. 18; and Ezek. 7) and that both Testaments speak mostly of a *duplex munus*, the twofold offices of king and priest (Zech. 6:13; Heb. 7; Rev. 5:10). However, he explains, this is because the prophetic function is considered to be *part of* the priestly office. Torrance integrates the three offices and their relation to the atonement of Jesus by correlating them with the three Old Testament aspects of redemption (*goel, kipper, padah*) that anticipate the redeeming work of Christ. The office of Prophet corresponds to the Word made flesh, Christ as advocate, which fulfills the *goel* aspect of redemption. The office of Priest corresponds to the *cultic-forensic* or *kipper* aspect of redemption—what Torrance calls *Christus Victima*, Christ the Victim. The office of King corresponds to the *Christus Victor* or *padah* aspect of redemption—salvation through the mighty act of God *sola gratia*, by grace alone.[3]

Hebrews certainly exalts Jesus as the Prophet of all prophets in various ways. For example, in chapter 3, the superiority of Jesus to Moses as prophet is

---

3. T. F. Torrance, *Atonement*, 58–59.

expounded. It is not even a fair comparison. It is not oranges being compared with oranges. Jesus is Son, Moses is servant. Jesus is the builder of the house of God, while Moses is just part of the house. The theme of hope from this passage in chapter 3 emerges again in the sixth chapter. The reality of the risen Son, who has entered the presence of God on our behalf as our advocate, is the hope of all in that "house" of the people of God. This prophetic advocacy is enfolded within his priesthood, however. We have this hope as an "anchor for the soul," the writer says, because Jesus "has become a high priest forever, in the order of Melchizedek" (Heb. 6:19–20). Again, in chapter 12, following the list of the people of faith, many of whom are prophets, the writer implicitly exhorts a contemplation of the supreme Prophet, the author and perfecter of faith, Jesus. However, the office of Prophet again merges with that of Priest in this passage. There is much to commend the view that it comes within the office of Priest.

There is a climactic nature to the paragraph in Hebrews 1:1–3. It ends with a statement that hints that the primary subject matter of the epistle will be Jesus's priesthood, a priesthood that does involve prophetic speaking, but one emphatically expressed by an all-atoning sacrifice for sins, and a priesthood in which he will forever carry and care for and comfort his people. And what brings him into the ongoing aspect of that office is an act of God, an act of resurrection and ascension and session at the right hand of God. It is to that seating, or session, of Jesus that we turn our attention.

In chapter 8, where the words "sat down" are repeated, the writer actually sums up the entire epistle. In doing so, he brings together the session and the intercession aspects of the priesthood of Jesus: "Now the main point of what we are saying is this: We do have such a high priest, who *sat down* at the right hand of the throne of the Majesty in heaven, and who *serves* in the sanctuary, the true tabernacle set up by the Lord, not by a mere human being" (Heb. 8:1–2, emphasis added).

These two aspects of the saving career of Jesus bring great comfort to the people of God. On the one hand, he has "sat down," a term that conflates the resurrection and the ascension and the coronation of Jesus and connotes a work that is finished. It has been said that in the Old Testament temple there were no seats, because the work of the priests was never finished. In the true tabernacle in heaven there is a seat—a heavenly throne at the right hand of the Father; and that Father has seated the Son there because the work of the reconciliation and the renewal of humanity and the cosmos is now complete. On the other hand, he "*serves* in the sanctuary." This is in the present tense. This is his unfinished work, by which he preserves his people to the end. We will return to this.

The third reference to Jesus's session is in Hebrews 10, where it emphatically signifies the finished nature of the atonement: "But when this priest had offered for all time one sacrifice for sins, he *sat down* at the right hand of God, and since that time he waits for his enemies to be made his footstool. For by one sacrifice he has made perfect forever those who are being made holy" (Heb. 10:12–14, emphasis added). These triumphant verses encourage us that because he has sat down, we are already decisively forgiven and are being progressively sanctified. These verses also make reference to the theme of something unfinished, for he waits for the final subjugation of all the enemies over which he won the decisive battle at the cross and in the resurrection.

In Hebrews 12 we have the final reference to the phrase "sat down":

Therefore, since we are surrounded by such a great cloud of witnesses, let us throw off everything that hinders and the sin that so easily entangles. And let us run with perseverance the race marked out for us, fixing our eyes on Jesus, the pioneer and perfecter of faith. For the joy set before him he endured the cross, scorning its shame, and sat down at the right hand of the throne of God. Consider him who endured such opposition from sinners, so that you will not grow weary and lose heart. (Heb. 12:1–3)

In this context, the triumph of Jesus after persevering through the sufferings of the cross is expressed in the "sat down." Here it is set before the people of God as incentive for their perseverance. The persecution-fatigued people of God to whom this writer addresses his epistle were to contemplate the Savior, and by participation in his life, they too would one day sit down. In Ephesians 2:6 Paul speaks of the believer as having already sat down with Jesus in the "heavenly realms," and of course this is true in a spiritual sense. Yet the writer of Hebrews urges a fixation on Jesus so that through his atonement and his intercession and their contemplative communion with Christ, they too will sit down, body, soul, and spirit, with Christ in heaven.

In Hebrews 6, the writer inspires the hope of the people of God by giving the most reassuring of descriptions about the security of the believer. He does so in light of the fact that Jesus has entered decisively ("sat down") and by assuring them that Jesus is there in an ongoing way. Having spoken of God's unfailing faithfulness to his covenanting promises, the writer concludes, "We have this hope as an anchor for the soul, firm and secure. It enters the inner sanctuary behind the curtain, where our forerunner, Jesus, has entered on our behalf. He has become a high priest forever, in the order of Melchizedek" (Heb. 6:19–20).

The Act of Resurrection and the Interceding of the King–Priest

We move now to focus on the ongoing priestly intercession of our Great High Priest. This is very relevant to the entire purpose of the letter of Hebrews, which is described by the author as a "word of exhortation" (Heb. 13:22) for the persecuted and suffering people of God. Before considering this aspect of Christ's work as distinct from the work he did before he "sat down," we need to consider how they relate to each other and how each relates to our atonement and preservation.

It is important, on the one hand, not to separate the sacrificial aspect of the atonement through the cross and resurrection, which is finished, and the ongoing work of intercession, which is ongoing. Puritan theologian John Owen devotes a chapter in his treatise *The Death of Death in the Death of Christ* to this theme: "Containing reasons to prove the oblation and intercession of Christ to be one entire means respecting the accomplishment of the same proposed end, and to have the same personal object." To support this union, Owen first illustrates that Scripture keeps them together, as for instance in Isaiah 53:12, which he quotes in this manner: "'He bore the sins of many' (behold his oblation!) 'and made intercession for the transgressors.'"[4] Romans 8:33–34 also features in support of keeping them together: "Who will bring any charge against those whom God has chosen? It is God who justifies. Who then is the one who condemns? No one. Christ Jesus who died—more than that, who was raised to life—is at the right hand of God and is also interceding for us." The gist of Owen's argument based on this text seems to be that the atonement accomplished by Jesus's death guarantees his intercession before the Father, which his presence there assures. Owen points to the verse preceding these verses to assist in interpreting them: "He who did not spare his own Son, but gave him up for us all—how will he not also, along with him, graciously give us all things?" (Rom. 8:32). On this verse he comments, "The love of God moved him to give up Christ to death for us all. From this, the apostle infers a kind of impossibility in not giving us all good things in him."[5] This interpretation is that the oblation and the intercession are related as the root of a tree is to its fruit.

Owen's second line of reasoning is that both the offering of sacrifice and intercession are functions of the priestly office: "To offer and to intercede, to sacrifice and to pray, are both acts of the same sacerdotal office."[6] He supports this copiously from the book of Hebrews and also from 1 John 2:1–2: "But if

---

4. Owen, *The Death of Death in the Death of Christ*, 32.
5. Owen, *The Death of Death in the Death of Christ*, 33.
6. Owen, *The Death of Death in the Death of Christ*, 33.

anyone does sin, we have an advocate with the Father, Jesus Christ the righteous. He is the propitiation for our sins, and not for ours only but also for the sins of the whole world" (ESV).

One of Owen's most telling arguments is the third one, in which he insists that the nature of the intercession that the High Priest Jesus engages in requires that there has already been an oblation that has atoned for sin. Here we hear Owen's voice at its best:

> The nature of the intercession of Christ will prove no less than what we assert. It requires an inseparable conjunction between itself and its oblation. For as it is now perfected in heaven, it is not a humble dejection of himself, with cries, tears, and supplications. No! It cannot be conceived as a mere vocal entreaty. It is *real*. He presents himself, sprinkled with the blood of the covenant, before the throne of grace in our behalf.[7]

The presence of the nail-scarred real body of Jesus that appears in the presence of God for us (Heb. 9:24) is proof of the need for the oblation and of the prevailing nature of Christ's intercession. He is not interceding in heaven as our risen Priest to shore up an imperfect atonement. He is there as a constant sign that the guilt of sin has been removed. He is also there as an advocate when believers commit sins and confess them (1 John 1:7–2:3), granting them restoration of fellowship with the Father on that same ground. He is also breaking "the power of canceled sin"[8] until his people are home—that is, he is by his intercession and the work of the Spirit sanctifying his people until they are glorified. He has sat down *and* "he waits for his enemies to be made his footstool" (Heb. 10:13), and his intercession is crucial in the subjugation of the enemy of sin in his people. As Hebrews 10:14 indicates, "For by a single offering he has perfected for all time those who are being sanctified" (ESV).

But perhaps the most effective argument Owen offers in this context is "Christ United Them." He demonstrates this from John 17, the high priestly prayer of Jesus: "For there and then he both offered and interceded. He offered himself as perfectly, with regard to his own will and intention [v. 4], as he did on the cross; and he interceded as perfectly as he now intercedes in heaven." Pertinent to the theme of this book, Owen then uses the resurrection as a marker for the beginning of the intercession of Jesus, thereby emphasizing its importance. On the basis of 1 Corinthians 15:17 ("And if Christ has not been raised, your faith is futile, and you are still in your sins"), Owen concludes that

---

7. Owen, *The Death of Death in the Death of Christ*, 34.

8. This is a line in the hymn "O for a Thousand Tongues to Sing" (1739), lyrics by Charles Wesley (1707–1788).

"complete remission and redemption could not be obtained without our high priest entering into the most holy place to intercede for us (Hebrews 9:12)."[9]

In summary, to reflect Owen's words and to use my own, the sacrifice of Christ and his intercession may be distinguishable, but they are inseparable, and what unites them is that both occur within and by the *person* of Christ. I wish also to express that this ontological reality, the person of Christ, is the primary category above the actions of Christ in either sacrifice or intercession. Being—the ontological—must come first, and it is in the being of Christ that we find the resolution of an atonement accomplished and still being applied.

We turn now to consider this second aspect of Christ's priesthood as distinct from the work he did before he "sat down." The ongoing intercessory aspect of the priestly work of Christ may be summarized as (1) a sustaining work that guarantees the eternal security of the salvation of his people, (2) a shepherding work that involves the impartation of his sympathy and his strength to his people, and (3) a liturgical work that involves enabling and gathering up and presenting the preaching and worship and prayers of his people to the Father.

A Sustaining Work

The intercession of Christ for his people at the right hand of the Father would have been especially relevant to the audience of the Letter to the Hebrews. Many of them had been displaced. They had lost loved ones and property for the sake of Christ and were facing death themselves. The writer gives them assurance in chapter 7 of their continuance in light of the irrepressible resurrection life of Jesus. On what basis can he save his people forever? He has an indestructible life (Heb. 7:16). Death did not destroy his life, and in the power of an indestructible, endless life he sustains his people all the way to the end: "Because Jesus lives forever, he has a permanent priesthood. Therefore he is able to save completely those who come to God through him, because he always lives to intercede for them" (Heb. 7:24–25). Death would not destroy them either.

This aspect of the intercession is also a source of reassurance in light of the moral imperfections and sins of the people of God. In light of the 1 John 1 passage referred to above, we may be assured that when we confess our sins, God is faithful and just in forgiving us, precisely because in the atoning act of Christ we have been decisively forgiven all our sins, and his presence in a body that bears the marks of that atonement before the Father guarantees

9. Owen, *The Death of Death in the Death of Christ*, 35.

our forgiveness and the restoration of our fellowship with the Father. Our sins do not require a fresh justification, as if to crucify the Son all over again. They require restoration of fellowship through our interceding Great High Priest. That we have such a High Priest encourages us to confess openly and frequently, as a gathered people Sunday by Sunday and as individual persons living the life of prayer.

Yet in light of his finished work on the cross and in the resurrection, his presence there representing us woos us to come into his presence not with confession first but with worship. The Lord's Prayer does not begin with confession. It begins with God! It begins with worship, with submission to the reign of God. It even permits us to ask for bread before we confess our sins. Why might this be? To start our prayers with confession is to be self-focused rather than God-focused. We can approach the throne of grace with boldness, first because our Priest has offered one sacrifice for all time, and second because he himself now stands for us in the presence of God as testimony to that sacrifice and its ongoing efficacy. Don't leave your praying without confession, but don't become so preoccupied with your sins that your Savior in all his efficacy and majesty is eclipsed.

Let's return for a moment to John Owen's concern to keep the intercession and the sacrifice of Christ together. He writes,

> The main foundation of all the confidence and assurance whereof in this life we may be made partakers (which amounts to "joy unspeakable, and full of glory") ariseth from this strict connection of the *oblation* and *intercession* of Jesus Christ;—that by the one he hath procured all good things for us, and by the other he will procure them to be actually bestowed, whereby he doth never leave our sins, but follows them into every court, until they be fully pardoned and clearly expiated, Heb. ix. 26.[10]

A Shepherding Work

The shepherding work of Christ is a most heartwarming aspect of the work of the risen Christ for us at the right hand of the Father. The writer of Hebrews makes the point repeatedly that the risen Christ sympathizes with his people because he became human by the incarnation and because, as the risen One, he apparently continues to feel what he felt as a man and therefore can feel the feelings of and extend sympathy to his people. Whatever the discontinuities between the preresurrection and the postresurrection body of Christ, one continuity is the capacity to feel and to pass on sympathetic feeling.

10. Owen, *The Death of Death in the Death of Christ*, 35 (emphasis original).

There are three aspects to this shepherding ministry of Jesus: his sympathy, his strength, and the accompanying, coinherent work of the Holy Spirit with the Son in the imparting of this sympathy and strength.

The sympathy and the strength of the risen High Priest are expressed together in Hebrews 4:14–16: "Therefore, since we have a great high priest who has ascended into heaven, Jesus the Son of God, let us hold firmly to the faith we profess. For we do not have a high priest who is unable to empathize with our weaknesses, but we have one who has been tempted in every way, just as we are—yet he did not sin. Let us then approach God's throne of grace with confidence, so that we may receive mercy and find grace to help us in our time of need." This is one of the rich summary hinge passages in Hebrews. It begins with a hugely inspiring statement that we possess a Great High Priest who has ascended into heaven for us. The title the writer gives him here, "Jesus the Son of God," is precisely chosen, for he is a High Priest of sympathy, which is reflected in the human name "Jesus." Yet he is at the same time the all-powerful, divine "Son of God," with all strength to lift up and restore those who are growing weak and discouraged in the journey. The sympathetic nature of Jesus is then stressed in the following statement: "For we do not have a high priest who is unable to empathize with our weaknesses, but we have one who has been tempted in every way, just as we are—yet he did not sin" (Heb. 4:15). It is apparent here that the impartation of sympathy and strength is not only for the comfort of his people but also to galvanize them in the face of temptation to sin or to give up the pursuit of the Christian life. The passage then returns to the theme of the strength and resources of the Son of God. We are exhorted toward the life of prayer, the living of life in the presence of God, because in that sanctuary "we may receive mercy and find grace to help us in our time of need" (4:16). Mercy and grace flow only from one who is fully divine. And, again, they flow from someone who is fully human, who detects and discerns our crises, "our time of need."

The role of the Holy Spirit is not mentioned much in the Letter to the Hebrews, but the fact that it is through the Holy Spirit that the risen Great High Priest ministers his sympathy and strength to his people is implied in other writings of the New Testament. For example, both the Holy Spirit and the Son are called by the same name, Comforter, or *paraklētos* in Greek. The literal meaning of this term is "one who comes alongside to help." In John 14:16, this title is used of the Spirit and is translated as "comforter," "advocate," "helper," or "counselor" (also in John 14:26; 15:26; 16:7). In 1 John 2:1 it is used of Jesus himself: "But if anybody does sin, we have an advocate with the Father, Jesus Christ, the Righteous One." Earlier we noted how much the Holy Spirit was engaged in the life and death and resurrection of the Son.

If the Son has now poured out the gift of the Spirit from the Father to his church, then we may assume that the ongoing work of the Priest and that of the Holy Spirit are closely aligned.

Jesus reflected both the indivisibility and the distinctness of the comforting work of the Son and the Spirit in his speech to his disciples about the coming of the Spirit in John 14:18–20: "I will not leave you as orphans; I will come to you. Before long, the world will not see me anymore, but you will see me. Because I live, you also will live. On that day you will realize that I am in my Father, and you are in me, and I am in you." Jesus first affirms that the coming of the Spirit will mean that his leaving them at the ascension will not render them orphaned. The presence of the Spirit in them will mean the presence of the Son in them. Then, reflecting his own distinctive role as the Son, he informs them that they will not see him (once he has ascended), and then they will see him on resurrection day (14:19). Then Jesus assures them that by the coming of the Spirit they will be brought into three great unions that will assure them, among other things, that the presence of the Spirit in them means the presence of the Son also. They will know by the Spirit's revelation that the Son is in the Father (the union of the Trinity), that they are in the Son (the incarnational union of the Son with humanity), and that, by the Spirit, the Son is in them: "and I in you" (the pneumatological union of the believer with the Son).

That the works of the Son and the Spirit are indivisible is axiomatic for the trinitarian persons. Paradoxically, that each "appropriates" their distinctive roles is equally axiomatic. Each is *in* the other in both essence and act, yet each is *not* the other in their irreducible distinctiveness of personhood and act. In caring for the people of God, the Son and the Spirit cooperate together, each in their distinctive ways, the paraclete Priest by praying and being present before God, and the paraclete Spirit by imparting the presence and power of the Son. Yet they do these things completely concurrently and intertwined and with the same aim. This is real comfort for the people of God in every age.

A Liturgical Work

The third great work of our interceding Great High Priest has to do with leading the worship and prayers of the people of God. What does the resurrection of Jesus have to do with the worship service of the church, its liturgy, its Eucharist, its preaching, and its communal life together? What does it have to do with our corporate and personal prayers? It would perhaps not occur to many as they gather that the real preacher and the real worship leader is

Jesus, and that he is not just the object of our worship, with the Father and the Spirit, but also the subject, along with us.

One of the most important messages of the Epistle to the Hebrews is that our priesthood as worshipers has no meaning and no power apart from Jesus's priesthood. In chapter 8, the writer begins by referring to this liturgical or worship role of our Great High Priest: "Now the main point of what we are saying is this: We do have such a high priest, who sat down at the right hand of the throne of the Majesty in heaven, and who serves in the sanctuary, the true tabernacle set up by the Lord, not by a mere human being" (Heb. 8:1–2). What does the serving role of our Priest mean here? It is the word *leitourgos* in Greek. It describes the role of Jesus as the new Head of humanity, the High Priest of a new priestly family who mediates and perfects our worship and offers it by the Spirit to the Father. Speaking of how Jesus translates our worship to the Father, a hymn of the church goes, "Much incense is ascending before the eternal throne; God graciously is bending to hear each feeble one; to all our prayers and praises Christ adds his sweet perfume, and He the censor raises their odours to consume."[11]

The following chapter of Hebrews contains a reference to the priestly ministry of all Christians: "How much more, then, will the blood of Christ, who through the eternal Spirit offered himself unblemished to God, cleanse our consciences from acts that lead to death, so that we may serve the living God!" (Heb. 9:14). The word "serve" here is also a liturgical word, *latreuein*, associated with service in the temple. The priesthood of all believers is an important truth for the church, and I believe we still await a full reformation of the church that takes the ministry of the whole people of God in and outside the church seriously. However, that priesthood means nothing apart from our priesthood in Christ's priesthood as our risen Head and Lord. The connection between his priesthood and ours is made explicitly in Hebrews 4:14–16: "Therefore, *since we have a great high priest* who has ascended into heaven, Jesus the Son of God, let us hold firmly to the faith we profess. For we do not have a high priest who is unable to empathize with our weaknesses, but we have one who has been tempted in every way, just as we are—yet he did not sin. *Let us then approach God's throne of grace with confidence*, so that we may receive mercy and find grace to help us in our time of need" (emphasis added). We have a Priest. Therefore, we are priests and can enter the presence of God.

At the level of our human need, we have great weakness when it comes to worship. The hymn referenced above also contains these apt words: "Though

11. "The Holiest We Enter" (1842), lyrics by Mary Bowley Peters (1813–56).

great may be our dullness in thought and word and deed, we glory in the fulness of Him that meets our need." Our concentration is scattered, our thoughts are often picayune,[12] our conception of the glory of God is infantile, our affections are often dull. We participate in worship as if it is *our* response to all that God has done for us, not realizing that we are woefully inadequate for the task and need an assist. Our worship is Pelagian in practice even if we are not so in theory. We deeply need an understanding that our worship has to be engraced, just as our salvation is engraced. Our worship is also functionally unitarian rather than trinitarian. We worship the one God as if we are unensconced in Christ and unassisted by the Spirit and undirected from and to the Father.

As the late Scottish theologian James Torrance assessed it, there are, broadly speaking, two different views of worship in the church today. "The first view, probably the commonest and most widespread, is that worship is something which we do—mainly in Church on Sunday." We may know that "we need God's grace to help us do it; we do it because Jesus taught us to do it and left us an example to show us how to do it. But worship is what *we* do." The upshot of this is that it makes our human priesthood the only priesthood, "the only offering our offering, the only intercessions our intercessions." As Torrance confirms, "It has no doctrine of the Mediator or the Sole Priesthood of Christ. It is human centered, with no proper doctrine of the Holy Spirit, and is basically non-sacramental. It engenders weariness." It is, he asserts, "what our forebears would have called 'legal' worship, and not 'evangelical' worship. It is what the ancient church would call 'Arian' or 'Pelagian,' and not truly catholic."[13]

By contrast, the second view is that worship is rather "the gift of participating through the Spirit in the incarnate Son's communion with the Father—of participating, in union with Christ, in what he has done for us once and for all in his life and death on the Cross, and in what he is continuing to do for us in the presence of the Father, and in his mission to the world."[14] Thus Torrance adds:

This second view is Trinitarian and incarnational. It takes seriously New Testament teaching about the sole Priesthood and Headship of Christ, the once-and-

---

12. This is a word I had never heard until J. I. Packer used it in grading an essay of mine on the Trinity in Jonathan Edwards many years ago when I was a student at Regent College. It means "small-minded" and therefore "trivial" or "of little value." It was used of a Spanish coin that was worth half a real.

13. J. Torrance, *Worship, Community and the Triune God of Grace*, 36–37.

14. J. Torrance, *Worship, Community and the Triune God of Grace*, 37.

for-all self-offering of Christ, life in union with Christ through the Spirit, with a vision of the church as the Body of Christ. It is fundamentally "sacramental"—but in a way which enshrines the Gospel of grace, that God in the gift of Christ and the gift of the Spirit, gives us what he demands—the worship of our hearts and lives. This is the heart of our theology of the eucharist.[15]

Our prayers, whether corporate or individual, are to be seen in the same way. Most Christians struggle with their "prayer lives" and are in need of a message that prayer is gift before it is task, that it is an engraced entry into a trinitarian communion going on all the time, an entry that begins with the prompting of the Spirit's intercession within us (Rom. 8:26–27) and is then facilitated by the intercession of the Son with the Father. It is listening prayer as the Father responds in the Son and through the Spirit. Paul gives a remarkable example in Ephesians 3:14–19 of a prayer that is profoundly trinitarian. He prays to the Father, thereby invoking the Spirit, who imparts the fresh indwelling of the Son in order that those prayed for may be filled with the fullness of God.

The preaching of the church is likewise to be seen first as the preaching of Jesus through the human preacher to his church. In John 20, when Jesus stands in the midst of his disciples to form them as the church that would continue his sentness on earth, he first speaks as that risen One. His message is one of shalom: "Peace be with you!" (John 20:19, 21). If what John is doing in this passage is giving us his image of the church, then what constitutes that community is the preaching of the Word. When Peter describes what that looks like in the early church, he says, "If anyone speaks, they should do so as one who speaks the very words of God" (1 Pet. 4:11). Preaching in the church is theo-participatory. When preachers have seriously engaged the written Word in faithful and skillful exegesis in the power of the Spirit until they have encountered the living Word in the written Word, and when preachers stand up to deliver their expository, gospel-focused, and Christ-centered preaching, they can by faith assume that the risen Christ is speaking in their speaking. This is affirmed in the Second Helvetic Confession of the Protestant Reformation, which says, "The preaching of the Word of God is the Word of God." This is the ongoing prophetic ministry of the exalted Jesus, putting a spotlight on an entirely different aspect of preaching. It brings relief and joy to the preacher to know that God is at work as the preacher is at work. The preacher doesn't need to do God's work for him. But at the same time, this perspective compels the preacher to study the written Word carefully, for it is

15. J. Torrance, *Worship, Community and the Triune God of Grace*, 22–23.

only to the extent that the preacher is expressing faithfully the intent of the Word (expository preaching) in the power of the Spirit (empowered preaching) that the reality of Christ speaking is possible. This is both a profoundly sacred and a deeply joyful understanding of preaching. Relevance to the culture is important, but the exposition of the text itself is the relevance. This is where the living Christ is encountered.

Notably, James Torrance also includes mission within this concept of high priestly and trinitarian worship: "Our mission to the world and ministry to the needs of humanity, are they not the gift of participating in Christ's mission to the world and his ministry to human needs? Is this not the meaning of life in the Spirit?"[16] These sentences communicate profoundly how the worship and prayers of the church are in fact the mission of the church—before a hungry person is fed or an inquiring person is evangelized.

What does the resurrection of Jesus have to do with worship and prayer and mission? Pretty much everything!

Discussion Questions

1. The world of high priesthood and of Melchizedek may seem strange to us. Sum up what role the resurrection plays in Jesus's priestly ministry under the headings of "session" and "intercession."

2. What could be done in the church to make people more aware of the engraced nature of their personal and corporate prayers and worship, as assisted by the high priesthood of Jesus? What would be the payoff of this?

3. If worship and prayer are indeed a participation in the communion of the Trinity, how do we signal in our liturgy that we are aware of this and that we need the aid of this communion?

16. J. Torrance, *Worship, Community and the Triune God of Grace*, 23.

9

The Resurrection as the Reaffirmation of Creation

The New Testament writers speak as if Christ's achievement in rising from the dead was the first event of its kind in the whole history of the universe. He is the "first fruits," the "pioneer of life." He has forced open a door that has been locked since the death of the first man. He has met, fought, and beaten the King of Death. Everything is different because He has done so. This is the beginning of the New Creation: a new chapter in cosmic history has opened.

—C. S. Lewis[1]

In this chapter we explore what Jesus's resurrection in a body means for creation. Does it have something to say about how God thinks of his creation? Does it in some way signal God's reaffirmation of creation? Does it in fact reassure us of God's ongoing commitment to his creation? Does it reaffirm the message of the incarnation that matter is good, that matter matters in the cosmos? If creation is reaffirmed by the resurrection of Jesus, if it says something about the created order, what does this mean for ethics, and what does it mean for the study of science and the arts? And does the resurrection of Jesus in a body also reaffirm God's commitment specifically to the human body?

1. Lewis, *Miracles*, 237.

The Reaffirmation of Creation

The possibility that the resurrection of Jesus in a body has something to say about God's commitment to the goodness of the created order is not something the Scriptures directly assert in any one particular text. It is nevertheless a fair and logical inference from all the biblical data concerning what the resurrection is and what it means. The resurrection of Jesus in a body certainly inaugurates the new creation. In fact, the resurrected body of Jesus is the very essence of the new creation from which the whole new creation springs. Since the new creation does not arise from the destruction of the old creation but rather is the product of the reconciliation and regeneration of that creation, we may say that the resurrection is the reaffirmation of creation.

A passage in John's Gospel that communicates this message is 20:19–23, in which Jesus appears to his disciples on resurrection Sunday, on the evening of the first day of the week. At first glance, Jesus appears simply to comfort and reassure his bewildered and fearful disciples and then to endow them with his great trinitarian mission, in which they will participate by the Spirit breathed upon them. But in John's typically metaphorical way, he is saying more. If this is John's metaphorical description of the church being formed, and I think it is, then the church is described in a creational context. The church is constituted as the new humanity in a new creation. The church has been formed, but the creation has been reaffirmed. We have already referenced the dynamics of creation and new creation in this passage:[2] the first day of the week, the wind, the breathing of God into humanity—all this tells us that John is crafting a picture not only of transformed disciples but of disciples who now constitute a new humanity in a new creation that has continuity and discontinuity with the old. The resurrection has formed a new humanity, but it has also reaffirmed the creation, forming a new creation.

The apostle Paul also makes the connection between the death and resurrection of Jesus, the outpouring of the Spirit, and the reaffirmation of creation. He also provides some insight into what the old creation needed since it was a victim of the fall of its human head. In Romans 8, he states that "the creation waits in eager expectation for the children of God to be revealed. For the creation was subjected to frustration, not by its own choice, but by the will of the one who subjected it, in hope that the creation itself will be liberated from its bondage to decay and brought into the freedom and glory of the children of God" (Rom. 8:19–21). Although the resurrection has already accomplished creation's liberation, creation, like the children of God,

---

2. See "The Resurrection and the New Creation" in chap. 5.

awaits the full manifestation of that liberation, and so "the whole creation has been groaning as in the pains of childbirth right up to the present time" just as "we ourselves, who have the firstfruits of the Spirit, groan inwardly as we wait eagerly for our adoption to sonship, the redemption of our bodies" (8:22–23). This passage assures us of God's continued commitment to what he first created as "good." What was good but incomplete has in one sense already been completed through the incarnation, life, death, and resurrection of Jesus, the last Adam and the divine Creator. Yet in another sense it awaits full completion at the culmination of the eschaton.

In his most majestic christological passage, Colossians 1:15–20, Paul seals the issue. All creation has been reconciled to God and has a place in God's eschaton, his future, which is already breaking in. Should we doubt the value of creation, Paul tells us that "the Son is the image of the invisible God, the firstborn over all creation" (1:15)—that is, he is its true ruler by virtue of his having become the ultimate image of God, the Man who is God. The first Adam is transcended by the last Adam. In a way that the first Adam could never be, the last Adam, after his incarnation, was the image of the invisible God in visible form. He was the fullness of deity in bodily form (v. 19), whereas the first Adam was a reflection of God in bodily form. Paul's point here seems to be that the Son of God, who became human for us, has gained the right to fulfill the reign over creation that the first Adam forfeited. Most important for our purpose here is that the realm of the reign of Christ, as a result of his becoming incarnate and his saving history, is a reaffirmed creation, not a discarded one. The advent of the incarnate and risen One leads to a reign over creation. It does not lead to the demise of creation.

In verses 16–20, Christ's right to reign over the reaffirmed creation is elucidated. First, in verses 16–17, that right comes from the fact that he created the creation in the first place. It was already his by virtue of the fact that he was its Creator: "For in him all things were created: things in heaven and on earth, visible and invisible, whether thrones or powers or rulers or authorities; all things have been created through him and for him. He is before all things, and in him all things hold together." But then, crucial to our point here that the resurrection of Jesus means the reaffirmation of creation, in verse 18 Paul speaks explicitly of Christ as the risen One and, as such, the source of a resurrected community, the church, of which he is the Head. Given the antecedent creational context and the coupling of the realities that Christ is both Lord of creation and Head of the church, the implication is that the community of the church in union with its risen Head is a community that shares in his reign over creation. "And he is the head of the body, the church; he is the beginning and the firstborn from among the dead, so that in everything he might have the supremacy" (v. 18). The final two verses of this great christological passage bring the themes of creation and redemption together in a compelling manner: "For God was pleased to have all his fullness dwell in him, and through him to reconcile to himself all things, whether things on earth or things in heaven, by making peace through his blood, shed on the cross" (vv. 19–20). The fullness of the essence of God became one with a created human body, and by that incarnation, by the reconciling blood of Christ, and by his resurrection in a body, God and humanity are reconciled—but so are God and the entire creation, both terrestrial and celestial.

The tendency of popular Christianity to separate creation and redemption, and therefore to lean toward a dualistic worldview, must come under serious scrutiny in light of the fact that redemption is the redemption *of* creation, not the redemption of believers *out of* creation, both now and in the future. Speaking of the "salvation of souls" is unfortunate language, for example, if by souls we mean disembodied persons. God is saving persons (the correct translation of "souls" in both Testaments)—that is, whole persons, embodied persons—for habitation in a new creation in which heaven comes to earth. Dualistic ways of viewing work are also cured by this perspective—that is, a separation between the work we do in church, and especially what pastors do in church, and what we do Monday through Friday. There is often an implicit understanding that church work matters more than work as a teacher or contractor or accountant, that the calling and work of a pastor are of higher value than those of a carpenter. This is dualistic thinking that must be eliminated by God's reaffirmation of the creation through his redemption and resurrection. All work done for the glory of God matters to God and is a participation in the new creation. The work of the chemist who gives creation a voice and explains the book of creation is just as valuable as the work of the theologian who explains the written book of Scripture. Work is not something we do outside the realm of God's presence and the kingdom of God—not something we get through in order to get to the really important work we do on Sundays when we worship. One aspect of the gathered "life together" of the church is that every believer offers up to God the work they have done all week, even if it feels incomplete and flawed. The risen Christ gathers it up and offers it as a fragrant offering to the Father on our behalf. It has often been pointed out that what we partake of in the Lord's Supper every Sunday is not wheat and grapes but bread and wine, symbolizing the completed work of Christ on our behalf but also the reality that, by grace, our work is caught up into his work in the world.

In sum, along with the incarnation, in the resurrection we see God's ongoing commitment to the created order. It loudly echoes the words God spoke about the goodness of creation when he created it at the beginning. It cries out that matter matters; that matter is good, not evil; that it is not of lesser value than spirit, as in Greek philosophy. The first creation was declared "good" by God in the account of creation in Genesis 1. However, it was not complete. It was eschatological. God passed the baton of the care and completion of creation to the first Adam, the first humanity. However, the last Adam actually will complete it through his resurrection and his new resurrection humanity. The resurrection recapitulates humanity in Jesus as the last Adam, enabling regenerate humans to live out the cultural mandate, to recover what it means to know human flourishing, to be fully human, caring for creation. It means the end of all dualism with respect to Christian life and mission. It makes science worth studying. It gives art its ultimate meaning. It also reasserts the moral order present in creation, implying the possibility that the ethics of creation and the ethics of reconciliation are one. It also implies that ethics, formation, and justice for the people of God are also for all humanity and that the church is called to be an influence on these things, in an evangelical rather than a legal manner. This means pointing to the fact that God does not give his commands to make life dull or joyless, but rather because they bring the shalom he desires for human beings. It also includes the church in offering alternatives that make following the way of God possible for people. Above all it means to present Christian ethical perspectives in a way that is filled with grace and not condemnation, with civility and not disrespect.

We now consider the relationship between the resurrection and the reaffirmation of creation as it pertains to science, art, and ethics.

Science and the Resurrection

If the resurrection means that matter matters, then this is of course a strong encouragement for humanity to study what matter is and what it does. In other words, the pursuit of the natural sciences finds strong justification and incentive in the resurrection of Jesus. The development of science in the West was actually facilitated by a Christian understanding of creation as a created good that was reaffirmed as such by the incarnation of God in a material human body and by his resurrection in that human body. Cultures with a low view of matter, such as some strands of ancient Greek culture, had little interest in science. Such cultures showed great interest in mathematics, which could be done without getting one's hands dirty with experimentation. Matter was inferior to intellect and to spirit and so was not worth studying. At the other end of the spectrum were cultures that sacralized creation to such an extent that fear prevented empirical engagement with creation.

The Christian faith, grounded in a doctrine of creation, affirms that creation is good but that it is not God. A doctrine of creation that was vindicated
by the incarnation and the resurrection of the Son of God was ideal for the development of science. A Christian way of seeing the world meant that matter
could be explored without fear. A Christian way of being meant that matter
should be explored because it was God's creation, over which humans had a
vocation of caring stewardship. An attitude of curiosity and wonder about
science should be part of the Christian *habitus*, or lifestyle, for everyone, even
if not all of us can be high-level scientists. Intellectual dwarfism with respect
to science is not a virtue for any Christian. It does not honor the resurrection.

The advancement of science undergirded by these Christian sentiments
is indeed borne out in history. The most eminent scholar in our time of the
history of the development of science and of religion, Peter Harrison, has
shown convincingly in his book *The Territories of Science and Religion* that
not only were science and religion not opposed, but they were actually consis-
tently in a mutual or symbiotic relationship up until the seventeenth century.
Science, birthed within the church, became a rebellious teenager in modernity.
The stark separation of fact and values drove the disciplines apart. Postmodernity has made us aware that the idea of the purity of reason is a fallacy
and that it is impossible to separate the investigator from the experiment. In
this particular sense (but not in all matters), Christianity and postmodernity
have some overlapping interests. In our time, it has become clear that there
is a close relationship between how we know what we know in science and
how we know what we know in Christian theology. Both the valuing of reason
and an awareness of the limits of reason have always been a hallmark of the
Christian tradition, which has affirmed since Augustine and through Anselm
a "faith seeking understanding" approach to epistemology. There has been a
humble awareness that, apart from the incarnation, by which God has been
revealed, and apart from the illuminating work of the Holy Spirit and the
communal reception of theology by the church throughout the ages, our
knowledge is limited. We know only within a hermeneutical circle of divine
triune revelation. Though not articulated as such until recently, this may be
described as a form of critical realism. With respect to the resurrection, as
indicated in chapter 1, Christians do not seek absolute proof in a way that
smacks of the naive separation of reason and faith within modernity. We noted
that both science and historical studies are governed not by logical positivism,
or verificationism, but by falsificationism or "truthlikeness," that which best
corresponds with the evidence.[3]

3. See "What Can Be Proved?" in chap. 1.

The polarization of reason and faith within modernity stands in contrast not only to premodern sensibilities but also to how early evangelicals viewed this matter. It would never have dawned on John Wesley, for example, that theology or biblical studies was done by faith whereas science was done by reason. In his writing on hermeneutics, Wesley affirms that the primary mode of interpretation in all intellectual pursuits, including theology and biblical studies, is reason, which, he suggests, "God has given us . . . for a guide." In an affirmation of reason's role in all aspects of knowledge, he writes, "Reason can assist us in going through the whole circle of arts and sciences; of grammar, rhetoric, logic, natural and moral philosophy, mathematics, algebra, metaphysics. . . . If you ask, what can reason do in religion? I answer, it can do exceeding much, both with regard to the foundation of it, and the superstructure."[4] There is also an acknowledgment of the need of the Holy Spirit and faith in these endeavors too, but this, for Wesley, was not in opposition to reason. The use of reason when it came to interpreting Scripture also led him to affirm that the purpose of the Scriptures was not to be a scientific textbook, since its purpose is primarily salvific. He articulates that it is a mistake to make the Scriptures say what the author did not intend to say, especially with respect to scientific matters. Within that framework of the proper understanding of the nature and purpose of Scripture, Wesley encouraged the interpreter to draw upon all resources available, including scientific ones, in the search for truth.[5]

The resurrection of Jesus as historical fact is vital to the Christian faith in general, but it is also a marker of the fact that the Christian faith is a historical faith grounded in a Man who is God! The union of God and humanity in the Son and the continuance of this union in the resurrection might be considered to be a heuristic for the union of theology and science. The resurrection of God the Son in a body declares that the domain of science and theology is one, yet differentiated. I have argued elsewhere, with T. F. Torrance and others, that theology and science are in fact coinherent, just as the divine and human natures of the risen Son are coinherent.[6] This means that each is in the other, yet each is not the other. Mutuality and particularity are what characterize the hypostatic union: the divine nature and the human nature are both true

4. Wesley, "The Case of Reason Impartially Considered."

5. Consider Wesley's integration of scientific discovery and theology: "We say, the moon moves round the earth; the earth and the other planets move round the sun; the sun moves round its own axis. But these are only vulgar expressions: for, if we speak the truth, neither the sun, moon, nor stars move. None of these move themselves: They are all *moved* every moment by the almighty hand that made them." See Wesley, "Spiritual Worship," Sermon 77, I.6 (*Works of John Wesley*, 3:92–93).

6. See Hastings, *Echoes of Coinherence*, and references therein.

and full in the Son. They interpenetrate each other to some extent, yet each is distinct and unmixed or unconfused. In fact, it was the divine *person* of the Son who assumed a human nature, and therefore the divine nature has precedence, as Chalcedon asserted. Similarly, revealed conciliar theology is the queen of the sciences. Nevertheless, science, even if it is subject to credal theology for Christians pursuing science, must be respected in its own right. Theologians should not tell scientists how to conduct their guild. Yet there is a deep mutuality of these disciplines in which each can be enriched by the other. It is hoped that scientists will in fact develop a second order theology of science as they reflect theologically on their science. Union with differentiation is present in the Son of God, and indeed it is the very essence of the triune God. Each of the persons is in the other, yet each is not the other. This is then echoed in many aspects of the cosmos and in the pursuit of knowledge about God (theology) and about creation (science).

In addition to the recognition of the consonance of theology and science with respect to knowing, there is a profound ontological overlap inherent in these disciplines, as suggested precisely by the presence of both God and humanity in the incarnate Son of God and as this was reaffirmed in the resurrected Christ. God's decision in eternity past to enter his creation in the incarnation of the Son was an eternal decision. The Son was *incarnandus*—that is, oriented toward becoming human even before the incarnation—and after it he is forever incarnate. Today, humanity is still in the Godhead in the person of the risen, exalted Son at the right hand of the Father in the communion of the Holy Spirit. Nothing conveys more graphically the union of the pursuit of the knowledge of God in theology and the pursuit of the knowledge of his creation through science. God is not the same as his creation, despite popular pantheistic notions of "mother earth" and "the universe has spoken." God has come into his creation in the incarnation in a way that does not confuse or confound God and humanity. He did so in order to redeem humanity and creation, in order to show his commitment to his creation, in order that humanity might play its proper earth-keeping role in creation. There can never be a dualism of the spiritual and the physical in Christian theology. Knowledge of God and knowledge of his creation go together. When Jesus rose from the dead, creation was reaffirmed in its goodness, and humanity in Jesus was reconciled and regenerated in order to fulfill its stewarding role. Part of that stewarding is knowing who God is and who we are as human image bearers and knowing what creation is and how it functions. Jesus rose from the dead as the God-Man. That is theology. He rose from the dead to reaffirm creation and reconstitute a humanity devoted to caring for creation. That is science. Yes, the resurrection matters!

And if God is the Creator, we might even expect to see some ontological resonance of who he is within creation. This involves humanity, which is the *image* of God, but also discovering aspects of the nonhuman creation as *traces* of the triune God. This might include, for example, the relationality of the triune God and the relationality of many aspects of his creation, as seen in chemical bonding, in quantum entanglement in the EPR (Einstein-Podolsky-Rosen) effect, in ecology, and so on. We might also expect that the beauty of the triune God, three persons in perfect harmony, might be echoed in the beauty of creation and the human capacity to appreciate beauty. This is an appropriate segue to speaking of the arts.

The Arts and the Resurrection

Whatever might the resurrection of Jesus have to do with the arts, with music, with painting, with sculpture, with drama and opera? There are two ways of thinking about this. Both relate to being, or ontology. Aesthetics relates to the divine being. First, if God the Creator is the "supreme Harmony of all," as Jonathan Edwards suggested,[7] then his beauty might be expected in his creation. Beauty is not something we ascribe to God; he defines it; he is beauty itself. All beauty perceived in creation is a reflection of his divine glory and "God-ness" (Ps. 19:1–6; Rom. 1:20). All humans have some capacity to appreciate beauty and therefore to create beauty in astonishing ways. Indeed, this may be one of the most important distinctives that define humans as image bearers. Yet it would appear that regenerate humans have a greater capacity to appreciate the source of beauty. When the psalmist says, "Worship the LORD in the beauty of holiness" (Ps. 96:9 KJV), the beauty of holiness does not mean much to those who have not yet gained what Edwards called a "new sense" of things. In 1740, he wrote retrospectively of his conversion, by which he gained a "new sense" of "the glory of the divine being" as specifically involving the Trinity: "God has appeared more glorious to me, on account of the Trinity. . . . It has made me have more exalting thoughts of God, that he subsists as three persons; Father, Son, and Holy Ghost."[8] The risen Christ is the fullness of the divine revelation of the Trinity and of beauty, and he is the means by which darkened human eyes are opened to see that beauty and the beauty of the world God created and the risen Son reaffirmed. This would seem to suggest that the worship of the church ought to be artistic, that the theological precision of worship should be accompanied by the aesthetic skill

7. See Edwards, *The "Miscellanies,"* no. 182 (*Works of Jonathan Edwards,* 13:329).
8. Edwards, "Personal Narrative," in *Letters and Personal Writings* (*Works of Jonathan Edwards,* 16:800).

and character of worship. The act of a woman in the Gospels epitomizes how worship should be expressed: "She has done a beautiful thing to me" (Mark 14:6). This would also suggest that the church should be the home of the arts, as it was in the High Renaissance.

There is, second, however, a particularly christological dimension to this, for the Son is often spoken of as the agent in creation, and the glory of God was made visible in the person of Christ. The revelation of God as Trinity is textured in the concreteness of the risen Son. That person is God in flesh, the paradigm of God's relationship to creation. Creation must therefore reflect something of the beauty of the Creator because creation is in union with God in the risen Son. The incarnate and risen Son was God manifest in flesh (John 1:14, 18). Whereas in Jesus's incarnate days prior to his resurrection and exaltation, that beauty or glory was veiled in his humble humanity, post-resurrection and especially postexaltation, the glory was unveiled. Prior to the cross in his high priestly prayer, Jesus prayed, "Father, glorify me in your presence with the glory I had with you before the world began" (17:5). It is a fair assumption that the risen Christ now radiates that iridescent glory. Glory and beauty are largely synonymous. Glory is the outshining of inner excellence. Now, since Christ is the Head of the church and the Lord of creation and the King of his kingdom, he surely imparts beauty and glory in every realm. He made all things with beauty, and the resurrection is the sign of the recovery and reaffirmation of beauty in the cosmos and an anticipation that the ugliness of disease and sin and death will one day be eliminated.

The arts are the product of the appreciation of beauty, and then they are the expression of that beauty in creations made by humans. Humans reflect the creativeness of the Creator in their creations, and they do so with varying degrees of beauty that reflect the Creator. The arts reflect the embodiment of humans and creation in ways that correspond to the wonderful affirmation given to the human body in Christ's risen body. The paintings and sculptures of Leonardo da Vinci and Michelangelo provide a notable example of appreciation of the human body, as Christian humanism was at its zenith in their era.

Ethics and the Resurrection

Though all events in the history of Jesus Christ, from incarnation to ascension, are vital to his saving work, Oliver O'Donovan has expressed the opinion that the resurrection should be emphasized when it comes to ethics in particular. Such a theological proposition is implied in various texts (Col. 3:1; 1 Pet. 1:3) and from the wider biblical story, in which the resurrection is seen to be "God's vindication of his creation and so our created life."[9] It derives especially from Paul's understanding of the significance of Christ's resurrection for humanity, particularly in his identity as the last Adam (1 Cor. 15:45). The initial purpose of the Creator before Adam sinned was to create a world in which humanity "has a place," and it is this purpose that the resurrection of the last Adam reaffirmed. Until resurrection morning, it may have looked as if God had given up on his creation. But when the Son, who had become one with creation and humanity, was resurrected, creation and the human place within it were reaffirmed. The fall of the first Adam, which threatened to "uncreate creation," was thwarted.[10] This is in keeping with the reality that Christ's redemption was not a redemption of humanity *from* creation (Gnosticism) but the redemption *of* creation.

How does this relate to ethics? The moral order placed within human persons made in the image of God by creation is one of the realities reaffirmed by the resurrection. This is realized increasingly in those who believe, but it is God's design for all humanity, suggesting that the church is to engage ethically with the world. This moral order includes a concept of the natural law, qualified by its presence in humanity through Christ and not by mere nature. For O'Donovan, ethics is therefore more than the "Command of God" ethics in Barth—that is, the Word of God heard from outside ourselves. It involves a moral order within the human person that is restored by the resurrection, one that enables the person in ethics to receive the Word of God and respond to it. While not neglecting the death of Christ and the Christian ethical life of participation with Christ in his death and resurrection, O'Donovan insists that the participatory aspects of personal ethics (involving mortification and vivification) and social ethics (involving criticism and revolution) can become negative if they are not understood from the perspective of "the centre," which is a "world-order" reaffirmed by resurrection.[11] This means that in both the mortification and the vivification aspects of union with Christ, the ultimate goal is *being human* as God intended this. O'Donovan argues that without the resurrection, the cross and the ascension would collapse "together without their centre" and "become symbols for a gnostic other-worldliness."[12]

As already suggested, O'Donovan sees the resurrection of Jesus as representative for *all* humanity, as 1 Corinthians 15:22 indicates: "All will be made alive." This broadens the scope of ethics and encourages the church to be in the public square—in an influential manner, as salt and light, not in an oppressive

---

9. O'Donovan, *Resurrection and Moral Order*, 13.
10. O'Donovan, *Resurrection and Moral Order*, 14.
11. O'Donovan, *Resurrection and Moral Order*, 14.
12. O'Donovan, *Resurrection and Moral Order*, 15.

or empire-building way. The created moral order was taken up into the Son by way of the incarnation, but its fate and the redemption and resurrection of humanity were assured by the resurrection of this representative man.[13] This gives evidence that God has been faithful to his creative order and that it will, in the end, have humanity in its proper place within it.

What does this mean for ethics? Most obviously, the resurrection makes ethics evangelical—that is, of the gospel, of the resurrection of Jesus. Ethics flows from union with the risen Christ and is empowered by the Spirit. It implies that ethics arises from a God who is *for* humanity and who commands what brings humans into shalom and human flourishing. Second, the resurrection unites creation and kingdom ethics together as one. In opposition to those who make a distinction between kingdom ethics and creation ethics, O'Donovan states that the resurrection event, which was the sign of the kingdom, was also the sign of the reaffirmation of creation. If kingdom ethics was entertained in opposition to creation, this would be a fundamentally dualistic eschatological kingdom bearing no resemblance to that of the New Testament. And creation ethics considered apart from the kingdom of God would not be evangelical ethics, since the good news that God had acted to fulfill his purpose for creation would fail to be heard. O'Donovan asserts that in "the resurrection of Christ, creation is restored and the kingdom of God dawns."[14] It reaffirms the moral order of creation, which is the realm of the kingdom of God.

Third, because of the resurrection, ethics is public, pertaining to all humans, and not esoteric or mystical. The idea that such a moral order exists runs counter to the voluntarist nature of Western moral thought since the Enlightenment. Morality has since then been seen as a function of the human will, a matter not of thoughtful public reason but of free human self-determination, something necessary for order in individual and social life.[15] This describes the ethical way of being in most Western democracies today—the individual and autonomous choices prevail in ethical dialogue. This explains why there is no way forward in resolving ethical issues in any objective manner in such societies. Christians have often capitulated to the same presuppositions and so remained aloof from the ethical arena, assuming that the moral law has no place in a secular society. Since according to this viewpoint ethics is seen to be esoteric and only for people of "faith," Christians believe they can lay no claim on those who are not Christians, who, after all, don't care about ethics.[16]

13. O'Donovan, *Resurrection and Moral Order*, 15.
14. O'Donovan, *Resurrection and Moral Order*, 15.
15. O'Donovan, *Resurrection and Moral Order*, 16.
16. O'Donovan, *Resurrection and Moral Order*, 16.

Since non-Christians often reflect good ethics in many aspects of human life, this latter view is obviously wrong—because it fails to take creation into account and with it "the reality of a divinely-given order of things in which human nature itself is located."[17] This is what the resurrection has reaffirmed. It is an ontological reality of human being. This is not to deny the fact that humanity has rebelled against this order or that human nature is fundamentally flawed. "Yet," says O'Donovan, "this order stands over against us and makes its claim upon us." It is objective, simply something "there," and since humanity has a place within it, it issues its summons to every human person. The moral order is not something that either the Christian or the non-Christian can choose to opt into or out of since it is a reality God has given and then reaffirmed in the resurrection of Jesus in a created, human body.[18]

In sum, the evangelical, kingdom-creational, public nature of resurrection ethics urges the church to engage, not withdraw, drawing upon the ethics of its own ethos as the community of the risen Christ and emanating this goodness to the world nonoppressively as a *communio in ekstasis*, like the Trinity.

The Reaffirmation of Embodiment

In addition to reaffirming creation, and the human place in creation, the resurrection of Jesus in a body reaffirms the goodness of the human body, the potential for its misuse and abuse, and the theo-anthropological reality that the body is not peripheral but central to human identity and personhood. The fact that the past resurrection of Jesus as the Man for all humanity in a human body is the guarantee and harbinger of the future resurrection of the bodies of all human persons (1 Cor. 15:22) confirms this. The greatest chapter in the Bible on the theme of the resurrection is 1 Corinthians 15, and it should be seen not just as a source of hope for the future but as an apologetic for the importance of the body. In fact, this chapter is not to be seen in isolation from the rest of the epistle, in which Paul is correcting a notion derived from the Greek Corinthian culture that what you do with your body does not matter, morally and ethically speaking. Corinthian culture was as sexualized as ours is today. This had infiltrated the Corinthian church to such an extent that the immorality within the church outdid even that in the surrounding society (1 Cor. 5:1–5). Paul makes an appeal in chapter 6 for sexual holiness, indicating that having sex with someone other than your spouse is not just to share bodily

17. O'Donovan, *Resurrection and Moral Order*, 16.
18. More detail on ethics and its relation to the resurrection may be found in Hastings, *Theological Ethics*, 120–48.

fluids but to be united as persons, and that to do so is to desecrate the body, which is the temple of the divine Third Person of the Trinity. But the root of the moral compromise was the fact that some in the Corinthian church had imbibed a Greek philosophical—perhaps Platonic, perhaps pre-Gnostic— view that the body was inferior to the soul or spirit. First Corinthians 15 is thus a great apologetic for the body, one that is grounded in the fact that Christ rose again in a body and that therefore all humans will also have their bodies resurrected. If this is the case, stewarding that body now and keeping it free from sexual sin now really matters.

In fact, already in the midst of his exhortation on the life of sexual holiness in chapter 6, Paul signals the key dynamic that he will develop fully later: the resurrection and therefore the importance of the body in human life and ethics.

> The body, however, is not meant for sexual immorality but for the Lord, and the Lord for the body. By his power God raised the Lord from the dead, and he will raise us also. Do you not know that your bodies are members of Christ himself? Shall I then take the members of Christ and unite them with a prostitute? Never! Do you not know that he who unites himself with a prostitute is one with her in body? For it is said, "The two will become one flesh." But whoever is united with the Lord is one with him in spirit.
>
> Flee from sexual immorality. All other sins a person commits are outside the body, but whoever sins sexually, sins against their own body. Do you not know that your bodies are temples of the Holy Spirit, who is in you, whom you have received from God? You are not your own; you were bought at a price. Therefore honor God with your bodies. (1 Cor. 6:13–20)

There is rich and profound theology of the body in this passage:

1. The body is in profound mutual relationship with the Lord ("for the Lord, and the Lord for the body" [v. 13]).
2. The body is a member of Christ himself; here Paul speaks of the body as a person.
3. The body is integral to personhood—union of human bodies is a union of human persons; in other words, there can be no union of bodies that is not also a union of human "spirits."
4. The body, which includes sexual organs, is a sacred moral location, making its violation in sexual sin more ontological and therefore more serious than other sins.
5. It is the very temple of the Holy Spirit.

However, the foundation of this teaching on the sacredness and centrality of the body is the resurrection of Jesus in a body: "By his power God raised the Lord from the dead, and he will raise us also" (v. 14).

All of this biblical data points toward a theological anthropology in which the body and the inner being of a person are to be viewed as profoundly integrated. The popular usage of the term "soul" to describe part of the human being runs contrary to the biblical usage, in which it describes the whole person. In that sense also, the popular phrase among evangelicals, "getting souls saved," is only correct if the whole embodied person is being referred to. The future of human persons is not ultimately to be disembodied souls in heaven; it is to be resurrected, embodied persons in heaven come to earth. This idea of integrated anthropology, which may be expressed in the words that we are "embodied souls" or "animated bodies," reflects a *traducian* anthropology, which is the idea that the soul is not created and endowed upon a developing fetus at some stage of its development; rather, it is propagated from parents and is communicated via DNA. This stands in contrast to both the *creationist* view of the soul (the soul is created separately from the body during pregnancy and given either at conception, animation, or birth) and the *Platonic* view (the soul is eternal and given to the body from which it is separate; the value of the body is underplayed). The integrated view has many implications for questions posed by medicine, psychology, and brain science. Specifically, the question of the relationship between consciousness and the brain arises. The discussion as to whether the brain *emits*, *transmits*, or *permits* human consciousness, engaged in chapter 6, comes into play here. The "emits" opinion, also called the materialist position, is not prevalent even among secular philosophers.[19] Among theologians, the location of the soul or spirit synonymously—that is, as an inner part of a person—when they die and before the resurrection is a matter of debate with significant pastoral consequences, as will be seen in the following chapter. Suffice it to say here that all orthodox theologians can agree that the end state or telos for believers in Jesus is an embodied one, at the resurrection.

Contemporary society in North America and Western Europe, and indeed globally through the influence of the West, reflects a very Greek, disembodied view of human persons. Ironically, while paying so much attention to our bodies and what they look like, we often have a total disregard for what we do with our bodies sexually or how we treat our bodies as we approach the end of life. Promiscuity in our culture reflects a disregard for the view that your

19. See Goff, *Consciousness and Fundamental Reality*, for an introduction to this topic. See "Pastoral Questions" in chap. 6.

body is not what you have but who you are. The idea of being a virgin before marriage is now cause for scorn and laughter on reality shows and in popular media. How we make decisions about our sexual orientation is all about how we feel, not what our bodies are. Gender, a social construct, has replaced sex or sexed-ness in these decisions. Granted, there are physical, hormonal, and psychological complexities, especially in the case of people who are tragically born intersex, that require great compassion. But whims of fancy and experimentation often uproot the bodily anatomy in this culture of unconditional acceptance. What I do with my body when the end of life approaches has become—in my Canadian culture at least, through MAID (Medical Assistance in Dying)—a matter of voluntarism and crass individualism. This reflects a complete disregard for the divine prerogative over our lives, including over our human bodies and when they die. Yet if O'Donovan is right, the true nature of the human body and our accountability to God for what we do with it stand over our culture and in human consciences in ways that cannot be salved apart from the grace of God and the reconciliation and shalom found in the life, death, and resurrection of Jesus. There is always hope of new life.

A few years ago I was visiting Bogotá, the capital of Colombia. I was taken to the art gallery that features the sculpture and paintings of Fernando Botero. I was already inquisitive about his art, as my wife, Tammy, had some samples of it. I was curious about why Botero makes most of his sculptures oversized or bloated. This is in fact his signature style, known as "Boterismo." Human persons and animals are depicted with an exaggerated volume. I was really keen to find out why. I asked rather boldly to see the curator of the gallery. Whereas I expected her to say what some of my reading had indicated—that it is Botero's form of political critique and farce, or just humor, or that he himself is not sure why he likes that form[20]—the curator actually said it is because he wishes to emphasize the embodiedness of persons and things! My theologian's heart sang!

In an educational climate in which we are thankful for technologies that allow us to continue in our educational missions even during a pandemic, I am nevertheless certain that this is a secondary "good" that can never replace or compete with embodied communal learning in a classroom. In an increasingly disembodied world where we spend too much time looking at screens, and in which even our grandchildren know how to flip the screen of an iPhone when they are one-year-olds, we need a strong reminder of our embodied nature as human persons, both now and in the eschatological future—which is our next topic.

20. Memory McDermott, *Tea for Two*, 167.

Discussion Questions

1. How do we make the connection between the resurrection of Jesus in a body and God's reaffirmation of creation, or the reaffirmation that matter matters?

2. Not all Christians can be scientists, but we all can and should be engaged with creation. We should care for it and develop a curiosity and sense of wonder about it. What practices might encourage that curiosity and wonder?

3. Not all Christians have the same level of artistic ability, but we can all develop the creativity centers of our brains. Constant technological stimulation makes this difficult in our time. What practices, both of avoidance and of engagement, are necessary for you to develop a more creative way of life, reflecting the beauty of the triune God in your worship and life?

10

The Resurrection and the Nature of the Second Coming

But Christ has indeed been raised from the dead, the firstfruits of those who have fallen asleep. For since death came through a man, the resurrection of the dead comes also through a man. For as in Adam all die, so in Christ all will be made alive.

—1 Corinthians 15:20–22

This final chapter on the theology of the resurrection naturally concerns the resurrection of humanity, which the resurrection of Jesus made possible. But given that the resurrection is the reaffirmation of the entire creation, space must be given to a discussion of what it means for the new creation—that is, the entire cosmos. With respect to both the future of human persons and the future of the new creation, eschatology is both realized and future. The new creation has dawned but has not yet fully come. The kingdom has come but has not yet fully come. Our salvation is both complete and being worked out. In light of this, two main subjects will be considered: the resurrection as the center of realized eschatology, and the resurrection as the center of and the guide to future eschatology.

That the resurrection of Jesus is the key that unlocks all of eschatology is not surprising, given, for example, Peter's expression of this very thing in 1 Peter 1: "Praise be to the God and Father of our Lord Jesus Christ! In his great mercy he has given us new birth into a living hope through the resurrection of Jesus Christ from the dead, and into an inheritance that can never perish, spoil or fade" (1 Pet. 1:3–4). The intention of this chapter is to show the relationship between the event of the resurrection of Jesus, the person of the resurrected Jesus, and the future of humanity and the new creation. The primary text concerning the resurrection as the center of realized eschatology is Acts 1. The texts concerning the nature of the future of the believer in light of the resurrection are 1 Corinthians 15 and 1 Thessalonians 4. The nature of the new creation as depicted in various biblical texts will be discussed with a special emphasis on Revelation 21 and the climactic interweaving of creation, covenant, and community in the vision of the future.

The Center of Realized Eschatology

What is the significance of the resurrection of Jesus for eschatology? First we consider the resurrection as the center of realized eschatology.[1] Here we celebrate the reality that by the resurrection, the work of regeneration has been accomplished in the lives of believing humans, and the work of transformation has begun in anticipation of the day when the risen Christ is seen and transformation is complete and glorification has begun. Here we celebrate the reality that the resurrection is the beginning of the new creation, even before it actually comes in its completeness.

Nowhere in the New Testament is there greater evidence of the resurrection as the inauguration of the end, or eschaton, than in Acts 1. The early verses give a summary of Jesus's postresurrection appearances to his disciples and their general purpose, and then suddenly in verse 4 Luke dives down to describe one particular meeting that turns out to be the last meeting between the risen Jesus and the disciples. Eugene Peterson's paraphrase, *The Message*, expresses what is implicit in this story: "These were his last words" (Acts 1:9). This is a watershed passage, therefore. Surrounding that meeting and following it, we learn about the dynamics of the kingdom come that the risen One inaugurated and are given a picture of what the future coming of Christ and the kingdom fully come will be like.

What dynamics were at work in this remarkable event that were so transformative for the beleaguered apostles and early followers of Jesus? The imagination runs wild as we try to imagine the events and the words of Jesus that are rhetorically dramatized here by their ultimacy. The gravity and grandeur

---

1. The term "inaugurated eschatology" is sometimes used to describe the tension of holding realized eschatology and future eschatology together. I use the term "realized eschatology" with a similar understanding that it is not fully realized until future eschatology unfolds.

and glory of Jesus's postresurrection, pre-ascension ministry and climactic ascension make it a compelling piece. Whatever happened was utterly transformative. I would love to know what it was that finally awakened these Christ followers.

At the very core are a few couplets that are descriptors of Jesus in his inaugurating work. The first places Jesus in his suffering and in his resurrection at the center of things: "After his suffering, he presented himself to them and gave many convincing proofs that he was alive" (Acts 1:3). In a pithy way, Luke describes the passion of Christ: "after his suffering." No doubt he had in mind its salvific nature, but perhaps, in the missional context of Acts, he wishes to emphasize that this is the mark of the Christ and therefore of the Christian who will bear witness to him. Even if not many or any of us are martyred, the mark of the cross is upon us, and that means possible persecution, inevitable personal pain, and being baptized into the pain of a suffering world. This is what the inaugurated kingdom looks like, on the one hand. Pretty much every single leader I have known in any realm, church or marketplace or academy, has been hurt, has been deeply wounded, has suffered in their vocation and ministry and yet is still committed to the cause.

This is because of the second part of the couplet Luke gives us in describing Jesus as the center of the kingdom. This is his resurrection: "He presented himself to them and gave many convincing proofs that he was alive" (Acts 1:3). Resurrection is the foundation of the faith and the other keynote of the kingdom. In interpreting T. F. Torrance's view of the resurrection, Paul Molnar writes that "any eschatology minus the actual resurrection would have no relevance to on-going world history."[2] Suffering and resurrection are inseparable in our formation in union and communion with Jesus's death and resurrection, and in our grace-filled journey toward ministry to others.

But as these disciples are together for the last time, I notice that Jesus puts together two additional realities that define the inaugurated kingdom: the mission of the church *and* the empowering by the Spirit; they were not to go until the Spirit came. Acts 1:4 makes the explicit connection between the Spirit and mission in a negative sense: "On one occasion, while he was eating with them, he gave them this command: 'Do not leave Jerusalem, but wait for the gift my Father promised, which you have heard me speak about.'" Verse 8 makes it in a positive sense: "But you will receive power when the Holy Spirit comes on you; and you will be my witnesses in Jerusalem, and in all Judea and Samaria, and to the ends of the earth." There is no explanation for what became the remarkable witness of the apostles apart from the coming of the

2. Molnar, *Thomas F. Torrance*, 240.

Third Person of the Trinity to indwell and empower them. This great passage in one sense marks the passing of the baton of mission from one person of the Holy Trinity to another. This is the very essence of the kingdom for Luke: the presence of the Spirit, who has been given from the Father through the risen, ascended Lord. The work of the Spirit in and upon Christ in Luke's Gospel is now about to be correspondingly in and upon his church.

But in between the two expressions of the necessity of the Spirit for witness, there is a specific question from the disciples about the nature of the kingdom of God. It indicates they were still not quite ready for world mission: "Then they gathered around him and asked him, 'Lord, are you at this time going to restore the kingdom to Israel?'" (Acts 1:6). We often say as educators that there are no bad questions. But this question from the apostles must have filled the Lord Jesus with despair. As John Calvin comments, "There are as many errors in this question as words."[3] The verb, the noun, and the adverb each indicate a misunderstanding in their thought. The verb "restore" betrays the fact that they were expecting a political and territorial kingdom. Understanding the relationship of the Spirit to the kingdom would help them get this straight. Jesus's words in verse 8 would let them know that they needed spiritual power, not weapons, and that the nature of the kingdom is in fact his rule in the lives of his people by the Holy Spirit. As John Stott puts it, "It is spread by witnesses, not by soldiers, through a gospel of peace, not a declaration of war, and by the work of the Spirit, not by force of arms, political intrigue or revolutionary violence." And then he wisely adds,

> In rejecting the politicizing of the kingdom, we must beware of the opposite extreme of super-spiritualizing it, as if God's rule operates only in heaven and not on earth. The fact is that, although it must not be identified with any political ideology or programme, it has radical political and social implications. Kingdom values come into collision with secular values. And the citizens of God's kingdom steadfastly deny to Caesar the supreme loyalty for which he hungers, . . . which they insist on giving to Jesus alone.[4]

This is our calling still today as the apostolic people of the kingdom.

The noun "Israel" shows that they were expecting a national kingdom and that they were still deeply affected by ethnic prejudice. God's aim is to make for his Son a community "from every nation, tribe, people and language" (Rev. 7:9). And then there is the adverb "at this time." They expected an immediate establishment of Christ's kingdom, perhaps by military force. Two things

---

3. Calvin, *Commentary upon the Acts of the Apostles*, 43.
4. Stott, *The Spirit, the Church and the World*, 42.

would help them gain a right perspective here. The first was *epistemological*—knowing what they could and could not know. Between Pentecost and the parousia, they were to be engaged in worldwide mission on behalf of the ascended King, not the resolution of "times and seasons." They were to announce that the King had come and what he had achieved in his first coming and to call people to repent and believe in preparation for the second coming so they could participate in the new creation. Second, their perspective would be changed by a right understanding of the flow of history—that is, *eschatological* clarity was needed. In the last of the couplets in this text, two events shape the disciples: they see Christ ascend, and they hear a commentary from the angels on the nature of his second coming.

Let me first express the underexposed glory of the ascension and its significance to our salvation and to our sense of mission. It is mysterious, but it is a crucial salvific event that describes the ultimate act of theosis that Christ accomplished in his vicarious humanity for us: here we see a Man being taken up to the right hand of the Father. Humanity is taken up into the Godhead at the incarnation, but it is taken up expressly as a humanity that has been purified in the person and salvific acts of Christ and now glorified in the ascension. The language Luke uses to describe the ascension is expressive: "He was taken up" (Acts 1:9). It assumes the pleasure of the Father, who is satisfied with Jesus's atoning life and death. The taking up "in a cloud" is also expressive, not only because it corresponds to the clouds with which he will come again (Matt. 24:30) but because it may signify the Shekinah cloud of the Old Testament, which both revealed the glory of God and veiled it so the people would not be consumed. Perhaps Christ's glorification had begun on the way up.

And what does Jesus do when he gets to heaven? Acts is about Christ's ongoing mission on earth through the church, by the Spirit; Hebrews is about his reign as the unique King-Priest after the order of Melchizedek. Hebrews, the masterful expounding of the atonement and of the high priesthood of Christ, describes two main aspects of Jesus's role as ascended King-Priest: his session and his intercession. His *session* signifies his completed atoning sacrificial work and that he is triumphant conqueror over sin and death and Satan. "After he had provided purification for sins, he sat down at the right hand of the Majesty in heaven" (Heb. 1:3)—that is, he sits as a King! Acts 1 suggests a "now but not yet" dimension to the kingship of Jesus when it brings together ascension and parousia, and this is also found in the book of Hebrews. It is expressed in Hebrews 10 by his being seated as "he waits for his enemies to be made his footstool" (v. 13). This is reflected in the continuous work of sanctification expressed in 10:14: "For by one sacrifice he has made perfect forever those who are being made holy." But it also has creational and cosmic associations. The kingdom has come but not yet fully come. The creation still groans awaiting the consummation associated with the full redemption of the people of God.

This intermediate season in the divine calendar explains the second aspect of the high priesthood of Christ, his *intercession*, which sustains our lives and worship until that consummation. This is his ongoing work of sympathizing with us in our sufferings, imparting strength to us, and above all praying for us and enabling even our response to God in worship and in prayer so that it is delightful to the Father. I commend his sessional and intercessory work as your Great High Priest to carry you all the way through your life and mission here, no matter what may befall you.

Recalling the comment of T. F. Torrance that life between the ascension and the return of Jesus is lived within an "eschatological reserve created by the ascension"[5] leads us both to live with a sense of triumph in light of the kingdom come and to live with realism in recognition that it has not yet fully come. Even our work in the kingdom is therefore always fallible, and yet it has a sense of significance to it that anticipates the renewal of all things.

In sum, the resurrection of Jesus, in its coupling with the cross, in its movement on to ascension and the outpouring of the Spirit, and in its anticipation of the second coming, provides the core to our understanding of the kingdom come, of the eschaton already inaugurated. It is a realm of joy and yet tension, of expectancy with realism, of hope for what is yet to come and mission until he comes.

But what of this second coming, our surprising hope? Luke provides us with some basic information.

The Center of and Guide to Future Eschatology

In this second section we specifically address the matter of the resurrection as the center of and the guide to *future* eschatology in its various aspects, human and cosmic. We begin by considering Luke's clues about that event. In Acts 1 he describes what happened when Jesus ascended to heaven: "They were looking intently up into the sky as he was going, when suddenly two men dressed in white stood beside them. 'Men of Galilee,' they said, 'why do you stand here looking into the sky? This same Jesus, who has been taken from you into heaven, will come back in the same way you have seen him go into heaven'" (Acts 1:10–11).

5. T. F. Torrance, *Space, Time and Resurrection*, 157.

As is often the case in Luke's Gospel, Luke mentions the presence of angels to interpret important events in the career of Jesus. Here is no exception. Their words contain implicit rebuke. The disciples were not to stand there scanning the sky any longer. "No more stargazing," they said. Why? Because Jesus is coming again, and in the meantime their task was not to stare into the sky but to go to the ends of the earth on mission. The remedy for unprofitable stargazing and speculative studies of "times and dates" in eschatology is a Christian theology of history. It is an understanding of the broad strokes of what God has revealed: first, the ascension, the return of Jesus to heaven; next, the coming of the Holy Spirit at Pentecost; then the church going out in mission to the world; and lastly, the return of Christ at his second coming, or parousia. We need to hear the words of the angels so that we are ready for mission and so we don't lose perspective in kingdom community business. I might summarize the angelic message this way: "You have seen him go. You will see him come, and he will come as you saw him go—that is, personally and visibly. All the details and when, you don't need to know. What you do need to know is that between his going and his coming, there is another coming, the Spirit's, and his coming is so that you can go—into all the world to receive the kingdom community of Christ." Two things were to guide their kingdom mission: they were to go both "to the ends of the earth" (Acts 1:8) and "to the very end of the age" (Matt. 28:20). The church today must not stop until both ends have been reached.

The three most important pieces of information about the second coming of Christ that Luke gives us are in fact expressed in these words of the angels: "This same Jesus, who has been taken from you into heaven, will come back in the same way you have seen him go into heaven." "This same Jesus" is the first. He "will come back" is the second. He will do so "in the same way you have seen him go into heaven" is the third. In other words, he will come back personally, he will come back certainly, and he will come back bodily and visibly. The same risen and now glorified Jesus will come; he will come even though it seems as if he has been gone for a long time, and it will be sudden, at a specific point in time; and he will come still embodied and therefore visibly. "Every eye will see him," as Revelation 1:7 says.

It is a matter of personal concern for me that the church in our time does not speak much of the second coming. Perhaps this is an overreaction or course correction for an evangelical church that, even thirty years ago, was obsessed with eschatology and the "signs" of the second coming, and in which there was tireless and acrimonious debate about chiliasm. There was much debate about the millennium and whether one should be premillennial, amillennial, or postmillennial, and if one was premillennial, whether one should be

pretribulational, midtribulational, or post-tribulational! If the church were
to focus on the fact that Jesus *is* coming, personally and visibly and suddenly,
if they were to gain hope from it, and if they were to spread that hope in a
deeply disturbed world, watching their lives and not watching for signs, the
second coming would retain its balance and effectiveness as a doctrine. Silence
about this subject is unforgivable in these times.

There are two opposite errors in the doctrine of eschatology that cen-
teredness on the resurrection of Jesus corrects. The first is making it too
earthly. This is an error of the political hope of the church establishing utopia
on earth prior to the second coming. This is where the "restoration of the
kingdom to Israel" translates into political activism and restorationism. The
second is making his return too *heavenly*. This is the error of the pietist who
stargazes and dreams only of heaven, as if to escape the body and fly with
angel wings for eternity. The remedy for both false activism and false pietism
is to bear witness to Jesus in the power of the Spirit, which implies both
earthly responsibility and heavenly enabling! It is to realize that although the
resurrected and exalted and returning body of Jesus is a real, earthly body,
it also has heavenly orientation and suitability. He is the Man from heaven,
and our experience of the kingdom of God or the new creation will have a
heavenly character to it. The coming of the kingdom is such that his will is
going to "be done on earth as it is in heaven." Conversely, the body of Christ
in which he ascended and will one day descend is a real human body, and,
correspondingly, we are to engage in mission in our real bodies; we are not
to seek to escape a life that is truly human nor seek spiritualities that are
disembodied and disengaged from real life.

There are two other very important passages that inform us about the
nature of the second coming of Christ. Each depends upon the resurrection
of Jesus for its assertions. The first is 1 Thessalonians 4:13–18, which brings
reassurance that when Christ returns he will resurrect Christians who have
died and not just welcome those who are alive at that time. But all the assur-
ances for grieving people that Paul gives are grounded in this statement: "For
we believe that Jesus died and rose again, and so we believe that God will
bring with Jesus those who have fallen asleep in him" (v. 14). The resurrection
is the ground for the parousia.

Then in 1 Corinthians 15, Paul elaborates on the great theme of the hope of
the resurrection of dead humans at the second coming. This hope is based on
the fact that the One human who has become one with humanity, and is our
representative Head, has died and risen again. That foundation is expressed
right at the outset of this majestic passage. It is in fact the very heart of the
Christian gospel: "For what I received I passed on to you as of first importance:

that Christ died for our sins according to the Scriptures, that he was buried, that he was raised on the third day according to the Scriptures" (1 Cor. 15:3–4). His apologetic for general resurrection is Christ's resurrection, and vice versa (vv. 12–19). At a crucial point Paul turns from an apologetic approach to one of positive proclamation: "But Christ has indeed been raised from the dead, the firstfruits of those who have fallen asleep. For since death came through a man, the resurrection of the dead comes also through a man. For as in Adam all die, so in Christ all will be made alive. But each in turn: Christ, the firstfruits; then, when he comes, those who belong to him" (vv. 20–23). Grounded in the union of the Son with real humanity, Paul establishes that Christ's risenness has become the ground for the risenness of all humans one day.

In verses 35–49, Paul then uses the body of the risen Christ as the model for what our risen bodies may be like on that day. Then comes the climactic doxological ending of the chapter, in which Paul celebrates that the second coming will bring about the change in our humanity from mortal to immortal, from perishable to imperishable, in ways that are analogous to the risen body of Jesus. Just like Jesus, we will be continuous with who we were before the resurrection with respect to identity and personhood and being truly human. But just like Jesus in his postresurrection body, there will be a certain discontinuity related to the heavenly orientation of our new existence. As verse 51 declares, "Listen, I tell you a mystery: We will not all sleep, but we will all be changed." We will be changed, presumably by our seeing Jesus. We will be changed with respect to the presence of sin in our lives, and we will be changed with respect to the longevity of our human personhood, as we will be changed from mortal to immortal, from perishable to imperishable.

Personal Eschatology

Consideration has already been given in chapter 6 to the state of deceased believers on resurrection day, and before that in the intermediate state. We noted that death in Paul's view means that we are immediately, in both a temporal and a spatial way, in the presence of Christ, consciously, forever. With regard to the nature of the resurrection, in which the body and the soul are reunited, we discussed the elements of continuity and discontinuity between the body before and after the resurrection, drawing on the nature of the body of Jesus before and after. God, who knows our DNA and our unique history of relationships, will not struggle to raise bodies and reconstitute whole persons from graves and oceans and hills where their ashes have been scattered.

The relative clarity around the final resurrection state of redeemed humans relates to the notion that our end state is an embodied one and that this body-soul integrated union is the truly human way of being, just as was the truly human resurrection body-soul of Jesus. Not all has been revealed about this way of being. Jesus makes plain that there will be no marrying and giving in marriage, suggesting that the nature of the relationship we have with the person who was our former spouse will, in the new creation, perhaps reflect what we enjoyed spiritually, intellectually, and affectively in the here and now. This prompts the question as to the importance of sexuality or even its existence in the new glorified humanity, and the question of the importance of sexuality to human identity now. The making of humanity in the image of God clearly and explicitly included the maleness of the male and the femaleness of the female and the complementarity of each to the other. The sexing of humans had a contemplative purpose, driving humans, whether single or married, to find in God their deepest intimacy and satisfaction. It also had a communal and procreation purpose within marriage. Whatever it is about sexuality in humans that images the triune God—mutuality, personhood, ecstatic delight in the other—will apparently be fulfilled in other unknown ways in the kingdom fully come. Its joy will surely transcend that of genital sex. It will provide a greater degree of ecstasy in communion with God and other glorified humans.

Communal and Cosmic Eschatology

Turning now to the communal and cosmic aspects of eschatology, we recall that Jesus's resurrection in a body reaffirms the created order. We recall also that Jesus's ascension in a body to the right hand of the Father as the *eschatos* Adam implies the renewal of all creation, and that his return in a body anticipates the day when heaven will come down to earth, as Revelation 21 indicates. The beauty of the consummated new creation will be resplendent with the glory of God. We will participate in that day, and even our work will somehow find a place of value in it. Giving a full account of future eschatology is not our purpose here. Keeping the resurrection and the resurrection life of Jesus in focus, I will offer a few comments on the picture John gives us of the new heaven and the new earth in Revelation 21 that will suggest what the day of resurrection will look like.

> Then I saw "a new heaven and a new earth," for the first heaven and the first earth had passed away, and there was no longer any sea. I saw the Holy City, the new Jerusalem, coming down out of heaven from God, prepared as a bride beautifully dressed for her husband. And I heard a loud voice from the throne saying, "Look! God's dwelling place is now among the people, and he will dwell with them. They will be his people, and God himself will be with them and be

their God. 'He will wipe every tear from their eyes. There will be no more death' or mourning or crying or pain, for the old order of things has passed away."

He who was seated on the throne said, "I am making everything new!" Then he said, "Write this down, for these words are trustworthy and true."

He said to me: "It is done. I am the Alpha and the Omega, the Beginning and the End. To the thirsty I will give water without cost from the spring of the water of life. Those who are victorious will inherit all this, and I will be their God and they will be my children. But the cowardly, the unbelieving, the vile, the murderers, the sexually immoral, those who practice magic arts, the idolaters and all liars—they will be consigned to the fiery lake of burning sulfur. This is the second death." (Rev. 21:1–8)

Reading Revelation 21 and 22 is like taking a sneak peek at the last pages of a mystery novel to see how things turn out when curiosity overtakes us. Only in this case, this is a sneak peek at the end of the saga of all sagas, the story of God's work in the world from creation to this consummation. Revelation 21, along with chapter 22, provides a glorious conclusion not just to the book of Revelation, not just to the New Testament, but to the entire Bible.

First, these last two chapters together function as one bookend to Revelation. They correspond to the themes of the first chapter. The prologue in 1:1–6 is answered by the epilogue in 22:12–21 with respect to both prophetic content and liturgy. In similar fashion, the vision of the majestic Christ walking among the seven urban churches in 1:9–20 seems to foreshadow the presence of God and the Lamb in the new city (21:1–22:5). Furthermore, promises made to the seven churches and to the martyrs of chapter 7 are now fulfilled in the new creation, the new Jerusalem of chapters 21–22. If the subtitle of this book of the Bible might be something like *Following the Lamb into the New Creation*, as Michael Gorman has suggested, the way of the Lamb that has been followed by the faithful throughout this book is here vindicated, and by contrast, the way of the beast and those who follow it now stands condemned. As Gorman states, "The unholy triumvirate of Satan, the Beast from the Sea, and the beast from the land has been defeated, along with the idolatry and evil they perpetrate on the human race in the name of the divine. The harlot of Babylon—the supposedly eternal empire, *Roma Aeterna*, the *Imperium Aeternum*—is gone, replaced by the risen Lamb's bride, the new Jerusalem, which will actually last forever."[6]

Second, with respect to how these chapters function in the New Testament, they reveal that the incarnation of God in the one Man Jesus, which is where the Gospels begin, is now reenacted with God and the risen Lamb dwelling

6. Gorman, *Reading Revelation Responsibly*, 160–61.

with all humanity forever. God has become one with humanity in order that humanity might become relationally one with God. The great summation of the church fathers with respect to the meaning of salvation has reached its fulfillment. These chapters also bring to fulfillment the kingdom of God that was inaugurated by the presence and saving work of Jesus as narrated throughout the New Testament. The throne of God and of the Lamb and its irresistible sway in the new creation tell us that the kingdom that had come but was not yet fully come between the resurrection and the second coming of Christ (implicit here) has now fully come. The risen Christ is truly the Alpha and the Omega, the Beginning and the End.

But third, the whole of divine revelation in the Holy Scriptures climaxes here in a threefold way: with reference to creation, to covenant, and to the community of the people of God.

Creation. The grand narrative that began in Genesis with creation is completed in the new creation. The garden into which the first Adam brought curse and death is now an urban garden in which the risen last Adam presides, where it seems that people from all of history who have expressed faith in Jesus Christ now live in a state of flourishing and peace, and all suffering has gone. It is a new order of things, which it is hard for us to grasp given that, at least for animals and plants, death is part of the cycle of life. The climactic words of Revelation 21:6 ("He said to me: 'It is done'") are reminiscent of the Lamb's cry on the cross ("It is finished!"). They imply that the creational act of God has been brought to completion. The expression of the final vision of the completion of the grand narrative here in a new creation is culminative also in the sense that its content echoes very similar language in the Old Testament prophets. The vision of magnificence and beauty and true healing and hope of human flourishing in the immediate presence of God echoes some of the great eschatological texts in the Old Testament, especially the late chapters of Isaiah. Isaiah 65:17–19 provides one example:

> See, I will create
>   new heavens and a new earth.
> The former things will not be remembered,
>   nor will they come to mind.
> But be glad and rejoice forever
>   in what I will create,
> for I will create Jerusalem to be a delight
>   and its people a joy.
> I will rejoice over Jerusalem
>   and take delight in my people;

> the sound of weeping and of crying
>> will be heard in it no more.

The only shifts when this is interpreted in Revelation 21 are that the new Jerusalem is now the bride of the Lamb, which refers to all the faithful in Christ who have conquered the beast, and that instead of an actual temple, God and the Lamb *are* the temple (21:22).

Covenant. Second, the allusions to covenant express another revelation-climactic piece in Revelation 21. When we hear words like "I saw the Holy City, the new Jerusalem, coming down out of heaven from God, prepared as a bride beautifully dressed for her husband" in verse 2, and words like "'Look! God's dwelling place is now among the people, and he will dwell with them. They will be his people, and God himself will be with them and be their God" in verse 3, and words like "Those who are victorious will inherit all this, and I will be their God and they will be my children" in verse 7, we are hearing echoes of God's expression of covenant all through the biblical narrative. The old covenant was expressed in this language of reciprocal belonging between God and his people: "I will take you as my own people, and I will be your God" (Exod. 6:7). The new covenant was prophesied in these terms: "My dwelling place will be with them; I will be their God, and they will be my people" (Ezek. 37:27). And these words are owned by the writer of Hebrews in chapter 8 as the new covenant finds its fulfillment in the people of the risen and ascended Priest. Jesus is God's covenant partner on our behalf, the only one able to keep it, and the new covenant gets truly and fully fulfilled only in him and in all who rest in his faithfulness. That faithful community in Christ is here depicted as the bride of the Lamb, which leads us to the third aspect of the biblical narrative that is finding closure here.

Community. The culmination of God's community is expressed here. This is suggested in Revelation 21:2–3 also. The mention of "bride" immediately conjures up the notion of covenant. Creation and covenant come together in God's community, in the bride and the risen Bridegroom together. They are his people whom he has always loved in both the era of the old covenant and that of the new. The presence of this new *humanity* is the key also to the declared presence of the new *creation*, for they are those who reign in that new creation in Christ the last Adam, as God had first intended. And they are the people who come under God's gracious, unconditional covenant of redemption and grace. Who are these covenant people of God populating the new creation?

This community is depicted with two images. First, it is the new Jerusalem, which is contrasted with old Babylon. It is God's alternative to the empire of

Rome, which, with its motto that "Caesar is Lord," stood over against the kingdom in which, as was declared in the resurrection, "Jesus is Lord!" So we learn that first this community is being described as people of the risen King, people under the sway of the lordship of Christ. The crux of the Apocalypse is *allegiance* to the risen Lord!

Two additional things are suggested by this image of the new Jerusalem. First, its name suggests the continuity of the Old and the New Testament people of God. It is inclusive of the Old Testament people of God, and yet its newness lies in what is expressed later in Revelation 21, that *all* nations are included:

> I did not see a temple in the city, because the Lord God Almighty and the Lamb are its temple. The city does not need the sun or the moon to shine on it, for the glory of God gives it light, and the Lamb is its lamp. The nations will walk by its light, and the kings of the earth will bring their splendor into it. On no day will its gates ever be shut, for there will be no night there. The glory and honor of the nations will be brought into it. (Rev. 21:22–26)

Its inclusion of all peoples suggests that the missional nature and task of the church now is to embrace people of all nations, and especially refugees. The message of the Apocalypse is about embrace, or *hospitality*! This is emphasized by the fact that there are no closed gates in the city (21:25; Isa. 60:11).

Second, if it is inclusive of all the nations of all the generations of humanity, it must be pretty big. One of the ways in which John conveys that the new Jerusalem is "God's alternative to Rome's empire" and to Babylon in its successive incarnations[7] is its size: 12,000 stadia (1,500 miles) in length, width, and height means that the city "has a footprint approximately equal in size to the entire land mass of the Roman empire"—that it is "large enough to encompass . . . the world as John knew it."[8] Babylon, according to Herodotus, was a square.[9] But John goes even further: the city of God is a cube. This probably reflects the fact that the Holy of Holies was a cube, and it suggests that all the people of God in the new covenant are priests.[10] The Apocalypse is about the *wideness of God's mercy*. It is universal in scope— that is, with respect to desire and design, God wants all humanity to be saved. At the same time, he will not save those who will not be saved. The masses

---

7. Gorman, *Reading Revelation Responsibly*, 162.

8. Kraybill, *Apocalypse and Allegiance*, 177, 212, cited in Gorman, *Reading Revelation Responsibly*, 162.

9. Herodotus, *History* 1.178, cited in Gorman, *Reading Revelation Responsibly*, 162.

10. Gorman, *Reading Revelation Responsibly*, 162.

of people in the millennia of human civilization are perhaps the reason why this garden in Revelation is an urban garden or, better, a garden-city. Thus, civilization and urbanization are not wrong in themselves, but "babylonic distortions"[11] arise within human sociopolitical life from the practice of idolatry and from the sinful human condition. Richard Bauckham has said it this way:

> In the beginning God had planted a garden for humanity to live in (Gen. 2:8). In the end he will give them a city. In the New Jerusalem the blessings of paradise will be restored, but the New Jerusalem is more than paradise regained. As a city it fulfils humanity's desire to build out of nature a human place of human culture and community.[12]

The idea of a cube and its association with the temple, which is here inhabited by the immediate presence of God and the risen Lamb, conveys another striking feature of this future aspect of eschatology: the boundary between heaven and earth seems to disappear so that all is sacred space.[13] This is precisely anticipated in the risen person of Jesus, in whom it still may be said after his resurrection that "all the fullness of the Deity dwells in bodily form" (Col. 2:9). What Paul expounds in Colossians 1:19–20 ("God was pleased to have all his fullness dwell in him, and through him to reconcile to himself all things, whether things on earth or things in heaven, by making peace through his blood, shed on the cross") has now become true in Revelation 21. The Apocalypse is marked by *God's perpetual, perceptible presence*—a state of permanent incarnation, so to speak. This is in fact the most significant characteristic of the new Jerusalem: divine presence in all its fullness and glory (Rev. 21:3, 22; cf. Ezek. 37:26–27). What glory that will be!

The second image that John uses to describe the new covenant community in the city is the bride of the Lamb. This metaphor is not new to John. Paul uses it in Ephesians 5 of the church, which Christ loved and gave himself up for. It assumes covenant, and it assumes faithful covenant love. The community of the new creation lives in the awareness of the magnanimous and intimate love of God. In the Beloved, they are deeply loved. But with respect to this metaphor, what strikes me most is that the community comes down from heaven "prepared as a bride beautifully dressed for her husband" (Rev. 21:2). What is remarkable is both its presence in heaven before coming down

11. Gorman, *Reading Revelation Responsibly*, 164.
12. Bauckham, *The Theology of the Book of Revelation*, 135, cited in Gorman, *Reading Revelation Responsibly*, 164.
13. Gorman, *Reading Revelation Responsibly*, 178.

to earth and the fact that there in heaven it has been prepared for this moment of revelation or apocalypse, presumably by the consummation of its salvation through seeing Jesus face-to-face in the beatific vision. This seems to validate what 1 Thessalonians 4 asserts—that the living and the resurrected saints will rise to meet the Lord in the air at his second coming before they return to earth as the glorified saints in the new Jerusalem.

One is of course tempted to see how this fits into various eschatological schemes. Pretribulational and midtribulational premillennial positions have the church raptured to heaven for some time before it returns at the second stage of the second coming. So it fits! Post-tribulational or historical premillennialism has the saints raptured and then immediately coming back down to earth with Christ. So it fits! It also fits the amillennial view, in which the second coming involves an ascent of the living saints along with those raised from the dead and then a descent. On one account, the postmillennial position alone sees the second coming primarily as metaphorical—that is, it envisions that all the saints at the final eschaton will be there because they have been regenerated from heaven. This seems unlikely in light of the personal and literal nature of the ascension and the equivalence anticipated for the second coming in Acts 1.

The people who comprise the bride of the Lamb are characterized by the satisfaction of their thirst in Christ, who as the ascended Bridegroom is the source of the water of life, over against those who satisfy their deep soul hunger with idols, counterfeits. They are also characterized by their faithfulness, which has overcome the beast and the narratives of the secular city. Their risen Bridegroom, who is also their Great High Priest, living in the power of an endless life, has faithfully saved them all the way to the end by his intercession (Heb. 7:24–25), and at the same time, they have proved their election by their perseverance to the end.

This bridal community is also contrasted with another community that is headed for another destiny altogether: "But the cowardly, the unbelieving, the vile, the murderers, the sexually immoral, those who practice magic arts, the idolaters and all liars—they will be consigned to the fiery lake of burning sulfur. This is the second death" (Rev. 21:8). Is there a literal, conscious hell (Reformed, Puritan, Catholic), not just a grave of annihilation? Or might the open gates of the city suggest that all will one day enter, given the desire of God that all be saved and the superabundant provision of atonement in the all-sufficient offering up of the life of the Son of God in a human body? It is clear that those who are going to the "fiery lake" are those who habitually and unrepentantly and defiantly followed the course of these behaviors. It seems reasonable to say that those who give evidence that they do not want to be in heaven will not be forced to go there. They go into the fiery lake, refusing to accept God's desire for all to be saved. They go refusing to accept the verdict of God that in Christ humanity has been justified. The philosophical difficulty with an eternal hell in which humans will be suffering in torment forever seems incompatible with a cosmos in which all has been reconciled. How will rejoicing saints in heaven be feeling about their loved ones who are off somewhere else in the universe suffering in hell?

The annihilation view has some advantages, to be sure.[14] This involves the idea that punishment is eternal in consequence but not in duration. Another possibility is the Roman Catholic mainstream view that whereas some will indeed go to an eternal hell of conscious suffering, others will endure a season of purgation by the blood of the Lamb in order for them to believe and be made fit for heaven. Some annihilationists seem to be referring to the moment of the death of an unbeliever, who simply ceases to exist then. Others, in keeping with the fact that the unrighteous and the righteous are both raised again (John 5:29), believe the annihilation is what occurs at the final judgment when the wrath of God will consume the unrighteous. What ought to prompt us to take hell seriously, however, is how much Jesus spoke of it and the way he spoke of it—with deadly seriousness. This factor, along with the justice of God, weighs in to suggest that even though we may not fathom now the metaphysical and moral realities of hell, and even though the concept of an immortal soul is more Platonic than Christian, and even though all that God has created is good, hell should be taken seriously. After all, when the Son of God has died and risen for humanity, the gravity of rejecting him cannot be underestimated. Our view of the risen, conquering Son as *Pantokrator*, Jesus Christ as the risen Lord of the universe, urges us to take the judgment that has been committed to him and the possibility of hell seriously.

A few final summary observations may be made regarding Revelation 21. In light of the risen Christ, there is reason for hope in a world that seems upended right now. In light of the cosmic outworking of the resurrection of Jesus, there is no sea in the eschatological city. The "sea" in the book of Revelation depicts chaos and evil. In the present time, when we struggle so much with illness and death and loss, we may lift up our heads, for in the city of the risen One where we are going, there is no death and no mourning and no more tears. In the present time, when we struggle so much with the presence

14. See https://www.afterlife.co.nz/articles/john-stott-and-annihilationism/. See the dialogue between John Stott and J. I. Packer in this regard in Packer, "Evangelical Annihilationism in Review." It may also be found at https://www.the-highway.com/annihilationism_Packer.html. See also Packer, "The Problem of Eternal Punishment," 23.

of sin and its consequences, we may lift up our heads, for there is no sin in the new creation. In the present time, when creation seems so fragile and polluted, we may lift up our heads, for God has not abandoned his creation in the risen One! It will be transformed, not eradicated, and our task in light of Christian hope is to live as embodied persons under the last Adam, the risen Lord of all, exercising stewardship of God's good creation. Eugene Peterson bemoaned that "new heavens and new earth" is often reduced to "heaven" and then completely misunderstood. He states, "The frequency with which St. John's vision of heaven is bloated by make-believe into an anti-biblical fantasy is one of the wonders of the world."[15] N. T. Wright has added weight to this: he calls Revelation 21–22 "the marriage of heaven and earth . . . the ultimate rejection of all types of Gnosticism, of every worldview that . . . [separates] the physical from the spiritual. . . . It is the final answer to the Lord's Prayer (thy kingdom come)."[16]

There is cause for individual hope based on Revelation 21, but there is especially cause for communal and cosmic hope. Individual hope for deliverance from death is legitimate. Hope of reunion with loved ones is also legitimate. Hope of individual resurrection is legitimate. But this picture of future eschatology is much more about reconciliation of nations and the formation of the one people of Christ whose members are equal and equally loved and yet apparently still diverse, a people living in harmony with God in a whole new cosmos.

Above all else, this hope of the future concerns "God and the Lamb." The incarnation of God in the person of Christ is the very center of this eschaton. God cannot be separated from the Lamb. God as Trinity is not just how he has been revealed—it is who God is. And God has permanently taken humanity into the communion of the Godhead in Christ, the divine-human Son. His humanity and what he accomplished in that representative humanity cannot be denied. The Lamb of God, who is risen but will also always be thought of as freshly slain (Rev. 5:6: "Then I saw a Lamb, looking as if it had been [freshly] slain, standing at the center of the throne, encircled by the four living creatures and the elders"), is the center and object of our eternal worship.

> Worthy is the Lamb, who was slain,
>   to receive power and wealth and wisdom and strength
>   and honor and glory and praise! (Rev. 5:12)

15. Peterson, *Reversed Thunder*, 171.
16. Wright, *Surprised by Hope*, 104.

Discussion Questions

1. What is meant by "realized eschatology" and "future eschatology," and what role does the resurrected Christ play in each?

2. There is a lot we know and a lot we don't know about the future. What do we truly know about the return of Christ and the things that will transpire after that?

3. We might sum up the future state of the world by saying it will be earthly, yet earthly with a heavenly presence and a worshipful orientation. We could say that we will have *occupations* as earthly human people but that our *preoccupation* will be worship of the risen Lamb. That actually sounds quite a bit like how Paul urges us to live now: "Since, then, you have been raised with Christ, set your hearts on things above, where Christ is, seated at the right hand of God. Set your minds on things above, not on earthly things" (Col. 3:1–2). The goal of Christian maturity seems to me to be the development of a preoccupation with the risen Christ in heaven that transforms our occupations here on earth. How can we be formed this way? The great reality is that the triune God is already at work in us toward this telos, and we grow into it by participation in the work of the Father, who raised the risen Son by the power of the Spirit.

Conclusion

Remember Jesus Christ, raised from the dead, descended from David. This is my gospel, for which I am suffering even to the point of being chained like a criminal. But God's word is not chained. Therefore I endure everything for the sake of the elect, that they too may obtain the salvation that is in Christ Jesus, with eternal glory.

—2 Timothy 2:8–10

In summing up the theology of the resurrection, it seems vital to me to recapitulate its message, to urge the people of God to live into the reality that is already real, and to exhort the whole church of God, whether pastors or laypeople, to preach it with passion—no matter the cost.

The Core of the Core of the Gospel

If you were challenged to say what the essence of the Christian gospel is in a nutshell, what would you say? In this exercise you are not allowed to go to the historic creeds or any of the confessions, because they are too long! It seems to me that when the biblical authors choose to do this "nutshell" kind of writing, they inevitably mention the resurrection of Jesus. How about Paul in the passage in 2 Timothy above? What is the gospel, Paul? "Remember Jesus Christ, raised from the dead, descended from David" (2 Tim. 2:8). There's a sound bite for you! The gospel is first and foremost centered in the person of Jesus Christ, and it is in particular focused on the resurrection of that person from the dead. The core of the core is the resurrection.

Again, what is the gospel, Paul? We get what seems like a slightly longer version of 2 Timothy 2:8 in Romans 1:1–4, in what appears to be some kind of a repetition of a theological formula that Paul used. The "gospel of God" (Rom. 1:1) is this: "the gospel he promised beforehand through his prophets in the Holy Scriptures regarding his Son, who as to his earthly life was a descendant of David, and who through the Spirit of holiness was appointed the Son of God in power by his resurrection from the dead: Jesus Christ our Lord" (Rom. 1:2–4). The descent from David mentioned in both passages emphasizes the humanity of Jesus and his fulfillment of the Jewish messianic promises of the Old Testament. The resurrection declares the Son to be the authoritative Son of God in power, both the messianic Son of God of the Davidic covenant (2 Sam. 7; Pss. 2; 89) and the essentially divine Son of God.

What if we ask Peter, "What is the gospel, Peter?" When he preaches on the day of Pentecost (given the sermonic format, we can allow him a few more words), his answer focuses on three or four references to the resurrection of Jesus, which identifies Jesus as Lord and Christ: "But God raised him from the dead, freeing him from the agony of death, because it was impossible for death to keep its hold on him. . . . He [David] spoke of the resurrection of the Messiah, that he was not abandoned to the realm of the dead, nor did his body see decay. God has raised this Jesus to life, and we are all witnesses of it. Exalted to the right hand of God, he has received from the Father the promised Holy Spirit and has poured out what you now see and hear" (Acts 2:24, 31–33). Then, when Peter gives his pithy summary of the gospel in his first epistle, the resurrection is again prominent—even preeminent: "Praise be to the God and Father of our Lord Jesus Christ! In his great mercy he has given us new birth into a living hope through the resurrection of Jesus Christ from the dead" (1 Pet. 1:3).

The fact that in this pithy form Peter mentions the resurrection and not the death of Jesus does not imply that the cross matters less than the resurrection. Rather, the death of Jesus is implicit in or included with the resurrection. At the risk of stating the painfully obvious, there could be no resurrection if Jesus didn't first die. In fact, I suggest that Paul may be using something like a literary device called "synecdoche," in which a part represents the whole. So, for example, when the captain of a ship says, "How many hands on deck?" he is using the hand to represent the whole person, asking how many sailors he has at work. Similarly, Paul is using the term "resurrection" to refer to the entire event of the death and resurrection of Jesus. And in any case, Paul's other great summation of the gospel in 1 Corinthians 15:3–4 contains explicit reference to Christ's death and his burial, as well as his resurrection.

Having said that, the fact that the gospel is boiled down to the resurrection as the core of the core does remind us of one major theme of this book: the atonement, our salvation and our future resurrection and glorification, and the renewal of all creation all have their efficacy because they have been accomplished in the *person* of Jesus, the One who became one with us in the incarnation in order to act on our behalf in life and in death and to remove death from us in the resurrection. In that sense, perhaps Paul includes the entire incarnational history of Jesus in the phrase "raised from the dead." It functions as a caption over the entire salvific history of Jesus.

Living Into the Reality That Is Already Reality

Having recapped the content of the theology of the resurrection, emphasizing that it is the very core of the gospel, I, with the heart of a pastor, want to urge you to live into resurrection reality. Christ is risen! And in Christ, *so are you*! This is what is most really real about you. You are in union with Christ in accordance with the premundane electing purposes of God in Christ. Paul, in a similar summarizing, pithy expression of the gospel in the first chapter of 2 Timothy, says, "This grace was given us in Christ Jesus before the beginning of time, but it has now been revealed through the appearing of our Savior, Christ Jesus, who has destroyed death and has brought life and immortality to light through the gospel" (2 Tim. 1:9–10). In union with Christ, you have been regenerated in the risen One. In his death and resurrection, you have died and your life is now hidden with Christ in God (Col. 3:1–3). The *ordo historia* of Jesus is now the *ordo salutis* of your life! The risen One now lives in you by the presence and the power of the Holy Spirit.

However, what is really real about us in God's eyes needs to be embraced in the depth of our consciousness. Paul repeatedly and systematically urges the people of Christ to live into, to appropriate, to practice the great reality that we have died and are now risen with Christ. Indeed, Paul himself never arrives at this matter of experiential participation in Christ through mortification and vivification. Philippians 3, written toward the end of his life, expresses the deep hunger he still experienced, the never-satisfied desire to know more of Christ in both resurrection life and passion sufferings: "I want to know Christ—yes, to know the power of his resurrection and participation in his sufferings, becoming like him in his death, and so, somehow, attaining to the resurrection from the dead" (Phil. 3:10–11). The "somehow" of verse 11 should be interpreted not as a matter of doubt but of wonder—the wonder that the people of God might one day, at the parousia, enter into the fullness of their resurrection life in Christ. The purpose of this book will be unfulfilled unless it creates a hunger for people to know Christ in both the power of his resurrection and the fellowship of his sufferings, to engage in practices that are cradles of grace for mortification and vivification. Why does Paul go contrary to chronological order in this text? Why does "the power of his resurrection" come before "participation in his sufferings"? There is a pastoral reason for this. The people of God need the hope of resurrection in order to bear the sufferings that go with faithfulness to Christ. This brings me to a final word on proclamation, for it is in the context of sharing the gospel in our ecclesial life and boldly proclaiming the uniqueness of Jesus Christ the risen Lord in the power of the resurrection that we enter into sufferings with Christ.

Preaching Hope for the Hopeless, No Matter the Cost

Even the context of Paul's gospel-in-a-nutshell statement in 2 Timothy 2 convinces us that the suffering and death of Christ are implied in the phrase "raised from the dead." He immediately follows up with a summary of the gospel of resurrection: it is that "for which I am suffering even to the point of being chained like a criminal. But God's word is not chained. Therefore I endure everything for the sake of the elect, that they too may obtain the salvation that is in Christ Jesus, with eternal glory" (vv. 9–10). Clearly, what brings on the suffering in Paul's life is his faithful and fearless proclamation of the gospel he has summarized. If only he would just stop preaching, his sufferings would go away!

The same pattern of thought is present in 2 Timothy 1:11–12. After a pithy summary of the gospel in verses 9–10, in which the resurrection is again prominent, Paul says, "And of this gospel I was appointed a herald and an apostle and a teacher. That is why I am suffering as I am. Yet this is no cause for shame, because I know whom I have believed, and am convinced that he is able to guard what I have entrusted to him until that day." In these words, Paul expresses the desire of my heart—for my own life and for every church and every child of God. It is that we may joyfully proclaim the power of the resurrection, knowing two realities: first, that the risen Jesus is the only hope for the brokenness, sinfulness, and ultimate cosmic hopelessness of every person and every culture in every country of the world; and second, that in declaring this to people, even when we do so wisely and respectfully, we will experience some suffering. We will experience the suffering of entering into the sufferings of the world and the added suffering of being misunderstood and even hated if we proclaim the risen, unique Son of God faithfully in a fragmented culture characterized by secularism, naturalism, consumerism, ethnocentrism, individualism, religious pluralism, moralism, libertinism, modern scientism, and postmodern despair. Preach the risen Christ, the hope of the nations! Preach the risen Christ, and the power of the resurrection will sustain you through your participation in his sufferings.

Bibliography

Alfeyev, Hilarion. *Christ the Conqueror of Hell: The Descent into Hades from an Orthodox Perspective*. Crestwood, NY: St. Vladimir's Seminary Press, 2009.

Athanasius. *On the Incarnation of the Word*. https://www.ccel.org/ccel/athanasius /incarnation.ix.html.

Barth, Karl. *Church Dogmatics*. Edited and translated by Geoffrey W. Bromiley and Thomas F. Torrance. 4 vols. New York: T&T Clark, 2009.

Bauckham, Richard. *The Theology of the Book of Revelation*. Cambridge: Cambridge University Press, 1993.

Bender, Kimlyn J. *Karl Barth's Christological Ecclesiology*. Burlington, VT: Ashgate, 2005.

Billings, J. Todd. *Calvin, Participation, and the Gift: The Activity of Believers in Union with Christ*. Oxford: Oxford University Press, 2007.

Blomberg, Craig. "Where Do We Start Studying Jesus?" In Wilkins and Moreland, *Jesus under Fire*, 17–50.

Boersma, Hans. "Justification within Recapitulation: Irenaeus in Ecumenical Dialogue." *International Journal of Systematic Theology* 22, no. 2 (April 2020): 169–90.

Bruce, F. F. *The Epistle to the Hebrews*. New International Commentary on the New Testament. Grand Rapids: Eerdmans, 1990.

———. *The Gospel and Epistles of John*. Grand Rapids: Eerdmans, 1994.

Buechner, Frederick. *The Alphabet of Grace*. New York: Harper, 1970.

———. *The Longing for Home: Recollections and Reflections*. San Francisco: HarperSanFrancisco, 1996.

———. *Wishful Thinking: A Theological ABC*. New York: Harper & Row, 1973.

Calvin, John. *Commentary upon the Acts of the Apostles*. Vol. 1. Edited by Christopher Fetherstone and Henry Beveridge. Grand Rapids: Eerdmans, 1965.

―――. *Institutes of the Christian Religion*. Translated by Ford Lewis Battles. Grand Rapids: Eerdmans, 1959.

Claypool, John. *The Light within You*. Waco: Word, 1983.

Clement of Rome. *1 Clement*. http://www.earlychristianwritings.com/text/1clement -lightfoot.html.

Craig, William Lane. *Assessing the New Testament Evidence for the Historicity of the Resurrection*. Lewiston, NY: Mellen, 1989.

Crisp, Oliver D. "Federalism vs Realism: Charles Hodge, Augustus Strong and William Shedd on the Imputation of Sin." *International Journal of Systematic Theology* 8, no. 1 (January 2006): 55–71.

―――. "On Behalf of Augustinian Realism." *Toronto Journal of Theology* 35, no. 2 (Fall 2019): 124–33.

Crossan, John Dominic. *Jesus: A Revolutionary Biography*. San Francisco: Harper-Collins, 1991.

Dunn, James D. G. *Remembering Jesus*. Vol. 1 of *Christianity in the Making*. Grand Rapids: Eerdmans, 2003.

Dunnam, Maxie. *Alive in Christ: The Dynamic Process of Spiritual Formation*. Nashville: Abingdon, 1982.

Edwards, Jonathan. *Dissertation I: Concerning the End for Which God Created the World*. In *The Works of Jonathan Edwards*, vol. 8, *Ethical Writings*, 405–536. Edited by Paul Ramsey. New Haven: Yale University Press, 1989.

―――. *Letters and Personal Writings*. Vol. 16 of *The Works of Jonathan Edwards*. Edited by George S. Claghorn. New Haven: Yale University Press, 1998.

―――. *The "Miscellanies," a–500*. Vol. 13 of *The Works of Jonathan Edwards*. Edited by Thomas A. Schafer. New Haven: Yale University Press, 1994.

―――. "Observations concerning the Scripture Oeconomy of the Trinity and the Covenant of Redemption." In *Treatise on Grace and Other Posthumously Published Writings*, edited by Paul Helm, 77–98. Cambridge: James Clarke, 1971.

―――. *Religious Affections*. Vol. 2 of *The Works of Jonathan Edwards*. Edited by John E. Smith. New Haven: Yale University Press, 2009.

Elowsky, Joel C., ed. *John 11–21*. Ancient Christian Commentary on Scripture: New Testament 4b. Downers Grove, IL: InterVarsity, 2007.

Flett, John G. *The Witness of God: The Trinity, Missio Dei, Karl Barth, and the Nature of Christian Community*. Grand Rapids: Eerdmans, 2010.

Foley, Marc. *The Ascent of Mount Carmel: Reflections*. Washington, DC: ICS, 2013.

Fuller, Reginald H. *The Formation of the Resurrection Narratives*. 2nd ed. Philadelphia: Fortress, 1980.

Garcia, Mark A. *Life in Christ: Union with Christ and Twofold Grace in Calvin's Theology*. Milton Keynes, UK: Paternoster, 2008.

Goff, Philip A. *Consciousness and Fundamental Reality*. Oxford: Oxford University Press, 2017.

Gorman, Michael J. *Reading Revelation Responsibly: Uncivil Worship and Witness; Following the Lamb into the New Creation*. Eugene, OR: Cascade Books, 2017.

Guthrie, George H. *Hebrews*. NIV Application Commentary. Grand Rapids: Zondervan, 1998.

Habermas, Gary. *The Risen Jesus and Future Hope*. Lanham, MD: Rowman & Littlefield, 2003.

Habermas, Gary R., and Michael R. Licona. *The Case for the Resurrection of Jesus*. Grand Rapids: Kregel, 2004.

Harrison, Peter. *The Territories of Science and Religion*. Chicago: University of Chicago Press, 2017.

Hart, Trevor. *Regarding Karl Barth: Essays Toward a Reading of His Theology*. Carlisle, UK: Paternoster, 1999.

Hastings, W. Ross. *Echoes of Coinherence: Trinitarian Theology and Science in Conversation*. Eugene, OR: Cascade Books, 2017.

———. *Jonathan Edwards and the Life of God: Towards an Evangelical Theology of Participation*. Minneapolis: Fortress, 2015.

———. *Missional God, Missional Church: Hope for Re-evangelizing the West*. Downers Grove, IL: IVP Academic, 2012.

———. *Theological Ethics: The Moral Life of the Gospel in Contemporary Context*. Grand Rapids: Zondervan, 2021.

———. *Total Atonement: Trinitarian Participation in the Reconciliation of Humanity and Creation*. Minneapolis: Lexington Books / Fortress Academic, 2019.

Hebblethwaite, Margaret. *The Way of St. Ignatius: Finding God in All Things*. London: Fount Paperbacks, 1990.

Hendricksen, William. *New Testament Commentary: Exposition of the Gospel according to John*. Grand Rapids: Baker, 1954.

Holcomb, Justin S. *Know the Creeds and Councils*. Grand Rapids: Zondervan Academic, 2014.

Irenaeus of Lyons. *Against the Heresies Book 3*. Translated by Dominic J. Unger. Mahwah, NJ: Newman Press, 2012.

Jenson, Robert. *America's Theologian: A Recommendation of Jonathan Edwards*. New York: Oxford University Press, 1988.

Kraybill, Nelson. *Apocalypse and Allegiance: Worship, Politics, and Devotion in the Book of Revelation*. Grand Rapids: Brazos, 2010.

Ladd, George Eldon. *A Theology of the New Testament*. Grand Rapids: Eerdmans, 1993.

Lane, William L. *Hebrews: A Call to Commitment*. Vancouver: Regent College Publishing, 1985.

Lewis, C. S. *God in the Dock: Essays on Theology and Ethics*. Edited by Walter Hooper. Grand Rapids: Eerdmans, 1970.

———. *Mere Christianity*. London: Collins, 1952.

———. *Miracles*. San Francisco: HarperOne, 2001.

Longman, Tremper, III. *How to Read Genesis*. Downers Grove, IL: IVP Academic, 2005.

Luther, Martin. *Luther's Works* (American edition). Edited by Jaroslav Pelikan and Helmut T. Lehmann. 55 vols. Philadelphia: Fortress; St. Louis: Concordia, 1955–86.

Mangina, Joseph L. "Mediating Theologies: Karl Barth between Radical and Neo-orthodoxy." *Scottish Journal of Theology* 56, no. 4 (2003): 427–43.

McCheyne, Robert Murray. *Memoir and Remains of the Rev. Robert Murray McCheyne*. Edinburgh, 1894.

McCormack, Bruce L. "*Justitia Aliena*: Karl Barth in Conversation with the Evangelical Doctrine of Imputed Righteousness." In *Justification in Perspective: Historical Developments and Contemporary Challenges*, edited by Bruce L. McCormack, 167–96. Grand Rapids: Baker Academic, 2006.

McDermott, Gerald. Review of *The Sermons of Jonathan Edwards: A Reader*, edited by Wilson H. Kimnach, Kenneth P. Minkema, and Douglas A. Sweeney. The American Religious Experience. December 1999. http://are.as.wvu.edu/mcderm.htm.

McDermott, Memory. *Tea for Two: Nature's Apothecary*. 3rd ed. N.p.: PublishAmerica, 2005.

McGrath, Alister E. *Iustitia Dei: A History of the Christian Doctrine of Justification*. Cambridge: Cambridge University Press, 1986.

McKirland, Christa L. "Sexual Difference in Christian Theology: Male, Female and Intersex in the Image of God." *Journal of Psychology and Theology* 44, no. 1 (Spring 2016): 99–100.

Migliore, Daniel. *Faith Seeking Understanding: An Introduction to Christian Theology*. Grand Rapids: Eerdmans, 2004.

Miller, David L. *Hells and Holy Ghosts: A Theopoetics of Christian Belief*. New Orleans: Spring Journal, Inc., 2004.

Moffett, Samuel H. Review of *Christ outside the Gate*, by Orlando Costas. *Theology Today* 43 (1984): 214.

Molnar, Paul. *Thomas F. Torrance: Theologian of the Trinity*. Aldershot, UK: Ashgate, 2009.

Muller, Richard. *The Unaccommodated Calvin: Studies in the Foundation of a Theological Tradition*. New York: Oxford University Press, 2000.

Newbigin, Lesslie. *The Gospel in a Pluralist Society*. Grand Rapids: Eerdmans, 1989.

O'Donovan, Oliver. *Resurrection and Moral Order: An Outline for Evangelical Ethics*. Grand Rapids: Eerdmans, 1986.

Owen, John. *The Death of Death in the Death of Christ: A Treatise in Which the Whole Controversy about Universal Redemption Is Fully Discussed.* In *The Death of Christ*, vol. 10 of *The Works of John Owen.* Edited by William H. Goold and William H. Gross. London: Johnstone & Hunter, 1850–53. https://www.apuritansmind .com/wp-content/uploads/FREEEBOOKS/TheDeathofDeathintheDeathofChrist -JohnOwen.pdf.

Packer, J. I. "Evangelical Annihilationism in Review." *Reformation & Revival* 6, no. 2 (Spring 1997): 37–51.

———. "The Problem of Eternal Punishment." *Crux* 26, no. 3 (September 1990): 18–25.

Peterson, Eugene. *Reversed Thunder: The Revelation of John and the Praying Imagination.* New York: Harper & Row, 1988.

Polkinghorne, John. *Science and the Trinity: The Christian Encounter with Reality.* New Haven: Yale University Press, 2004.

Popper, Karl. *Conjectures and Refutations: The Growth of Scientific Knowledge.* London: Routledge, 1963.

Ramelli, Ilaria L. E. *The Christian Doctrine of* Apokatastasis*: A Critical Assessment from the New Testament to Eriugena.* Leiden: Brill, 2013.

Smail, Thomas A. *The Giving Gift: The Holy Spirit in Person.* Eugene, OR: Wipf & Stock, 2004.

Stevens, R. Paul. *Doing God's Business: Meaning and Motivation for the Marketplace.* Grand Rapids: Eerdmans, 2006.

———. *The Other Six Days: Vocation, Work, and Ministry in Biblical Perspective.* Grand Rapids: Eerdmans, 2000.

Stott, John R. W. *The Spirit, the Church and the World: The Message of Acts.* Downers Grove, IL: InterVarsity, 1990.

Strauss, David. *A New Life of Jesus.* 2 vols. Edinburgh: Williams and Northgate, 1879.

Tappert, Theodore G., ed. *The Book of Concord: The Confessions of the Lutheran Church*, 292. Philadelphia: Fortress, 1959.

Torrance, James. *Worship, Community and the Triune God of Grace.* Carlisle, UK: Paternoster, 1996.

Torrance, T. F. *Atonement: The Person and Work of Christ.* Edited by Robert T. Walker. Downers Grove, IL: IVP Academic, 2009.

———. *The Mediation of Christ.* Colorado Springs: Helmers and Howard, 1992.

———. *Space, Time and Resurrection.* Edinburgh: T&T Clark, 1998.

Webster, John. "'The Firmest Grasp of the Real': Barth on Original Sin." *Toronto Journal of Theology* 4 (Spring 1988): 19–29.

Wesley, John. "The Case of Reason Impartially Considered." Sermon 70 in *Sermons on Several Occasions.* https://www.ccel.org/ccel/wesley/sermons.vi.xvii.html#vi .xvii-p0.3.

———. *Sermons III: 71–114*. Vol. 3 of *The Works of John Wesley*. Edited by Albert C. Outler. Nashville: Abingdon, 1986.

Wilkins, Michael J., and J. P. Moreland, eds. *Jesus under Fire: Modern Scholarship Reinvents the Historical Jesus*. Grand Rapids: Zondervan, 1996.

Willard, Dallas. *The Spirit of the Disciplines: Understanding How God Changes Lives*. New York: HarperCollins, 1991.

Wright, N. T. *John for Everyone, Part 2*. London: SPCK, 2002.

———. *The Resurrection of the Son of God*. Vol. 3 of *Christian Origins and the Question of God*. Minneapolis: Fortress, 2002.

———. *Surprised by Hope: Rethinking Heaven, the Resurrection, and the Mission of the Church*. New York: HarperOne, 2008.

Yamauchi, Edwin. "Jesus outside the New Testament: What Is the Evidence?" In Wilkins and Moreland, *Jesus under Fire*, 207–30.

Subject Index

Scripture and Ancient Sources Index

DATE DUE